MW00450292

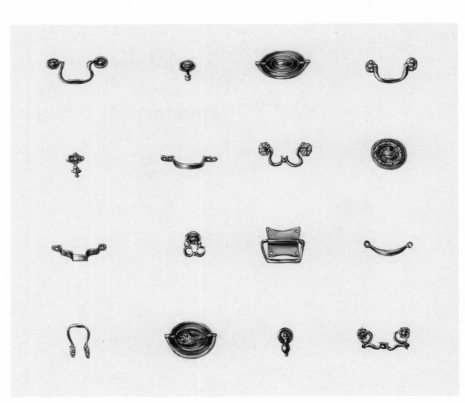

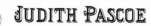

JUDITH PASCOE

THE HUMMINGBIRD CABINET

A RARE AND CURIOUS HISTORY
OF ROMANTIC COLLECTORS

CORNELL UNIVERSITY PRESS
ITHACA AND LONDON

Frontispiece: Lisa Milroy, *Handles* (1988). Copyright © Lisa Milroy. By kind permission of the artist and the Board of Trustees of the National Museums Liverpool (Walker Art Gallery).

Copyright © 2006 by Cornell University

All rights reserved. Except for brief quotations in a review, this book, or parts thereof, must not be reproduced in any form without permission in writing from the publisher. For information, address Cornell University Press, Sage House, 512 East State Street, Ithaca, New York 14850.

First published 2006 by Cornell University Press
Printed in the United States of America

Design by Scott Levine

Library of Congress Cataloging-in-Publication Data

Pascoe, Judith, 1960-
    The hummingbird cabinet : a rare and curious history of romantic collectors / Judith Pascoe.
        p. cm.
    Includes bibliographical references and index.
    ISBN-13: 978-0-8014-4362-6 (cloth : alk. paper)
    ISBN-10: 0-8014-4362-8 (cloth : alk. paper)
    1. Collectors and collecting—England—History—19th century.
    2. Romanticism—England—History—19th century. 3. English poetry
—19th century—History and criticism. I. Title.
    AM343.P37 2006
    821'.709145—dc22
                                                            2005016064

Cornell University Press strives to use environmentally responsible suppliers and materials to the fullest extent possible in the publishing of its books. Such materials include vegetable-based, low-VOC inks and acid-free papers that are recycled, totally chlorine-free, or partly composed of nonwood fibers. For further information, visit our website at www.cornellpress.cornell.edu.

Cloth printing   10 9 8 7 6 5 4 3 2 1

for Perry

CONTENTS

ILLUSTRATIONS

❧ ACKNOWLEDGMENTS ❧

A year-long fellowship from the National Endowment for the Humanities and a Faculty Scholar fellowship from the University of Iowa gave me time enough to get lost in the archives and time enough to find my way back out. These institutions had faith in me and I am grateful to them.

Two works of distinguished scholarship serve as touchstones for my book: *The Shows of London* by Richard Altick (Harvard, 1978) and Naomi Schor's "*Cartes Postales:* Representing Paris 1900" (*Critical Inquiry* 18 [1992]: 188–244). Library copies of Altick's compendious account of eighteenth- and nineteenth-century popular exhibitions grow shabby from overuse, and the book's price shoots upward in the used book market. This is to say that *The Shows of London* should be permanently in print. Schor's elegant meditation on postcard collecting, which I first heard as a lecture at University College, London, thrilled and inspired me. It has lost nothing upon multiple rereadings.

I am also happy to thank the many curators, librarians, and archivists who fielded my requests for obscure books and material oddities. They include, closest to home, the unflinching Interlibrary Loan librarians and helpful Special Collections staff at the University of Iowa. Farther afield, I owe thanks to the staff of the British Library, the London Library, and the British Museum archives; Sheila de la Bellaigue and Pamela Clark, Registrars, Royal Archive; Frances Dimond,

Photography Curator, Royal Archive; Bridget Wright, Bibliographer, Royal Library; Christopher Lloyd, Surveyor of the Queen's Pictures, the Royal Collection Trust; Karen Lawson, Senior Picture Library Assistant, Royal Collections Enterprises; Clemency Fisher, Curator of Birds and Mammals, Liverpool Museum, National Museums and Galleries on Merseyside; Ann Datta, Zoology Librarian, the Natural History Museum (London); Alison Harding, Assistant Librarian, Ornithology and Rothschild Libraries (Tring); Michael Walters, Curator of Eggs, Bird Group, the Natural History Museum (Tring); Katrina Cook, Curator, Bird Group, the Natural History Museum (Tring); Rupert Calvocoressi, Image Management Executive, the Natural History Museum (London); Gina Douglas, Librarian and Archivist, the Linnean Society; Virginia Murray, John Murray (Publishers), Ltd.; Susan Giles, Curator of Ethnography and Foreign Archaeology, Bristol City Museum and Art Gallery; Caroline Ferris, County Archivist, Dorset Record Office (Dorchester); Kate Hebditch, Deputy Curator, Dorset County Museum (Dorchester); Kim Sloan, Assistant Keeper, Department of Prints and Drawings, British Museum; Bernard Nurse, Librarian, Society of Antiquaries (London); Bruce Barker-Benfield, Senior Assistant Librarian, Department of Special Collections and Western Mss., Bodleian Library; H. P. Powell, Assistant Curator, Geological Collections, Oxford University Museum of Natural History; Linda Birch, Librarian, Alexander Library, Oxford University; Simon Owens, Keeper of the Herbarium, Kew Gardens; Julie Anne Lambert, Librarian of the John Johnson Collection, Bodleian Library; Clive Hurst, Head of Rare Books and Printed Ephemera, Bodleian Library; Stephen Wagner, Curator, the Carl H. Pforzheimer Collection of Shelley and His Circle, the New York Public Library; Annette Fern, Research and Reference Librarian, the Harvard Theatre Collection; Kathleen Coleman, Curatorial Assistant, the Harvard Theatre Collection.

A version of part of chapter 1 appeared as "The Hummingbird Cabinet" in a special issue of *The Wordsworth Circle* (Winter 2004) focusing on natural knowledge in the romantic age. I am grateful to the editor of that issue, Noah Heringman, for including my work, and to Marilyn Gaull, the editor of *TWC*, for graciously allowing it to be reprinted here.

My thanks to Teresa Mangum, Kim Marra, Eric Gidal, and Ruth Lindeborg, each of whom commented on early versions of one or more of this book's chapters, and to Perry Howell, who commented on nearly every version of all of the chapters. I also thank Garrett Stewart, Stuart Curran, Margaret Higonnet, Michael Macovski, and Stephen Behrendt for writing letters in support of grant applications. Taylor Adkins provided last-minute research assistance. Claire Sponsler read the entire book in rough manuscript and made crucial chapter-shaping suggestions. Cornell University Press editor Bernhard Kendler enlisted perceptive and forbearing readers to review the manuscript; the comments of Cynthia Wall and Susan M. Stabile significantly influenced the evolution of this book. I also thank Amanda Heller, copyeditor extraordinaire, as well as senior manuscript editor Karen Hwa, who deftly guided the manuscript into print, and senior designer Scott E. Levine, who artfully constructed the book's physical form.

Finally, and most of all, I am grateful for the keen insight, rare enthusiasm, and bold example of Sara Levine.

THE LAST GUITAR
SHELLEY EVER PLAYED

In 1898, Edward Silsbee, an elderly American sea captain and self-proclaimed Percy Bysshe Shelley enthusiast, purchased a beautifully crafted Italian guitar that the poet once owned. Many people care about objects that once belonged to Shelley, and many objects that once belonged to Shelley have been lovingly preserved.[1] There are Shelley watch fobs and Shelley snuffboxes, a Shelley baby rattle and a Shelley raisin plate, Shelley hair and Shelley doodles. There may also be extant, or so it has been hoped, a volume of Keats's poems found in the drowned Shelley's pocket.[2] This sodden volume, which Edward Trelawny saw in Shelley's jacket when his body washed up on shore, was "doubled back, as if the reader, in the act of reading, had hastily thrust it away."[3] The book has fueled the longings of Shelley collectors everywhere. But neither the tragedy-laden Keats volume nor the surfeit of Shelley effluvia surpasses the Shelley guitar installed in the same fleece-lined wooden box in which it was encased when an infatuated Shelley gave it to Jane Williams. When Edward Silsbee bought the guitar from Jane Williams's grandson, he was asked to donate it to a British institution. And so Silsbee promised the instrument to Oxford, the university from which Shelley had been expelled.[4]

It is easy to understand why Shelley's guitar was, for Silsbee, a particularly resonant object, why its capture might stand as the pinnacle of a Shelley collector's career. A newspaper account of the Bodleian's acquisition of the guitar recognized its unique status among literary artifacts: "There is probably no other relic of a great poet so intimately associated with the arts of poetry and music, or ever will be, unless Milton's organ should turn up at a broker's, or some excavating explorer should bring to light the lyre of Sappho."[5] The guitar epitomized the musicality of Shelley's verse, the incantatory loveliness, for example, of "Lines: When the lamp is shattered," in which Shelley writes, "When the lute is broken, / Sweet tones are remembered not; / When the lips have spoken, / Loved accents are soon forgot."[6] The guitar also evoked the poet's romantic longings, his construction of an idealized romance as an escape from an increasingly complicated marriage, shadowed by the deaths of three children. In the poem "With a Guitar. To Jane," Shelley, writing as Ariel in *The Tempest*, describes the guitar as the dwelling of a "spirit" that would speak in "its highest holiest tone" only for Jane, figured in the poem as Miranda.[7] The guitar, in its physical substantiveness, conjured up Shelley's Shakespearean fantasy, as well as his own prematurely silenced poetic tones. Or, rather, it allowed the viewer to project all these associations upon it.

The newspaper account went on to describe the instrument's pristine state, a result of its having been "religiously preserved since Shelley's death." The chances of the guitar's being so preserved had been greatly enhanced as a direct result of this mythologized death. The legendary moment when Trelawny reached into the conflagration of Shelley's funeral bier in order to snatch Shelley's heart from the flames is etched in literary history as a morbid example of romantic sentimentality, but it anticipated and inspired subsequent instances of Shelley relic worship. The heart was eventually buried with the bodies of Mary Shelley and her parents in the Shelley family vault at Bournemouth, but not before it became the object of a custody dispute that ended with the relic residing in Mary Shelley's desk drawer.

Romantic era poets were particularly prone to having their hearts dried to a powder in a desk drawer or enshrined apart from their bodies.[8] They lived and died at a time when the notion that objects are imbued with a lasting sediment of their owners, one that can be kept in a box or encased behind glass, informed the public commemoration of fallen heroes such as Lord Nelson (whose body was pickled in alcohol so that it could be returned, intact, to England) and Napoleon (whose grave site's foliage was stripped clean of branches by souvenir seekers). This desire to possess material vestiges of the celebrated dead also influenced responses to living literary figures. A parade of tourists peered over Wordsworth's wall at Rydal Mount and gathered sprigs of laurel from the site as keepsakes. The Reverend Charles Valentine Le Grice, having successfully prised a walking stick from a reluctant Wordsworth in a manner unbefitting a clergyman, referred to his treasure "as if it were a piece of the true Cross."[9]

The kind of material longing that would cause a man to covet a poet's walking stick stands in striking contrast to the spiritual desire that is so often inscribed in romantic poetry. Shelley, when he sat down to write about his guitar, saw it primarily as a vehicle for a Spirit whose high holy tones served as an echo of its interlocutor's feelings. This Spirit is just one of many abstract emanations that circulate through Shelley's poetry and highlight the ephemerality of material—as opposed to spiritual or imaginary—things. In his "Hymn to Intellectual Beauty," Shelley courts the "awful shadow of some unseen Power," and this "various world" stands as an ephemeral stage set for encounters with the "Spirit of Beauty" which consecrates all that it shines upon. The actual world serves chiefly as a font of metaphors which Shelley employs as a means of describing a total abstraction that visits "with as inconstant wing / As summer winds that creep from flower to flower."[10]

Twentieth-century critics of romanticism speak of romantic poets as turning away from the physical world.[11] M. H. Abrams posits a shift in the romantic period from a view of poetry as a mirror reflecting the reality of the world to a conception of poetry as a lamp that, in William Hazlitt's terms, not only shows us an object but also "throws a sparkling radiance on all around it."[12] The physical object becomes less important than the way in which it is transformed by the poet's consciousness. In a bracing example of the New Historicist critical approach that dominated romantic studies in the 1980s and 1990s, Marjorie Levinson points out how the historical details of Tintern Abbey—the ruin, the air pollution, the impoverished hermits—get elided in Wordsworth's most celebrated poem.[13] Jerome McGann states that "the poetry of Romanticism is everywhere marked by extreme forms of displacement and poetic conceptualization whereby the actual human issues with which the poetry is concerned are resituated in a variety of idealized localities."[14] Mary Poovey refers to the romantic poets' "turn away from phenomenal particulars and toward the mind that contemplates those things" as the precursor of postmodern displacements of the stable fact.[15] Romantic poetry, accurately or not, has become known for enacting an escapist aesthetic, one that permits the poet to retreat from obdurate physical reality.[16]

We might reasonably view the activity of collecting as being severely at odds with the poetic value system of romantic poets. Wordsworth, a poet who, far more than Shelley, based his poetic practice on clear-eyed description, on a resolve "to look steadily at [his] subject," distances himself in his poetry from a too close attachment to material things, from the "getting and spending" of his day, but also from collecting practices.[17] One can detect a specific distaste for the collecting impulse in Wordsworth's professed inability to "class the cabinet" of his sensations in book two of *The Prelude*.[18] He faults those who create distinctions and then deem that these "puny boundaries are things / Which we perceive, and not which we have made" (2.218–19). But at the very moment when Wordsworth was writing these lines, romantic era collectors were amassing cabinets of books, birds, relics, antiquities, and fossils in greater numbers than ever before. If these collecting projects were motivated by the kind of calculating scientific impulse that Wordsworth condemns (the desire for mastery by way of totalizing classificatory systems), they were driven also by Wordsworthian modes of longing (for permanence, immortality, pleasure, recognition) which suffuse romantic poetry more generally. Romantic poetry's acute awareness of passing time and human loss contributed to, and reflected, a culture's new understanding of the past as an idealized lost world, partly salvageable through the recovery and preservation of old objects and documents. According to Stephen Bann, "more people came to share the passion for historical objects that had previously been confined to the antiquarian milieu" as history "became a substratum to almost every type of cultural activity."[19] This passion manifested itself in many forms; it led to the proliferation of antiquarian societies, the development of the historical novel, the rise of national libraries and museums—and the popularization of collecting.[20]

Long the exclusive bastion of the very rich, collecting became democratized during the early decades of the nineteenth century as opportunities for participating in this activity, directly or vicariously, proliferated. Periodical editors, for example, capitalizing on the public enthusiasm for collecting, equated magazines to museums or cabinets of collectible objects. The *Attic Miscellany* (a title that calls to mind preserved artifacts with both senses of the word "attic"), published in London from 1789 to 1791, included as part of its subtitle "The Correspondents' Museum." Other journals that constructed their readers as collectors included *The Cabinet Magazine or Literary Olio* (London, 1796–91); *The Lady's Monthly Museum, or Polite Repository of Amusement and Instruction* (London, 1796–1807); *The Cabinet; or, Monthly Report of Polite Literature* (London, 1807); *The Museum; or, Record of Literature, Fine Arts, Science, etc.* (London, 1822); *The Literary Museum* (London, 1828); and *The Lady's Magazine, and Museum of the Belles Lettres* (London, 1832–37). The journal titles depict the act of periodical reading as a form of connoisseurship.[21] Even those readers who could not afford their own collections could partake of a magazine museum.

The romantic period stands as a unique moment in collecting history—the halfway point between the princely private enthusiasms of the Renaissance wonder cabinet and the public institution of the Victorian museum—but it is a moment much less adequately historicized and theorized than the more familiar manifestations of collecting that serve as its temporal bookends. Recent cultural histories of wonder and curiosity, which address the phenomenon of collecting, have stopped just short of the romantic period. Lorraine Daston and Katharine Park's remarkable analysis of wonder focuses on medieval and Renaissance collecting; Barbara Benedict's exploration of the cultural status of curiosity in the eighteenth century encompasses the early nineteenth century, but not as a chief focus of interest.[22] Contributors to the burgeoning field of museum studies—for example, Annie E. Coombes in *Reinventing Africa*—understandably analyze in most detail the fully institutionalized museum of the Victorian period.[23] Studies of romantic poetry in the context of museum collections, such as *Poetic Exhibitions* by Eric Gidal and *The Sculpted Word* by Grant F. Scott, focus attention on poems that take museum objects as their subjects, using the politics of museum formation and the aesthetics of ekphrasis as suggestive explanatory contexts for literary works.[24] By contrast, I set out to focus on collected objects in the romantic period rather than on the poetry that addresses these objects, and to use romantic poetry as a means of explaining the popularization of collecting.

The spiritual longings of the romantic poets coexisted alongside early-nineteenth-century collectors' material pursuit of "rare" and "curious" objects, a pursuit so frenzied that Benjamin Robert Haydon attributed his contemporaries' acquisitiveness to a national character flaw. "Oh England, never were such a people," he wrote. "On every English chimney piece, you will see a bit of the real Pyramids, a bit of the Break Water, a bit of Stonehenge! a bit of the first cinder of the first fire Eve ever made, a bit of the very fig leaf which Adam first gave her."[25] At the same moment when romantic poets sought to escape the material realities of the actual world through a poetry that celebrated the transcendent power of the imagination, their contemporaries gathered, assembled, catalogued, and fictionalized the physical detritus of history. These seemingly diametrical pursuits—the displacement of history in romantic poems that glancingly engage actual places such as the ruins of Tintern Abbey, and the stockpiling of history by collectors who, given the opportunity, would have carried away bits of the ruin like marauding ants—are not unrelated. And these twinned romantic desires—to transcend the passage of time and to preserve the wreckage of its passage—influence us still.[26]

In the catalogue of the bicentenary Shelley exhibition at the Bodleian Library, there is a description of "Shelley's spy-glass"—the quotation marks signal the cataloguer's mild skepticism. The entry for this relic quotes Daniel Roberts on his successful salvaging of Shelley's boat. Out of a wreck "half full of a blue mud," Roberts claims to have "picked out Cloths of all sorts (mostly rotten) books & spy glass broken." The catalogue entry points to this reference as "presumably" the context for the small spyglass "now preserved—after repair?—amongst the family relics," before concluding, "If the identification is correct, Shelley may have looked through it on his last voyage."[27] How we long to believe that the buffed and polished spyglass in the exhibition catalogue is the mud-caked broken spyglass that Roberts poignantly describes. One reads the cataloguer's last suggestive sentence and hears the slap of the waves. It is easy to glide past the cataloguer's qualifying "may" to conjure up a worried Shelley, scanning the coastline in a storm.

Edward Silsbee, the elderly American sea captain, was probably more susceptible than most people to this kind of imaginative supposing; in pursuit of Shelley relics, he insinuated himself into the Italian household of the elderly Claire Clairmont (Mary Shelley's half-sister and Byron's mistress), providing Henry James with the premise for *The Aspern Papers*.[28] Clairmont's home in Florence was a pilgrimage site for Shelley acolytes. When William Michael Rossetti visited her in June 1873, "she was a slender and pallid old lady, with thinned hair which had once been dark, and with dark and still expressive eyes." She was "more than moderately deaf," with a face "such as one could easily suppose to have been handsome and charming in youth," and a "clear, even-toned, and agreeable" voice.[29] Although Rossetti's intentions were scholarly—he sought to "ascertain distinctly what are Shelley's documents in Miss Clairmont's possession"—he was not immune to the allure of Shelley relics.[30] He was delighted to acquire, through Edward Trelawny's intercession, a sofa that Shelley had reportedly purchased for Leigh Hunt. At least that was the original story. The sofa took on more intimate associations, thanks to Trelawny's assurance that it had, in fact, been the one on which the poet had regularly slept at Pisa, and that Shelley had dozed on it before setting off on his doomed voyage in the *Don Juan*. The sofa was, therefore, as Rossetti was pleased to note, "the last couch Shelley ever slept on, which makes it extraordinarily interesting."[31]

When James turned Silsbee into a scholar-collector in *The Aspern Papers*, he might have modeled his fictional character after any number of Victorian scholars for whom the pursuit of a sofa on which Shelley once slept was a perfectly legitimate endeavor. By contrast, the attitude that present-day scholars adopt when they talk about collectors is very often one of condescension verging on disdain—this despite the fact that they, too, are collectors by avocation. The literary critic plucks extracts from literary works and reassembles them in the anthology of the critical essay.[32] The historian sifts through the flotsam of archives for usable details; as Carolyn Steedman writes, the historian's craft is "to conjure a social system from a nutmeg grater."[33] Still, we are reluctant to equate our own trolling for the perfect *aperçu* or revelatory object with the avidity of Shelley relic collectors. On the particular fascination with Shelley's heart, Sylva Norman writes, "Its treatment has been slightly absurd, a trifle vulgar, wholly sentimental—which is not to be wondered at, since, after leaving Shelley's body, it was handled by no one free from fanaticism, exaltation, misery, or some such abnormality of feeling towards Shelley."[34]

Norman's association of collecting with abnormal feeling is the legacy of Freud, whose writings overwhelmingly inform scholarly responses to this avocation. The Freudian collector is a sexually maladjusted misanthrope who hoards his quarry of books, stamps, or paintings as a means of compensating for a deficient self. The original Freudian collector, that is, Freud himself, kept a collection of antiquities—"amassed figures of Egyptian, Greek and Roman gods that lined the wall and swarmed over the desks and tables in [his] professional space."[35] These figurines likely faced him when he wrote the passages that would be used by others to pathologize the activity of collecting. "When an old maid keeps a dog or an old bachelor collects snuffboxes," Freud wrote, "the former is finding a substitute for her need for a companion in marriage and the latter for his need for—a multitude of conquests."[36]

There are comparatively few passages in Freud's writings that comment on the collector, but this small and tangential legacy has been expanded upon and popularized by Jean Baudrillard, among others. "In later life, it is men over forty who most frequently fall victim to this passion [of collecting]," Baudrillard writes, going on to describe collecting as "a regression to the anal stage, which is characterized by accumulation, orderliness, aggressive retention, and so on."[37] He calls the possession of objects and the passion for them a "*tempered mode of sexual perversion*," and compares the collector to the keeper of a harem: "Man never comes so close to being the master of a secret seraglio as when he is surrounded by his objects."[38]

The explanatory preeminence of Freudian collecting theory is partly a result of the eloquence of its latter-day proponents—most notably Susan Stewart, whose compelling *On Longing* is essential reading for any student of collecting— but it is also a function of the general, if also sexist, applicability of Freud's ideas.[39] Silsbee's acquisition of a guitar may seem easy to explain by way of psychoanalytic paradigms (phallic substitute, displacement, sublimation), but if we slip Silsbee into a Freudian case study folder and close the file drawer, some of his story's more interesting nuances fall away.

Silsbee longed to know the romantic poets in a tangible way. He quizzed Clairmont on her former acquaintances and took notes on her comments. His memoranda of these conversations reveal a preoccupation with how the romantic poets looked or sounded or moved. "Shelley's lips fine & not too thick," he noted, and "Shelley had the voice of *a child*—high *tenor from back of the head*." Silsbee's underscoring communicates his wonder at these intimate details, but also his awe of the woman who had communed with Shelley. "These were *her words*," Silsbee wrote.[40]

George Edward Woodberry recalled encountering the "Shelley-mad" Silsbee while breakfasting at the home of a Harvard professor and being permitted to hold a Shelley notebook, a "thin quarto bound in parchment" that Silsbee had acquired from Claire Clairmont. Eggs were allowed to cool and toast to harden as the "sacred relic" was displayed. Woodberry recalled the way Silsbee handled the volume, "carefully, fluttering the leaves as he picked out some of the more characteristic pages of the script, passing over others quickly, as if he felt a trust in his hands, and a privacy not to be lost sight of—something precious and intimate and inviolable."[41] Silsbee donated the notebook to the university in order to bring Shelley "near to the hearts and eyes and senses of Harvard youth" and to allow students to feel "the touch of Shelley's living hand upon the page." Woodberry, who was a Harvard senior when he met Silsbee over breakfast, shared the collector's vision of the volume's numinous power. "I can still feel the thrill in my fingers, as they moved over lines where Shelley's hand had hovered," Woodberry wrote years later, recalling that Silsbee's enthusiasms were "reduplicated from the fervors of my ardent youth."[42]

Silsbee's love of Shelley relics and manuscripts was accompanied by a possibly naïve but certainly heartfelt immersion in Shelley's poetry. According to Richard Garnett, the British Museum librarian who helped arrange the guitar purchase, Silsbee spoke chiefly of poetry and art, "on both of which he would utter deeper sayings than are often to be found in print. . . . He was the most enthusiastic critic of Shelley the present writer has known," Garnett continued, "but also the most acute and discriminating."[43] Describing Silsbee reciting Shelley verse, Woodberry wrote, "He had caught the magic by which the music in the verse brought the landscape emotionally, as well as objectively, before the mind and eye, the mood of the scene as well as its visual aspect."[44]

Silsbee was a primarily self-taught Shelley scholar whose chief credentials for fashioning himself as the poet's posthumous cup-bearer were an adventuresome past (he had voyaged twice around the world as a captain engaged in the East India trade) and a striking appearance. Garnett claimed that Silsbee resembled Edward Trelawny, who had styled himself after Byron's dashing Corsair. Another of Silsbee's contemporaries recalled him sitting "gloomily in an armchair, looking like some deep-sea monster on a Bernini fountain," while John Singer Sargent, whose portrait of Silsbee followed the guitar into the Bodleian's collections, described a man "dramatized by a buccaneering appearance and by a crop of piratical legends and tales."[45] Since Shelley's reputation was not particularly high in New England academic literary circles at that time, Silsbee could seem Shelley-like, that is, impassioned and iconoclastic, by virtue of his championing of Shelley's verse.

To understand Silsbee, we need to adopt something of his own affection for the objects he fleetingly owned, to hold collecting practice up to more than one light so that its nuances and contradictions can emerge. Silsbee collected Shelleyana, but, in the case of the guitar, he was able to do so only on the condition that it would immediately be placed where he would rarely have the opportunity to see it. Silsbee's love of Shelley relics was inseparably intertwined with his enthusiasm for Shelley's poetry, a poetry that advocates a lofty remove from earthly things. Silsbee sought to achieve a measure of immortality through association with a physical vestige of Shelley's verse, but what small fame he achieved came as a result of his story's being taken up by Henry James to demonstrate the deathliness of the collecting pursuit.[46]

Henry James shared Silsbee's belief in the power of Shelley's former possessions, and in the romantic past as a nobler era than his own. In his preface to *The Aspern Papers*, James writes, "I delight in a palpable imaginable *visitable* past—in the nearer distances and the clearer mysteries, the marks and signs of a world we may reach over to as by making a long arm we grasp an object at the other end of our own table."[47] When James heard the story of the "Shelley-worshipper" Silsbee's attempt to procure Shelley and Byron letters in Claire Clairmont's possession, he noted, "Certainly there is a little subject there: the picture of the two faded, queer, poor and discredited old English women—living on into a strange generation, in their musty corner of a foreign town—with these illustrious letters their most precious possession."[48] James was thrilled by the notion that he himself could have crossed the Clairmont threshold in Florence. He wrote, "The wonder of my having doubtless at several earlier seasons passed again and again, all unknowing, the door of her house, where she sat above, within call and in her habit as she lived, these things gave me all I wanted" (preface, viii).

James was most fascinated by "the fortunate privacy, the long uninvaded and uninterviewed state" of Claire Clairmont; it was this aspect of the Silsbee saga that he retained in his tale (preface, ix). In *The Aspern Papers*, the cloistered quality of Miss Bordereau's chamber, and of her life in Venice more generally, makes the collector's invasion seem all the more shocking. "Ah you publishing scoundrel," Miss Bordereau hisses when she discovers her tenant trespassing in her bedroom, his hand on the latch of her secretary cabinet. Newly unveiled, the extraordinary eyes of Miss Bordereau glare at James's narrator "like the sudden drench, for a caught burglar, of a flood of gaslight" (*Aspern*, 118). The narrator's publishing plans threaten the pristine isolation of the Aspern letters. Miss Bordereau's furious exclamation damningly associates the collector with a modern age in which, according to James, "photography and other conveniences have annihilated surprise" (*Aspern*, 49).

James's repeated allusions to photography as the form of technology that separated his own age from that of the romantics possibly stemmed from the threat it posed to the mysteriousness of the earlier era. The romantic poets were the last literary generation to go unphotographed, and so their faces are shrouded in a more opaque mystery than those of the literary figures who followed them. Claire Clairmont, the subject of James's and Silsbee's particular fascination, lived well into the age of photography, but her image was apparently never fixed on an iodized silver plate. *The Aspern Papers* portrays Miss Bordereau as the last person standing who is possessed of a "single pair of eyes into which his [the poet Jeffrey Aspern's] had looked," and a hand that his had touched (*Aspern*, 8). Marveling that she is still alive, James's narrator says, "It was as if I had been told Mrs. Siddons was, or Queen Caroline, or the famous Lady Hamilton" (*Aspern*, 5–6).

James's narrator celebrates the romantic period for its supposed remove from the pushy, aggressive modernism he associates with celebrity culture and technology (he does so in blithe disregard of the fact that the female icons he mentions were regularly featured in newspaper gossip columns). Of his elderly heroine Miss Bordereau, James writes in the voice of his awestruck narrator, "It was a revelation to us that self-effacement on such a scale had been possible in the latter half of the nineteenth century—the age of newspapers and photographs and interviewers" (*Aspern*, 8).

Shelley's guitar was photographed several times at the moment it was about to be handed from the guitar seller John Wheeler Williams to Silsbee, and then, immediately afterward, to the Bodleian Library. Williams believed in a relic's ability to serve as a bridge between the past and the present, to ennoble members of a later generation by association, and he had no squeamishness about the demystifying effect of photography or the intrusiveness of the press. He had photographs taken of himself with the guitar and sent prints to Garnett, writing, "Enclosed I beg to offer for your acceptance some photos of the Guitar & of myself that may be interesting to you. I have just had some done for a few friends specially interested in the Guitar & its history. . . . I had the one taken with the guitar as a reminder that I am the last link in the chain that connects the past with the present" (see fig. 1).[49] Williams wrote approvingly of Garnett's plan to write an account of the guitar transfer for the *Times:* "I have no doubt there are many people who would like to see the Guitar & thro' the medium of the

Fig. 1. Photo of J. W. Williams with guitar. Harry Ransom Humanities Research Center, the University of Texas at Austin.

'Times' will be able to do so." In a postscript to this letter, making reference to a popular tabloid, Williams added, "Should you like another photograph of guitar for Ill. London News I can send one."[50]

James's disparaging allusions to the advent of photography anticipate the writings of the philosopher and critic Walter Benjamin, who, like James and Silsbee, understood the allure of resonant objects and speculated about the impact of reproduction technology. Benjamin claimed that *"the technology of reproduction detaches the reproduced object from the sphere of tradition"* and that *"by replicating a work many times over, it substitutes a mass existence for a unique existence."*[51] The object, once photographed, loses something of its historicity and its originality, becoming less curious and rare as its facsimiles proliferate and spread.

Benjamin also shared with Silsbee and James a fascination with material objects. His sympathetic view of the collector stands in contrast to Freud's written comments on collecting, and it is tempting to attribute this difference to the disparity in their personal circumstances: Freud's collection of ancient artifacts made it safely from Vienna to London, where he had moved to escape Nazi persecution in 1938, two years before Benjamin, seeking to escape Nazi-occupied France, was turned back by Spanish border authorities. But that would be reading Benjamin's commentary on collecting through the dark lens of his final peripatetic days and his ultimate suicide at Port-Bou. Benjamin had already written what he had to say about collectors when he tried to cross the border into Spain;

he was carrying a large black briefcase possibly containing the manuscript of "Paris, Capital of the Nineteenth Century," a vast collection of quotations from which he was composing a cultural history of the Paris arcades.[52] Benjamin was exploring "the extent to which it is possible to be 'concrete' in the context of the philosophy of history."[53] He wrote to his friend Gerhard Scholem, "The issue here is precisely what you once touched on after reading *One-Way Street:* to attain the most extreme concreteness for an era, as it occasionally manifested itself in children's games, a building, or a real-life situation."[54] *One-Way Street* is an autobiographical montage consisting of short essays with titles such as "Chinese Curios," "Gloves," and "Toys." Sometimes these titles act as aids to memory, conjuring up objects that inspire musings on tangential topics, but sometimes Benjamin stays focused on the material world itself, as when he describes the collections of an untidy child: "His dresser drawers must become arsenal and zoo, crime museum and crypt. 'To tidy up' would be to demolish an edifice full of prickly chestnuts that are spiky clubs, tinfoil that is hoarded silver, bricks that are coffins, cacti that are totem poles, and copper pennies that are shields."[55]

In a section of *The Arcades Project* organized around the topic of collectors, Benjamin gives a nod to the Freudian stereotype of the collector in a convolute that conjures up an elderly hoarder stockpiling hairpins and bits of string. Benjamin, however, ends the passage with this exclamation: "But compare collecting done by children!"[56] Benjamin's child collector changes chestnuts into clubs, tinfoil into silver, cacti into totem poles. That is, the objects becomes launchpads for imaginative take-offs. No sooner does the collector handle the items in his showcase, Benjamin writes, than "he appears inspired by them and seems to look through them into their distance, like an augur."[57]

There are two photographs of Walter Benjamin working in the Bibliothèque Nationale in 1937. In one, he is consulting the *Grand Dictionnaire universel du dix-neuvième siècle*. "Walter Benjamin at the card catalogue of the Bibliothèque Nationale" reads the caption on the other photo; Benjamin is writing intently at a library table, with an ink pot in the foreground and a bank of card catalogue drawers behind.[58] In a passage of *The Arcades Project*, Benjamin writes, "Collecting is a primal phenomenon of study: the student collects knowledge," and in these photographs, Benjamin is preserved forever as the scholar-collector, bent over a dictionary or furiously transcribing notes, ideas, critical concepts.[59] The photographs raise the possibility that a critical work modeled on a collection might go on forever, that Benjamin, left to his own devices, might never have left the library. "For everything that matters is to be found in the card box of the researcher who wrote it, and the scholar studying it assimilates it into his own card index," Benjamin writes.[60]

In his work on the Paris arcades, Benjamin was innovating a mode of scholarly writing based on the juxtapositioning of quotations and reflections. Since Benjamin died before he could complete this project, and since it survives only in the form of notes that he arranged according to topic, it is a matter of debate whether the novelty of the work's structure is a product of deliberation or incompletion. Benjamin's American editors describe the work's discontinuous presentation as a determined effort to oppose traditional modes of argument, noting his preference for the montage form, "with its philosophic play of distances, transitions, and intersections, its perpetually shifting contexts and ironic juxtapositions."[61] But Benjamin's German editor compares the work's "oppressive chunks of quotations" to the "materials used in building a house, the outline of which has just been marked in the ground or whose foundations are just being dug."[62] We can read *The Arcades Project* as the playful innovation of a writer rebelling against the linear style of the academy or as the stillborn blueprint of a scholar stuck at the note-taking stage of research.

In a list of "Principles of the Weighty Tome, or How to Write Fat Books," Benjamin writes: "The typical work of modern scholarship is intended to be read like a catalogue. But when shall we actually write books like catalogues?"[63] In a catalogue, each separate entry is discrete; the white space separating one item from the next encourages the reader to stop or pause. One entry may be connected to the next in some way, or no such connection may exist; in either event, the reader is left to discover, or note the absence of, a link. In a work of modern scholarship, one idea leads directly into the next with only the smallest gasp of white space between chapters. Holes in arguments, whether as small as pinpricks or as large as manhole covers, get their edges tugged together by rhetorical force so that every idea seems perfectly defended. In his call for a scholarly book like a catalogue, Benjamin seeks to make overt the parallels between researchers' and collectors' avocations, to demonstrate how scholars pluck details out of their original contexts and mount them in display cabinets of their own construction.

Perhaps the reason why Benjamin's *Arcades Project* so fascinates is that it breaks the stylistic stranglehold of the scholarly monograph, its formal air of seamless certainty. Susan Sontag's work provides one testimony to the allure of Benjamin's critical method. In *On Photography*, Sontag describes photography's summing up of reality in "an array of casual fragments" as "an endlessly alluring, poignantly reductive way of dealing with the world." She characterizes Benjamin's collecting of quotations as a sublimated version of the photographer's activity, as manifesting "a disavowal of empathy, a disdain for message-mongering, a claim to be invisible." But despite these stern comments, she ends *On Photography* with a collection of untethered quotations, subtitled "Homage to W. B."[64]

Benjamin's method has a peculiar appeal for scholars approaching literary texts that are always already encased in layers of critical verbiage, a century's accretion of response and counter-response. The *Arcades* collage, in its interrupted and interruptive form, proposes letting words from the past speak on their own, without the din of scholarly paraphrase and qualification.

"What withers in the age of the technological reproductibility of the work of art is the latter's aura," Benjamin writes in his most famous essay.[65] And, in his "Little History of Photography," Benjamin asks: "What is aura, actually? A strange weave of space and time: the unique appearance or semblance of distance, no matter how close it may be."[66]

At his death, James, too, left behind an incomplete work, *The Sense of the Past*, a novel whose protagonist longs to revisit the past through its physical vestiges, and who manages to project himself from the year 1910 back to 1820 after inheriting a London town house containing a portrait of himself in that earlier era. Ralph Pendrel is a writer whose chief work, "An Essay in Aid of the Reading of History," has moved an elderly relative to bequeath his house to its author. The old man "had nowhere seen the love of old things, of the scrutable, palpable past, nowhere felt an ear for stilled voices, as precious as they are faint, as seizable, truly, as they are fine, affirm a more remarkable power than in the pages that had moved him to gratitude." James writes of his protagonist, "He wanted evidence of a sort for which there had never been documents enough, or for which documents mainly, however multiplied, would never *be* enough."[67]

Although James sympathized with Silsbee's belief in the resonance of poets' relics, and although he shared Silsbee's fascination with the romantic period, whose poets, however unwittingly, encouraged that belief through their celebration of authenticity and originality, James's version of Silsbee's story ends badly, with Miss Bordereau's papers burned and the collector left in possession of only a small portrait of Jeffrey Aspern. "When I look at it I can scarcely bear my loss," James's protagonist comments ruefully in the story's final line. This half sentence holds open the possibility that the collector may be mourning for something other than the destroyed papers, for his failure to associate honestly with living human beings, perhaps, or for his botched effort to commune with Jeffrey Aspern through material remains. But then the sentence swings closed on the hinge of a central dash. "When I look at it I can scarcely bear my loss—I mean of the precious papers" (*Aspern*, 143). James takes the more ennobling possibilities out of circulation.

The actual Silsbee suffered a different fate. Let us imagine the scene at the Bodleian Library on the day he was supposed to hand over the guitar: a scattering of librarians scared up for the occasion, and tea ladies standing ready to pour once the presentation ceremony was over. Since John Wheeler Williams, the guitar seller, was to transport it to Oxford, Silsbee may not yet have had an opportunity to touch the vine-scrolled face of the instrument or to tune the strings or to imagine himself as an infatuated poet strumming a chord. He might have done these things at the Bodleian—if he had ever managed to get there. An explanation for why he failed to show up for the ceremony is inscribed on the back of a letter that Lucy Derby Fuller wrote to the Bodleian librarian E. W. B. Nicholson.[68] Silsbee, unfamiliar with English train stations, and assuming that the ticket office was (as in the United States) close to the track, waited there for Richard Garnett. When the Oxford train left the station, Silsbee was still waiting at the ticket office. It is not clear whether Williams was also wandering around Paddington Station, finding or not finding Garnett, and catching the Oxford train to the Bodleian ceremony.

Silsbee at Paddington, waiting perplexed amidst purposeful commuters in dark suits and trilbies, stands as an emblem of the grandiloquence and futility of certain romantic longings, the desire to connect to the past and also the desire to achieve one's own immortality through this alliance. Silsbee saw himself as being uniquely suited for the role of Shelley acolyte. He took perhaps excessive pleasure in associating himself with Oxford through his gift of the guitar—"Oxford is what that vale in Greece was to the Egyptians," he burbled in a letter to Nicholson.[69] In penning an inscription for the glass case that was to hold the guitar he had donated, Silsbee crafted a piece of purple prose that Garnett diplomatically described as "far too eloquent for Oxford," hoping that the donor would "take a reasonable view, and leave the matter to the Bodleian."[70] Lucy

Derby Fuller later requested that the words "Salem, Massachusetts" be inserted after Silsbee's name in the inscription. "I knew how much he desired it—and that inscription is his only monument," Fuller wrote. Nicholson, with admirable frankness, noted in the margins of Fuller's letter, "I meant to do it anyhow," but he never honored this request.[71]

When James's narrator in *The Aspern Papers* looks back in time, he fondly imagines a society "less awake than the coteries of to-day . . . to tatters of old stuff and fragments of old crockery" (*Aspern*, 48). He imagines those who lived during the romantic period as loftier beings, removed from the grubby materialism of his own later moment. James's narrator is, of course, mistaken in this regard. What does one see when one looks into the museums, cabinets, libraries, and exhibitions of the early nineteenth century? An inordinate number of dead hummingbirds, for one thing, as chapter 1 demonstrates. Their feathered remains, still eerily iridescent, show how a collection might seem to stave off death without actually doing so. By gazing steadily at these specimens, and by examining the attachments collectors formed to particular birds, one begins to see how romantic aesthetics and collecting practice are intertwined, and also what Keats's immortal nightingale has in common with the dead husks of hummingbirds that, today, fill rarely opened museum drawers.

This book stands as an attempt to explore the potentiality and limitations of resonant objects, and to explain the popularization of collecting in the romantic period. The pages that follow focus on collectors from all walks of life, men *and* women who fashioned identities for themselves out of the compilation and arrangement of dead birds, books, botanical specimens, Napoleonic relics, Egyptian artifacts, and fossils. The range of people who collected each of these types of objects allows me to explore the uses of collecting for individuals who least resemble the stereotypical collector. I do not, for the most part, discuss renowned romantic era collectors—William Beckford, William Hamilton, Horace Walpole, Lord Elgin, George IV—all of whom have inspired museum exhibitions and elicited critical attention.[72] When I turn to the royal family, for example, as I do in chapter 2, I look to Queen Charlotte rather than her more famous collector husband and son. Although all the royal family members were, by turns, diverted and oppressed by their collections, Charlotte's forays into bibliophilic and botanical collecting were uniquely driven by queenly ennui. Her collecting practice allows me to challenge the too automatic association of collecting and imperialistic endeavor by revealing how Charlotte used an escapist version of this activity to reinvent herself as a humble cataloguer rather than a ceremonial figurehead. In general, my choice of collectors allows me to call into question oft-repeated tenets of collecting theory, critical commonplaces best suited for describing men rather than women, aristocrats rather than parvenus, archivists rather than entrepreneurs.

In this book I also set out to read romantic era collecting practice in the context of romantic poetry, to reveal the entanglement of literary and collecting aesthetics. Beginning in the mid-eighteenth century, and spurred by the rise of industrial manufacturing and by the reach of mercantile exploration, there was an explosion in the number and type of physical things—dishware, fabric, foodstuffs.[73] I am not the first to pursue links between romantic poetry and consumer culture. Elizabeth Jones shows the ways in which Keats employs in his odes "icons that once had meaning for political cultures, but that had become commodities in a market economy."[74] Andrea Henderson analyzes how, in Joanna Baillie's introduction to her *Plays on the Passions*, human passions "function as discrete items available for inventory, display, and sale."[75] Colin Campbell posits a causal relationship between the romantic ethos of transcendence and the culture of avid consumption that characterizes modern consumerism.[76] Building on this distinguished work, I set out to show how romantic poetic preoccupations—with immortality, pastoral escape, fame, sublimity, loss—underpin the accumulative practices of both early-nineteenth-century collectors and their likeminded descendants.

One sees, for example, in the widespread fascination with Napoleonic relics a peculiar instance of the romantic preoccupation with authenticity. The collectors and purveyors of these relics, intent on establishing their objects' credentials, sometimes went so far as to create authenticating stories for entirely inauthentic relics, narratives that served a variety of ends. In chapter 3, I explore the role that Napoleon's carriage, which had been captured at Waterloo, played in the imaginative self-constructions of Napoleon collectors such as William Bullock, who exhibited the carriage at around the same time that Byron was traveling across Europe in a replica of that vehicle. William Godwin's "Essay upon Sepulchres," in its curious preoccupation with the grave sites of fictional characters, provides us with a means of understanding how a facsimile of Napoleon's carriage enhanced Byron's peripatetic poetry writing, and also how the story of the actual carriage's capture served to legitimate objects far removed from Napoleon's last battle.

Another concern, which surfaces most overtly in the book's final chapters—in chapter 4, my account of the self-made Egyptologist Giovanni Belzoni, and in chapter 5, my discussion of the fossil–finder–turned–tourist attraction Mary Anning—is the obduracy of objects, the ways in which they refuse to cooperate entirely with the collector's and, ultimately, the scholar's best-laid schemes. One sees, particularly in the case of Anning's and Belzoni's scattered remains, how collected objects float free of their possessors and come to exist in inscrutable isolation, defying scholars' efforts to recast them as definitive evidence.

Directly or indirectly, all of the collectors featured in these pages had dealings with William Bullock. A hummingbird cabinet that may once have belonged to Bullock is the impetus for chapter 1. Queen Charlotte, the focus of chapter 2, donated a Japan peacock and a painted pheasant to Bullock's museum, gifts featured prominently in his catalogue.[77] Bullock was the mastermind behind the Napoleonic carriage exhibition, and Bullock's museum, remodeled as the Egyptian Hall, became the venue for Belzoni's exhibition of Egyptiana. Some of the fossils collected by Mary Anning passed through Bullock's hands when he served as the auctioneer for the collection of Thomas Birch, an Anning family benefactor. But if I were to follow the red thread that Bullock provides, I would risk winding up with an artificially linear and misleadingly coherent account of romantic collectors and their meandering obsessions.

This book is, in one regard, a romantic history of romantic collecting.[78] It takes seriously, and by necessity shares, the tendency of romantic histories to dwell upon their own fragmentariness, on the impossibility of capturing an intact history. Ann Rigney describes the history writing of Thomas Carlyle as "historiography in a negative key," since "what a historian could and should do [was] . . . constantly silhouetted against what for better or worse had been left out."[79] Hayden White, also writing on romantic historiographers such as Carlyle, comments that they looked to history "for neither understanding nor explanation but rather for inspiration—the kind of inspiration, moreover, that an older aesthetics called sublime."[80] This is a sublimity that derives from the impossibility of comprehending the enormity and obscurity of history. Because the collectors in whom I am most interested had a limited renown, or a fame that faded quickly after their deaths, what remains of their collections has been carelessly edited and destroyed over time. My narrative dramatizes that reality with its disjunctiveness; the fragmentary nature of my telling mirrors the fragmentary state of less well known collectors' surviving collections. Wordsworth wrote of the danger of trying to piece together the past from idiosyncratic remains, of overlooking "the large over-balance of worthlessness that has been swept away," and assuming that the best of the past is "typical."[81] My structuring method underscores the idiosyncratic aspect of the remains I examine, but it also pays homage to what has been swept away by making a place for what has disappeared and by questioning the forces behind the disappearance.

Despite increased scholarly interest in material culture, objects sometimes receive short shrift even in critical work that traffics in them.[82] Academic writing often does a poor job of capturing the sensuous appeal of particular objects, which may be one reason why collectors do not always receive judicious treatment. Benjamin (both as a sympathetic commentator on collecting and as a collector who has himself benefited from sympathetic commentary) is, of course, the exception to this generalization, particularly when he talks about himself as a collector of books. In a passage titled "Fancy Goods" in *One-Way Street*, he writes, "When a valued, cultured and elegant friend sent me his new book and I was about to open it, I caught myself in the act of straightening my tie."[83] In contrast to those who see the collector projecting himself onto everything he collects—"For what you really collect is always yourself," Baudrillard insists—Benjamin imagines the owner of an object courting its favor. He writes of collected objects, "We don't displace our being into theirs; they step into our life."[84]

This book traces the particular ways in which objects stepped into the lives of romantic collectors, and also the ways in which the objects moved on, leaving their collectors inevitably dead and almost as inevitably bereft of the forms of recognition they thought would accrue to them by association. The Shelley collector Edward Silsbee, both in his devotion to the poet's material remains and in his confidence that this devotion would win him a measure of immortality, stands as the inheritor of a constellation of romantic beliefs that fueled the practice of collecting.[85] In the pages that follow, I trace Silsbee's ardent and misguided pursuits back to their literary origins.

CHAPTER ONE

HUMMINGBIRD COLLECTORS AND ROMANTIC POETRY

Any day now, the hummingbirds in the London Natural History Museum may go missing. The birds are arrayed in a nineteenth-century glass cabinet the size of a circus car which may or may not have belonged once to William Bullock, the London Museum curator. They are faded from having spent so many years on display; it seems only a matter of time before they are relegated to deep storage along with decaying fossil mounts and fake dinosaur bones. Even second-rate hummingbird specimens, a little dull or loose in feather, have the power to fascinate, and one takes a guilty pleasure in looking at the gorgeous dead birds. Sapphire hummingbirds cluster in one area of the cabinet and ruby-breasted birds in another. Try to work out, in an ornithologically challenged kind of way, which birds might be "star-throats," and whether the orangey birds with the speckled tail feathers are "coquettes." You will feel confident only about the sword-billed hummingbirds; they must be the birds with beaks as long as swizzle sticks and slightly curved.

"There is not, it may safely be asserted, in all the varied works of nature in her zoological productions, any family that can bear a comparison, for singularity of form, splendour of colour, or number and variety of species, with this the smallest of the feathered creation," Bullock observed of hummingbirds in 1824.[1] Bullock described the appeal of the hummingbird for collectors in the early decades of the nineteenth century, a moment when the number of bird species known to English naturalists proliferated. The tenth edition of Linnaeus's *System Naturae*, published in 1758, identified only eighteen hummingbird species; by 1829, when R. P. Lesson began publishing his magisterial *Les trochildees ou les colibris et les oiseaux-mouches*, the first illustrated work devoted exclusively to "fly-birds," he described over a hundred species. To be a collector of hummingbirds in the romantic period was to experience the most inspirational collecting conditions: a seemingly endless supply of new types of birds, each potentially lovelier than the last. Racket-tailed hummingbird, fire-throated hummingbird, emerald-crested hummingbird—each flitted enticingly across the collector's field of vision.

In a surviving image of Bullock, he is dressed elegantly in a double-breasted half coat and ascot, his amiable expression calling to mind neither a rapacious collector nor a Barnumesque huckster. He was both. Bullock traveled to the Orkneys in order to hunt down one of the last surviving great auks. Paddling in a six-oared boat, he came close to catching one harried bird, but had to settle for purchasing its carcass from another hunter the following year.[2] He sought advice on whether he might put on show "the Head of Oliver Cromwell still intire with the flesh on" and fixed on a pike.[3] But no counsel prevented him from exhibiting a family of Laplanders as if they were reindeer antlers or leggings or any of the other Lapp accoutrements he featured in the same show.

Bullock learned his museum trade at the knee of his mother, the curator of "a most beautiful Cabinet of WAX FIGURES."[4] Mrs. Bullock molded effigies of famous dead people: the French royal family, Benjamin Franklin.[5] Her son became the impresario of a "Pantherion" of dead animals preserved by the magic of newly effective taxidermy techniques. Of all the creatures gathered in his well-stocked display cabinets, hummingbirds were heralded by Bullock as "the most splendid as well as the most diminutive creatures in this tribe of creation."[6]

Hummingbirds were for Bullock a focus of enduring fascination. His museum catalogues chart an upward trajectory in the resident hummingbird population, as if the stuffed birds procreated posthumously in the confines of his display cabinets. A case containing "24 species with their Nests" featured in the 1805 catalogue of Bullock's Liverpool Museum had expanded into a cabinet holding seventy hummingbirds by the time he moved his collections to London in 1810.[7] By 1812, Bullock boasted of having nearly one hundred various hummingbirds, "the finest collection in Europe."[8]

The hummingbird cabinet that survives in the Natural History Museum is positioned in close proximity to a beak exhibit featuring the severed heads of puffin, butcher bird, and hornbill. The signage in the gallery is defensive in tone. Posted next to the hummingbird cabinet, a small cardboard placard headed with the phrase "An Antique Collection" notes that the display "whilst being a fascinating artifact . . . is also a sad reminder of the price many birds have to pay for their splendid plumage." The Natural History Museum wants visitors to know that the specimens in this gallery are from the museum's historical bird collection, "which dates back over the last two hundred years." A card attached to a floor-to-ceiling case featuring beautifully plumed birds such as Lady Amherst's pheasant and Lawes's six-plumed bird of paradise concedes that "most people enjoy looking at beautiful specimen displays," but goes on to state that "the Museum no longer has an active collecting programme and would only display new specimens within rigorous conservation guidelines." The gallery's curators anticipate the opening of "a new, permanent bird gallery, presenting a contemporary view of bird biology, ecology and conservation using some of the latest techniques in multi-media display."[9]

The new gallery will be unlikely to shed any light on the longings and desires that were evoked by hummingbirds in the romantic period. It will not, I expect, help us to see how romantic modes of feeling fueled the pursuit of hummingbirds, or how they influenced the style of their display, or why they drove some admirers of the birds to a state of desolate despair. To understand those things, you are better off studying the antique hummingbird cabinet even though it uses one medium, presents an inaccurate view of bird biology, and has nothing to say about ecology and conservation, except that the blithe collecting that led to its creation predated any concern about bird population decline.

The hummingbird cabinet is large but easy to overlook; from a distance it looks like a neglected terrarium in which the foliage has been allowed to dry. But if you peer closely at this desiccated thicket, it blooms with hundreds of hummingbirds posed stiffly on every branch. Most people tend to glance at the hummingbird cabinet and move on, unaware that they are observing what Bullock called the crown jewels of the bird kingdom (see fig. 2).

We do not know whether Bullock ever read the *Lyrical Ballads*, but the museum-goer he depicts in his catalogue is a Wordsworthian being, recollecting in tranquility the pleasures of the museum visit. Bullock's "Companion" to the museum (as his catalogue was titled) promised to serve "in private" as "a pleasing resource" that would assist its possessors "in explaining to the circle of their friends, the gratification they have received; for, next to the enjoyment of beholding what is strange or beautiful, is the desire of recounting the wonders we have seen."[10] The Wordsworthian recollecting of emotion and the Bullockian recollecting of stuffed hummingbirds might seem to have little in common, but naturalists regularly embellished collecting manuals in the early nineteenth century with epigraphs from romantic poets. These literary flourishings emphasized "the legitimacy, intellectual worth, and spiritual potential of the activities they described."[11] Romantic poetry helped to distance the activity of collecting from the acquisitive, materialistic associations with which a romantic poet might have viewed this endeavor.

Fig. 2. Hummingbird cabinet. Copyright © The Natural History Museum, London.

There is possibly, however, a more integral link between romantic aesthetics and the rise of collecting as a popular avocation. Colin Campbell traces a connection between the spiritual longings we associate with romanticism and the rise of modern consumerism, which he characterizes as a self-delusory hedonism, a longing for imagined but unattainable sensations.[12] Modern consumers, like romantic poets, in Campbell's account, conjure up scenes in their imaginations that lead to pleasurable experiences of emotion, but these pleasurable states of mind cannot be matched by any experience in the actual world. The result is an inexhaustible desire for novelty, for new products, the experience of which promises to match the pleasurable imagined state. "It is largely novelty itself," Campbell writes, "that is being consumed, and since novelty is necessarily extinguished in the very process of its consumption, this serves to explain how it is that the generation of wants is endless."[13]

One can extend Campbell's argument: the fears and longings that were enacted in romantic poems, the overbearing sense of loss and ephemerality, also helped turn England into a nation of collectors. Hummingbirds elicited that trance of longing in which the collector constantly and pleasurably anticipates the latest new specimen to catch his attention. Just as any number of Keatsian characters are caught in a thrall of almost-bliss, the hummingbird collector lived in anticipation of the next, more beautiful bird to glint enticingly before his avid gaze.

There are surprisingly few hummingbirds in romantic poetry, and the ones that do make an appearance are far overshadowed by better-known birds—Coleridge's albatross, for example, or Shelley's skylark. The most famous romantic bird was the one Keats heard while sitting under a plum tree in Charles Brown's garden. Brown recalled: "In the spring of 1819 a nightingale had built her nest near my house. Keats felt a tranquil and continual joy in her song; and one morning he took his chair from the breakfast-table to the grass-plot under a plum-tree, where he sat for two or three hours." Brown credited his own foresightedness with rescuing Keats's "Ode to a Nightingale" from certain oblivion, his observation "that every short poem, which [the poet] was tempted to compose, was scrawled on the first piece of paper at hand, and that it was afterwards used as a mark to a book, or thrust any where aside." When Keats, having come in from under the plum tree, quietly shoved slips of paper behind some books, the keen-eyed Brown sought them out ("four or five in number"), puzzled over Keats's penmanship ("The writing was not well legible"), and arranged the scattered stanzas into "Ode to a Nightingale" ("a poem which has been the delight of every one").[14]

This account is very likely untrue. The manuscript of the poem consists of two half sheets, "neither of them a 'scrap.'"[15] Still, the story plays out the same tension between immortality and ephemerality that is written into the "Ode." "Thou wast not born for death, immortal Bird!" Keats writes in a stanza that has been fretting critics for years (281). Allen Tate calls this stanza the only one in Keats's ode that "contains a statement contradictory of our sense of common reality,"[16] and H. W. Garrod explains the contradiction by arguing that the nightingale goes from being a particular bird to a myth in phrases such as "light-winged Dryad of the trees."[17] It has also been suggested that Keats is thinking of the species, not the individual bird, when he makes the claim for its immortality, or that the nightingale's song represents "a universal and undying voice: the voice of nature, of imaginative sympathy, and therefore of an ideal Romantic poetry."[18] In a particularly ingenious reading—one can see the critic turning cartwheels to defend Keats against poetic weakness or false thinking—Andrew J. Kappel eloquently suggests that the bird's immortality is a result of its ignorance of death: "For the bird there is, in a stricter sense than usual, no tomorrow, only a series of todays, and the easy ecstasy of its singing can seem wasteful only to an ontology for which there is a tomorrow and which, hoping to live in it, invents conservation."[19]

The stuffed hummingbirds, by their very survival, seem to bear out Keats's line—even as they uncomfortably remind us of their own premature and unnecessary deaths. Since hummingbirds were New World birds which, in the early decades of the nineteenth century, had never been transported live to England, they seemed the most perishable of living things, delicate in flight, and doomed to die if removed from their natural habitat. But the hummingbird skins that made it to British ports in various states of preservation retained a colorful beauty which outlasted death and which stirred collectors to pursue more and better bird specimens.

The hummingbird owes its appeal to its shimmery plumage, a feature that caused admirers in the romantic period and ever since to compare it to jewels. "The precious stones polished by art, cannot be compared to this jewel of nature," wrote Bullock in his museum catalogue, quoting from the *History of Birds* of George-Louis Leclerc, the comte de Buffon. "The emerald, the ruby, and the topaz, sparkle in its plumage, which is never soiled by the dust of the ground."[20] This comparison of the birds' sparkly feathers to gemstones was constantly reasserted, especially in English nomenclature, which identified species of hummingbirds as garnets, rubies, sapphire-wings, sun-gems, sparkling-tails, emeralds, and brilliants. The hummingbird's iridescence is a structural feature, a permanent attribute caused by the fine anatomy of feather barbs and not by pigments—"Hence they do not fade however long they are exposed to light."[21] In describing the ruby hummingbird, Buffon noted that "the feathers of the throat are fashioned and disposed like scales, round and detached; which arrangement multiplies the reflections, that play both on the neck and the head of the fly-birds, among all their sparkling feathers."[22]

Buffon set the literary standard in scientific description, and Bullock cribs shamelessly from the ornithological volumes of Buffon's *Natural History*. The French naturalist's poetic elaboration of anatomy and behavior inspired lapidary descriptions of the birds, and a tendency toward both objectification and personification. Bullock described hummingbirds adding "to the high finish and beauty of the western landscape." In an account of the birds as nest builders, another hummingbird enthusiast wrote, "The nidification of the Humming-Birds is as singular as are the birds themselves." This same bird lover particularly praised the lavish decoration of the nests' outer walls: "With the utmost taste do these birds instinctively fasten thereon beautiful pieces of flat lichen."[23] Caught up in the spell of the hummingbird's splendid coloration and charming habits, the prose style of the natural historian took on a shimmery plumage of its own.

Collectors signaled the hummingbird's particular appeal as bijouterie by building display cases for them in isolation from other bird cabinets. The Philadelphia Museum curator Charles Willson Peale displayed a tree of hummingbirds under a glass dome on a stanchion in a gallery where bird cases were stacked four high along two walls. In Bullock's Liverpool Museum, the hummingbirds occupied a bell glass that stood upon "an elegant bronzed Egyptian tripod."[24]

Bullock's hummingbird cabinet, his gathering of dozens of birds in a snarl of branches, as if some important hummingbird conclave had just been called, represented a style of display that was in vogue during the early decades of the nineteenth century. William Swainson, in his 1836 *On the Natural History and Classification of Birds*, charts a trajectory from the custom of showing each species in a wooden case by itself to "the last and best" method of leaving the birds "in their skins" and arranging them in drawers. In between these two scientifically justifiable extremes lies Bullock's method, "the fashion of grouping the birds upon branches, fastened into large cases, on the back and sides of which were painted landscapes, &c.," a plan best calculated, according to Swainson, to produce "effect." "For those persons who merely possess a few splendid specimens for show, this is, perhaps, the best way of displaying them to advantage," Swainson wrote. For scientific purposes, however, it served little function, given "the comparative obscurity in which very many of the birds must be thrown."[25]

Although hummingbirds were not the only birds grouped together in decorative arrangements, the birds' size increased the enthusiasm for and the ease of creating these kinds of conglomerations. Commentators constantly remarked on the birds' tininess, lavishing their full descriptive powers on depictions of the minute. Listing the hummingbird's claims to being most worthy of notice, Bullock included its size, which he dramatized by pointing out that "some are so small that a cockchaffer would destroy them by collision in mid-air."[26]

Susan Stewart maintains that there are no miniatures in nature, that the miniature is a cultural product, the result of a certain way of looking at things, of manipulating the physical world.[27] Dollhouses are miniatures, and so are the miniature license plates or state flags you can buy at truck stops, because they have been specifically manufactured to charm the kind of person who likes imagining fanciful realms where a teapot the size of your thumb pad would be useful. Small natural objects, like acorns or fleas, are not miniatures, according to Stewart's argument, because they are not small replicas of something larger—they are merely small natural objects. It is tempting to think of hummingbirds as miniature birds, especially when you take into account the species known as "wood-stars," which are scarcely bigger than large bees; wood-stars, one might argue, are miniature versions of already miniature birds, but they are not miniatures in Stewart's sense of the term because they are not human constructs.

Romantic poets used the natural littleness of hummingbirds in the service of theatrical fantasies that do accord with Stewart's sense of the miniature as a realm apart. A poem titled "The Hummingbird," published as part of Charlotte Smith's 1804 *Conversations Introducing Poetry: Chiefly on Subjects of Natural History* (but most likely written by Smith's sister, Catherine Anne Dorset), begins by addressing the bird as "Minutest of the feather'd kind" and by describing the bird's "lovely fairy race" as "Beauty's epitome." The poem then proceeds:

> There, lovely Bee-bird! may'st thou rove
> Thro' spicy vale, and citron grove,
> And woo, and win thy fluttering love
> With plume so bright;
> There rapid fly, more heard than seen,
> Mid orange-boughs of polished green,
> With glowing fruit, and flowers between
> Of purest white.[28]

The poem transforms natural habitat into decorative ornamental realm and the bird into an ardent suitor. The hummingbird of the poem is an entirely human construct, one that seems better suited for a music box than any natural locale.

Keats, too, invokes the hummingbird to depict a fanciful realm that bears little resemblance to any actual bird habitat. One of his earliest poems, "On Receiving a Curious Shell, and a Copy of Verses, From the Same Ladies," begins with an address to an imaginary knight:

> Hast thou from the caves of Golconda, a gem
>> Pure as the ice-drop that froze on the mountain?
> Bright as the humming-bird's green diadem,
>> When it flutters in sun-beams that shine through a fountain? (10)

Keats's hummingbird flies into the poem only long enough to suggest the appropriate bird population for an entirely literary realm, a realm inspired, perhaps, by the "copy of verses" mentioned in the title: a transcript of "The Wreath and the Chain" by Thomas Moore. Of Moore's poetry, one reader enthused, "I never met with anything that carried me so completely away into the midst of Roses and . . . Perfumes and Hummingbirds and Jewels and all manner of Precious Stones."[29]

"What is more gentle than a wind in summer?" Keats begins "Sleep and Poetry," before he makes his second poetic reference to hummingbirds: "What is more soothing than the pretty hummer / That stays one moment in an open flower, / And buzzes cheerily from bower to bower?" (37). Although the hummingbird makes one appearance in the poem, it seems to reside subliminally throughout; the poem is full of hovering entities. Keats calls the bird to mind when he conjures up "shapes of light, aerial lymning," and the "soft floatings from a faint-heard hymning," this last in referring to thoughts of poetry. He addresses poetry as "ye whose charge / It is to hover round our pleasant hills!" and he writes that "imaginings will hover / Round [his] fire-side and haply there discover / Vistas of solemn beauty" (38, 42, 39).

The first lines of the poem link the hummingbird to bowers, those otherworldly realms which Keats often conflates with the remove of poetry. Just as the title of the poem associates poetry and a state of unconsciousness, so does the Keatsian bower promise a similar state of remove, the realm of imaginative pleasure, but one that is linked to death in its preternatural serenity. When, in "Sleep and Poetry," the narrator imagines a state of poetic apprenticeship for himself, he envisions a sensual retreat where, partnered by one of the "white-handed nymphs" (another group of hovering figures), he will reside "in the bosom of a leafy world." Together, they will rest in silence "like two gems up-curl'd / In the recesses of a pearly shell" (40). The images seem both beautiful and morbid, artistic and marmoreal.

The mummified remains of hummingbirds, birds that were known more than any other for their extraordinary liveliness—"little flutterers," Buffon called them—similarly invoked both perfection and deathliness.[30] Although the preserved birds had been granted a measure of immortality, their stillness could be unsettling. They looked as if they had been caught in some bird version of a game of statues. But if you touched one, it would fall over instead of flying away.

In his *Taxidermy*, William Swainson recommends that the bird collector set out early in the morning, equipped with fowling pieces, powder and shot, arsenical soap, pen knives, both sharp- and blunt-pointed scissors, cotton or tow, and a box made of tin to keep specimens cool. "In two or three hours," Swainson writes, "a sufficient number may be killed to occupy the collector during the rest of the day in stuffing."[31]

Bullock, too, was an enthusiastic proponent of do-it-yourself taxidermy. In his 1817 guide *A Concise and Easy Method of Preserving Objects of Natural History, Intended for the Use of Sportsmen, Travellers, &C. &C. to Enable Them to Collect and Prepare Such Curious and Rare Articles as They May Wish to Preserve, or to Transmit in Safety to Any Part of the World*, Bullock provided short and simple directions for stuffing birds. He breezily advised the amateur taxidermist to remove the bird's brain through an opening in its neck "by introducing a gouge, the handle of a tea spoon, or some such blunt instrument," after which, he instructed, the pupil should "cut away the tongue, and as much as possible of the flesh of the head and mouth." Finally, "care must now be taken to remove the eyes whole by the inside."[32] Bullock also supplied his readers with a recipe for preserving powder (one pound of arsenic, one pound of burnt allum, two pounds of tanners' bark, it began), which could be purchased ready-made at his museum. Sarah Lee, in her *Taxidermy; or, The Art of Collecting, Preparing, and Mounting Objects of Natural History, for the Use of Museums and Travellers*, detailed the most desirable technique for preserving hummingbirds, a strategy that involved making an incision through the breastbone, removing all soft parts with scissors, and filling the remaining cavity with cotton. There is no hint of squeamishness in Bullock's treatise or in Lee's directives on the proper way to eviscerate a hummingbird so as to retain "all the beauty and freshness of life."[33]

The romantic period corresponded with advances in taxidermy that made it possible, for the first time, to halt the progress of degradation in dead animal skins. The reason why there are no preserved dodo bird specimens extant is that the dodo suffered extinction before the taxidermist's arts became sophisticated enough to stop a dead bird from rotting away. The transition from an old method based on the use of sulfur and turpentine to a new reliance on arsenic as a preservative allowed birds, for the first time, to endure beyond death.

Bullock engaged the services of the professional "bird-stuffer" Josiah Nuttall, whose self-proclaimed artistry precariously survives in a few letters preserved in the holdings of the London Linnean Society. Detailing his pricing scheme to a potential customer, Nuttall wrote:

The small Birds I erected from the size of an Humming Bird to a Thrush—Mr Bullock gave me three shillings and sixpence each the price he told me had allways given. . . . I am now talking about good Birds and good work. Birds that I can dress without a shade and smooth as velvet and the very mind of the Bird—(wildly speaking) brought back again with action in the Limbs and in attitude easy—but if you would like them in the old goggle eye'd Rear'd up [Faker] way—I will do them at 2–6.[34]

The emphasis on naturalness, the attempt to position the bird's limbs as they would be in life, the effort to reveal its wild mind all echo the romantic appreciation of naturalness and authenticity; but the promise taxidermy held out of staving off the ravages of death, at the moment of its first successful realization in the early nineteenth century, was not entirely trustworthy.

Writing to William Swainson, Nuttall described the difficulty of "re-erecting" birds or rejuvenating old mountings gone bad. "Have in general found them the worst of subjects often moth eaten and the skins much broken," he wrote, presumably in reference to previously mounted birds requiring his services. "I once received from Mr Bullock one pound for the erection of a ground [Fyron] which is no larger than a Lark," he continued. "I had it to compose from single feathers." If Bullock was sending Nuttall clumps of feathers to turn back into birds, one can imagine that the visitor to his museum would have seen specimens in varying stages of decay. Swainson, in advocating the filing away of bird skins in drawers as the optimal mode of storage, noted that the exposure of plumage to light "entirely takes off the freshness and brilliancy of birds in the London collections in three or four years."[35]

Still, the precarious state of preservation did not dispel its wondrousness for those who first witnessed its promise. The curatorial woes of Charles Willson Peale, Bullock's American counterpart at the Philadelphia Museum, were mostly caused by "imprudent visitors" who insisted on manhandling the exhibits. "*Do not touch the birds, they are covered with arsnic Poison*," Peale warned on boards he posted in different parts of his museum. Yet, despite his best deterrent efforts, Peale lamented, "it has often been seen that persons while reading these precausinary notices would be stroking the Animals with their hands in a thought-less manner."[36]

A century later the enthusiasm of hummingbird spectators would become complicated by an awareness of collecting carnage. "Those pellets of dead feathers, which had long ceased to sparkle and shine, stuck with wires—not invisible—over blossoming cloth and tinsel bushes, how melancholy they made me feel!" wrote the naturalist W. H. Hudson in 1917 after he visited John Gould's collection of hummingbirds, crammed into that ornithologist's drawing room at 20 Broad Street, London.[37] But the melancholy that Hudson felt at the beginning of the twentieth century cannot be retroactively projected onto the collectors and would-be collectors who followed Bullock's directives. Romantic era viewers were apparently so caught up in taxidermy's magical ability to offset rot and decay that they were able to look at stuffed hummingbirds and marvel at getting to see birds in intimate detail, rather than shudder, like Hudson, at death gussied up with blossoming cloth and tinsel bushes. Hudson's negative reaction to the sheer volume of Gould's collection, its limitless seriality, would not have occurred to spectators newly impressed with collections and their orderly arrangements, and not yet troubled by thoughts of mass bird extinction.

For his 1805 exhibition catalogue, William Bullock described hummingbirds as having wings "so rapid in motion, that it is impossible to discern their colours, except by their glittering; they are never still, but continually visiting flower after flower, and extracting the honey."[38] Buffon wrote, "Their flight is buzzing, continued, and rapid."[39] Neither Bullock nor Buffon had seen a hummingbird fly when they wrote these descriptions. The bird-stuffer Nuttall, positioned at a remove from the South American forests where hummingbirds thrived, aspired in his work to a "naturalness" that was wholly imagined. Not having seen live birds, he would have had no way of knowing how closely the "attitude easy" of the birds he crafted approximated the poses of live birds. This disparity between the imagined live bird and the dead specimens epitomizes the romantic aspect of hummingbird collecting. The brilliant coloration of dead hummingbirds evoked the more animated brilliance of the living ones, holding out the tantalizing possibility that the next, more natural specimen might be able to satisfy the insatiable longing to see the bird in flight.

Bullock finally saw his first live hummingbird in early 1823 during a stop in Jamaica on his way to Mexico. He first heard, rather than glimpsed, the bird, which was emitting a "slight querulous note" as it perched in the highest branch of a breadfruit tree (*Travels in Mexico*, 266). He had auctioned off the contents of his London museum in 1819, but the trip rekindled his covetousness for hummingbirds. "In my former collection the variety of different species amounted to near a hundred, and every day brings us acquainted with more," he wrote, continuing, "In Jamaica I procured the smallest known, which is considerably less than some of the bees;—and in Mexico many new species, whose splendid colours glow with a brilliancy and lustre not surpassed by any with which we were previously acquainted" (*Travels in Mexico*, 263).

Bullock was facing all the familiar hummingbird collecting inducements—the allure of smallness, of jewel-like coloration, of splendor surpassing that of previously acquired specimens. But he was particularly transfixed by the living bird. "I often approached within a few feet, with pleasure observing his tiny operation of dressing and pluming, and listening to his weak, simple, and often-repeated note," Bullock recalled. "I could easily have caught him, but was unwilling to destroy so interesting a little visitant, who had afforded me so much pleasure" (*Travels in Mexico*, 265).

Bullock's hesitancy to collect live birds did not last. He embarked on a scheme to transport living hummingbirds to England, and, by offering a reward, accumulated nearly seventy, which he kept in cages. "Could I have devoted my whole attention to them, I have no doubt of the possibility of bringing them alive to Europe," Bullock wrote, although in actuality all his pent-up hummingbirds perished in a matter of weeks. Bullock furnished each cage with a small earthen cup half filled with sugar and water, and containing the yellow bell-shaped corolla of the great aloe—into which, he wrote, "the little prisoners were constantly inserting their long bifed tongues, and drawing up its luscious contents." Bullock marveled at the birds' constant flight, oblivious to the cruelty of the constraints he placed upon them. "It is true they are seldom off the wing, but never beat themselves against the case, nor the glass of a window; they remain, as it were, suspended in the air, in a space barely sufficient for them to move their wings, and the humming noise proceeds entirely from the surprising velocity with which they perform that motion by which they will keep their bodies in the air, apparently motionless, for hours together" (*Travels in Mexico*, 267–68).

Still, the experience of seeing the live birds cast a pall over his collection of dead ones. "Europeans who have seen only the stuffed remains of these little feathered gems in museums have been charmed with their beautiful appearance; but those who have examined them whilst living, displaying their moving crests, throats, and tails, like the peacock in the sun, can never look with pleasure on their mutilated forms," he wrote sadly. "I have carefully preserved about two hundred specimens, in the best possible manner, yet they are still but the shadow of what they were in life" (*Travels in Mexico*, 272–73).

John Gould also went to great lengths to bring a live hummingbird to England. A renowned publisher of books on natural history, Gould routinely sold his collections of particular species of birds when he had finished illustrating them, but he never parted with his hummingbird collection. "That our enthusiasm and excitement with regard to most things becomes lessened, if not deadened by time, particularly when we have acquired what we vainly consider a complete knowledge of the subject, is, I fear, too often the case with most of us," he wrote in his *Introduction to the Trochilidae, or Family of Humming-Birds*, going on to insist that "the pleasure which I experience on seeing a Humming-Bird is as great at the present moment as when I first saw one."[40]

Gould recounted his unsuccessful attempt to transport live hummingbirds, writing: "The little cage in which they lived was twelve inches long, by seven inches wide, and eight inches high. In this was placed a diminutive branch of a tree, and suspended to the side a glass phial which I daily supplied with saccharine matter in the form of sugar or honey and water, with the addition of the yelk of an unboiled egg." Gould's portable museum case made the birds available to spectators but curtailed the distinctive movement which was a chief impetus for collecting them alive. Gould, too, was particularly struck by the vibratory motion of the birds' wings—"exactly the opposite of what I expected"—but his carrier box cramped all movement.[41] We cannot know whether it was this confinement or the egg yolk diet that killed off the birds; only one made it as far as London and then succumbed the second day after arriving at Gould's house.

"They hang amidst *fuchsia* flowers, or float over beds of *bromelia*. . . . They dart long beaks into deep, tubular flowers, hovering beneath the pendant bells," wrote Charles Dickens about the specimens hanging from invisible wires in Gould's hummingbird exhibition, which drew 75,000 visitors to the London Zoological Gardens in 1851. "They poise themselves in the air, we hear not the humming of the wings, but we can almost fancy there is a voice in that beauty," he enthused.[42] In an effort to re-create the birds in flight, Gould displayed them in revolving cases, stage-lit so that the light would glint off their feathers. "It is impossible to imagine anything so lovely as these little Humming Birds," Queen Victoria wrote in her journal, "their variety and the extraordinary brilliancy of their colours."[43]

For at least one spectator, Gould's carefully staged birds in flight tragically evoked the more animated trajectories of living ones. After admiring Gould's hummingbird collection, John Ruskin lamented: "I have wasted my life with mineralogy, which has led to nothing. Had I devoted myself to birds, their life and plumage, I might have produced something myself worth doing. If I could only have seen a humming-bird fly, it would have been an epoch in my life."[44] Ruskin's existential crisis was likely provoked by the hummingbird's ambiguous status. Arrestingly beautiful artifacts, the birds in Gould's display conjured up even more beautiful, but also impossibly remote, live birds. The hummingbird

stationed in flight evoked a resplendent beauty of the most romantically unattainable kind.

W illiam Bullock stands as the materialistic alter ego of the romantic poets.
He was swept up in the same nexus of preoccupations with which their
poetry is infused, but he was moved to collect objects rather than to write
poems. One of Bullock's last schemes, a plan to develop his own town, tucked
into a curve of the Ohio River about two miles below Cincinnati, echoed the
more famous plan of Robert Southey and Samuel Taylor Coleridge, who, nearly
thirty years before, had dreamed of establishing a utopia in Kentucky. Their
community was transported, while still a theoretical construct, to the banks of
the Susquehanna, where Southey optimistically imagined he and Coleridge
would saw down trees while discussing metaphysics, part of a vision so innocent
of the harsh realities of agricultural labor and North American winters that it is
fortunate the two poets never wielded axes in the wilderness. The scheme
foundered for lack of funding, the aspiring commune dwellers fell out with each
other, and Southey and Coleridge's Pantisocracy (as Coleridge had named the
utopian society) became a resonant, if unfulfilled, epoch in the history of the romantic period, a gleaming instance of the visionary zeal and unworldly idealism
we commonly associate with that era's poets.

Bullock's more commercial plan for Hygeia, named after the goddess of
health, came closer to fruition than the Pantisocratic dream. Bullock purchased
property from a member of the Kentucky legislature; "Mr. Bullock's House" is
indicated cartographically by a block on the surviving map of the area. The map

also depicts four central squares inscribed in a circle of trees and bounded to the south by flower and vegetable gardens, in addition to three municipal buildings: a town hall, a library, and a museum (see fig. 3). Frances Trollope, who visited Kentucky in 1828, reasonably wondered at Bullock's decision to establish himself there: "It is impossible to help feeling that Mr. Bullock is rather out of his element in this remote spot, and the gems of art he has brought with him shew as strangely there, as would a bower of roses in Siberia, or a Cincinnati fashionable at Almack's." Trollope recalled Bullock showing his collection of engravings to "some gentlemen of the first standing, the very *élite* of Cincinnati," only to have one of them ask: "Have you really done all these since you came here? How hard you must have worked!"[45] The rage for collecting engraved portraits had long held London in its grip, but it apparently had not yet reached the Ohio Valley.[46]

By the time Bullock was pursuing the Hygeian scheme, Coleridge, his Pantisocracy long abandoned, was publishing "Constancy to an Ideal Object," a poem whose title calls to mind physical objects like the ones Bullock made a career of pursuing. Coleridge's ideal object, however, is not a material thing but rather the "Fond Thought" of a beloved other who lives only in the narrator's imagination, a figment of his obsessive devotion who is rendered perfect by his desire. The poem begins:

> Since all, that beat about in Nature's range,
> Or veer or vanish; why should'st thou remain
> The only constant in a world of change,
> O yearning THOUGHT, that liv'st but in the brain?[47]

The poem's "Object," that is, seems to exist in a different realm from the material objects Bullock collected and arranged in his museums. The poem's narrator addresses his illusory "loveliest friend," wishing that the "meed" of all his toils might be "To have a home, an English home, and thee!" Actual English homes in Coleridge's day were increasingly cluttered with stuff, most notably objects of their owners' peculiar collecting obsessions: cupboards of china, trays full of shells, and cabinets of stuffed birds. But the poem conjures up none of that material detritus in its mention of home. As quickly as the narrator evokes an En-

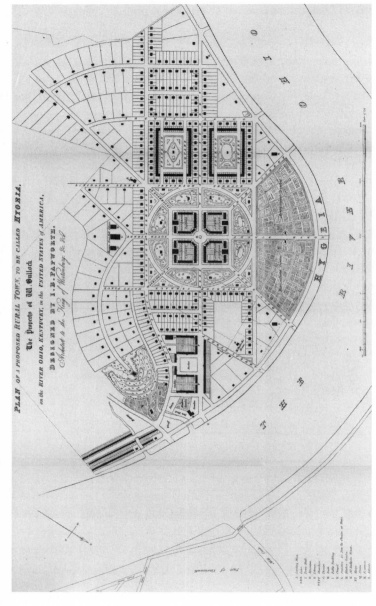

Fig. 3. Plan of a proposed rural town. By kind permission of the British Library. British Library catalogue no. 792.f.20.

glish home, he leaves that stolid entity behind, associating home, instead, with an imagined loved one rather than with a fixed locale:

> Vain repetition! Home and Thou are one.
> The peacefull'st cot, the moon shall shine upon,
> Lulled by the Thrush and wakened by the Lark
> Without thee were but a becalmed Bark,
> Whose Helmsman on an Ocean waste and wide
> Sits mute and pale his mouldering helm beside."[48]

The becalmed helmsman with his moldering tiller recalls the loitering knight of Keats's "La Belle Dame sans Merci," and Coleridge's birds, the thrush and the lark, toll us back to Keats's "Ode to a Nightingale." Coleridge, too, was inspired to write nightingale poems, the least noted of these a late untitled fragment which reads in its entirety:

> On the weak Spray of a Slim Ash,
> Whose few poor yearly Leaves
> Shook in the Gale and glitterd in the Spray
> Of a nigh Waterfall, I saw a Nightingale.
> And by the heaving plumage of her Throat and busy Bill
> That seemed to cut the Air,
> I saw he sang—
> And sure he heard not his own song or did but inly hear—
> With such a loud confused sound
> The Cataract spread wide around—[49]

These lines were originally written continuously as prose in one of Coleridge's notebooks. The ephemerality of the snippet's claim to being a poem mirrors the ephemerality of the world that Coleridge depicts within the poem. The "heaving plumage" and "busy Bill" of the nightingale stand out against the backdrop of the weak slim ash with its few remaining leaves. The bird in the poem, like the birds that were rounded up and mounted by collectors, holds out a promise of permanent vibrancy, but this permanency is threatened by the perishable nature of its surroundings. And just as "Constancy to an Ideal Object" takes the solid notion of home and transforms it into a spiritual attachment, so here the focus turns from the full-throated bird to its unbodied song, a tune even the nightingale itself can only "inly hear."

Bullock, by contrast, when he envisioned a home at Hygeia, focused on material goods. He imagined the town's inhabitants as museum attenders, or perhaps even collectors themselves, the kind of people who would appreciate the giant bone exhibit that he tried to wrest from a New Orleans museum curator at around the same time he was planning his retirement community. "I offered a considerable sum for these immense remains," Bullock recalled, "but the proprietor refused to part with them, assuring me that it was his intention to procure the remainder of them, and then take them to Europe."[50] Bullock did not last long in the American heartland. He traveled on to Venezuela, and back to London, then on to Berlin, where, in 1842, he wrote to Madame Tussaud's son in order to vouch for the authenticity of some Napoleonic relics. Before he embarked on his peripatetic final years, however, he had disencumbered himself of his hummingbirds.

The range and resonant associations of Bullock's hummingbird collection, its participation in the cluster of feelings we associate with romantic poetry, became most vividly apparent at the moment of its dissolution when the birds in Bullock's London museum were displayed for one last time and then sold at auction over the course of twenty-six days from April 29 to June 11, 1819, a few years before he traveled to Mexico.[51] The auction inspired rash behavior. A bidder for the University of Edinburgh planned to wait until the bidding was over and snatch up bargains in the aftermath, but, despite his caution, he found himself being swept along in the tide of specimens. "To day I have perhaps too many monkeys," he commented after the sixth day's sale."[52]

If you were not already a hummingbird collector, Bullock's auction might have turned you into one. His catalogue descriptions highlighted the rarity and charm of his birds. Who would not have been tempted to bid for the "Beautiful Blue Forked-tailed Humming Bird from Peru" or the "Bar-tailed Humming Bird of Shaw, from Mexico; a magnificent species, the only one in Europe"? Anyone might have felt a pang of remorse when the "Violet-eared Humming Bird" and the pair of "Red-breasted Humming Birds, with a nest" were carried off by other buyers. Many of Bullock's birds were "undescribed," the gathering of exotic birds having outpaced scientific typing. One could, therefore, purchase the "Large Blue-necked Humming Bird, undescribed," with the ambition that this bird would become the type specimen, the first-described example to which subsequently collected large blue-necked hummingbirds would be compared.[53]

The catalogue of Bullock's bird sales gave his hummingbird collection an afterlife that is captured most poignantly in the notebooks of George Loddiges, a famed nurseryman from Hackney whose horticultural business evolved symbiotically with his hummingbird obsession. Loddiges received shipments of orchids from South America accompanied by hummingbird skins. His hummingbird collection contained more than two hundred species "in all states of plumage and age, set up with his own hands, and disposed in a manner unrivalled for beauty and good taste," that is, arranged in cases positioned at each corner of his drawing room.[54]

Loddiges copied out the full description of Lot 92, a case containing "upwards of One Hundred specimens" of hummingbirds "absolutely unrivalled in any cabinet that exists." "Perhaps the whole of the Continental museums could not furnish as many as are together in this lot," the entry stated, and Loddiges could have judged the veracity of this claim, since he knew the continental hummingbird collections well. After a visit to Paris, he had made a note of the 143 hummingbirds he saw in a museum there, each with "the wings closed and

nearly all in the same position." "One looks to his next door neighbour," Loddiges wrote, "& the other returns the same compliment."[55]

Despite Bullock's wishes to the contrary, the Lot 92 cabinet was not sold intact but rather, according to Loddiges's notes, divided into lots which were
brought forth on the nineteenth day of sale.[56] Even cut asunder, however, they
did not entirely lose their association with Bullock. Twelve years after the auction, Loddiges noted that Mr. Swainson had brought him the two birds he had
requested, "namely the young one of lot 67 Bullocks Sale so that I now possess
both these."[57] He also illustrated a bird in Leadbeater's collection that had been
purchased in Bullock's sale with a charming color drawing (see fig. 4). Bullock's
auction created a sustained sense of loss *and* of heightened acquisitiveness, its
dissolution stirring other collectors to recall and to reincorporate the scattered
birds.

There are a few birds still extant that one can identify with certainty as having once belonged to William Bullock, most notably a White Swamp-hen that
was purchased by Lord Stanley on the seventeenth day of Bullock's auction. The
bird has a beak the color of a turkey wattle, and white feathers that go a little
scruffy in the neck region; it poses with one leg caught in mid-stride, perhaps
trying to evade the sailors who wiped out the entire population of White
Swamp-hens on the coast of Australia where this bird once lived.[58] They were
encouraged by the solicitations of collectors including Loddiges, who printed a
letter of instructions advising travelers how to keep birds dry during a voyage. If
the method—rolling them in bits of soft paper and placing them with camphor
or snuff of tobacco in a small box—proved too onerous, Loddiges was ready to
settle for less. "I would be very thankful, he wrote, "for Birds merely hung up by
a string through the nostrils, as soon as killed, till perfectly dry and stiff."[59]

Whether or not the hummingbird cabinet in the Natural History Museum
was ever in Bullock's London museum, there are almost certainly Bullock hummingbirds in the museum's bird archives, since George Loddiges's hummingbirds wound up there. The one thousand birds that Loddiges grouped in such
aesthetic categories as "Greens" and "Luminous Tailed" are now tipped on their
sides in metal storage cabinets.[60] Glued to their feet are bits of twig branches

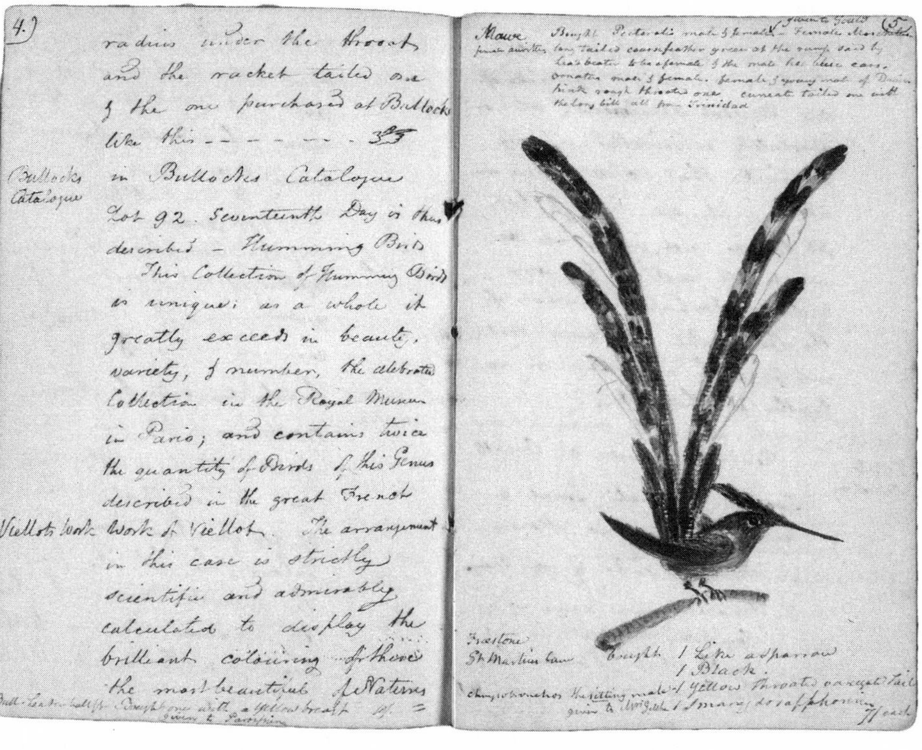

4.)
radius under the throat
and the racket tailed one
& the one purchased at Bullocks
like this - - - - - - - 3£
Bullocks Catalogue in Bullocks Catalogue
Lot 92 Seventeenth Day is thus
described – Humming Birds
This Collection of Humming Birds
is unique; as a whole it
greatly exceeds in beauty,
variety, & number, the celebrated
Collection in the Royal Museum
in Paris; and contains twice
the quantity of Birds of this Genus
described in the great French
Viellots Work Work of Viellot. The arrangement
in this case is strictly
scientific and admirably
calculated to display the
brilliant colouring of these
the most beautiful of Natures

Mawe
Trinidad

1 Like a sparrow
1 Black.
1 Yellow throated

Fig. 4. George Loddiges's notebook. Copyright © The Natural History Museum, London.

used in the original displays. There is a "Slender Sheartail" from case five, a very tiny bird with a purple breast in a circlet of white, and with a tail that forks off in two directions. There is a "Gorgeted Woodstar" with a dark green body and a pinky purplish throat. There are "Copper-bellied Puffleg" birds whose bellies do not look coppery at all, but who do have impressive white poufs around their ankles. My favorite bird is the type specimen of the *"Lesbia nuna gouldi,"* or "Green-tailed Trainbearer," a two-inch-long bird with swooping tail feathers that trail nearly six inches behind him (see fig. 5). It was named after John Gould, Loddiges's protégé, whose hummingbirds, all 5,378 of them, were purchased by the British Museum after his death, and now, like the Loddiges birds, are housed where no one can see them.[61]

No sounds emerge from their thousands of beaks, but these birds provide mute testimony to their collectors' insatiable longings, romantic desires fueled by the impossibility of fulfillment. The superannuated hummingbirds have staved off death with their arsenic-laden stuffing and survived to epitomize the romantic pursuit of perfect and permanent beauty. They show how the loftier ideals of the romantic poets became intertwined with collectors' materialistic pursuits and were realized in diminished fashion—not levitating in glittery splendor, but stuck on a branch or stiffly prone in a cabinet drawer.

Fig. 5. *Lesbia nuna gouldi*, Green-tailed Trainbearer, George Loddiges collection. Copyright © The Natural History Museum, London.

CHAPTER TWO

QUEEN CHARLOTTE, COLLECTOR AND COLLECTIBLE

In 1788 an addled King George III removed from the wall of his room Johann Zoffany's *Tribuna of the Uffizi*, a virtuoso painting of the Medicis' octagonal art gallery which had been commissioned by Queen Charlotte eight years before (see fig. 6).[1] In Zoffany's rendering, a crazy quilt of tiny Rubenses and Raphaels lines the walls of the room, while the foreground is strewn with the gallery's overflow, a litter of busts and plaques and medallions, the detritus of avid collecting. At the time he took down the painting, the king had developed a settled aversion to his wife, who was a collector of paintings, prints, ivory furniture, pottery, botanical specimens, and books. We can only surmise why the *The Tribuna of the Uffizi* displeased him. Robert Fulke Greville, who provides the account of its removal, noted merely that "the Q: was now in no favour," and that George took down the painting with his own hands: "He had it immediately off the Nails on the Floor, before He was perceived to be busy with it."[2]

Johann Zoffany was a prolific painter of Queen Charlotte and her children. He

Fig. 6. Johann Zoffany, *Tribuna of the Uffizi* (1780). The Royal Collection © 2001, Her Majesty Queen Elizabeth II.

painted the royal family grouped under a colonnade on the edge of a wooded park. He painted Queen Charlotte sitting on a bench in a rustic setting and surrounded by her husband and children. He painted the two eldest princes in satin Van Dyck costumes with rosettes on their shoes. He painted the Princess Royal and Prince William standing on a stone ledge with a dog jumping toward them. He helped to burnish the royal family's public image with his paintings of their domestic life.

Zoffany also painted a portrait of Queen Charlotte at her dressing table with her sons George and Frederick (see fig. 7). With its depiction of a French clock,

Fig. 7. Johann Zoffany, *Queen Charlotte with Her Two Eldest Sons* (1771). The Royal Collection © 2001, Her Majesty Queen Elizabeth II.

Chinese figures, a Flanders lace table cover, and a German silver-gilt toilet service, *Queen Charlotte with Her Two Eldest Sons* portrays Charlotte as an imperial queen, surrounded by the wealth of many nations.[3] Outside the queen's window, an ibis spears the lawn with its curved bill. Charlotte maintained a menagerie whose stock was augmented by "recent discoveries in the Southern Ocean."[4] Her personal elephant wore an elegant headband embroidered with crowns, and was cared for by two East Indian attendants. As queen of England, Charlotte had the world's plunder at her fingertips. In a diary entry dating from 1789, the queen writes, "Governor Perry of Barbadoes made me a present this Morning of a most beautiful Peroquet the Plumage of which is Orange blue & Green tipped with red."[5] But Charlotte's delighted mention of this gift stands in stark contrast to the rest of the diary's entries, which chronicle a routine of sedate pastimes. When the queen was not accepting exotic gifts, she was mostly keeping to her room and reading sermons to the princesses.

Zoffany's *Tribuna of the Uffizi* does not depict Queen Charlotte, but it provides a good starting point for a discussion of her collecting, with its male connoisseurs casting proprietary gazes upon an array of paintings and statues, mostly of women. The gallery painting invites us to think about Charlotte's complicated relationship to connoisseurship. Charlotte involved herself most intensely with collecting in a realm removed from her official status as queen, a pastoral zone in which she and her daughters used curatorial busywork to imagine themselves as purposeful workers rather than bored denizens of court. Zoffany's gallery painting, both as a reminder of King George's addled loathing and as a depiction of the gendered nature of connoisseurship, draws our attention to the ways in which collecting turned Charlotte into a queen, but also to how this activity allowed her to escape that sometimes tedious role.

Charlotte first landed on British soil in 1761 as the teenaged German third cousin of her husband-to-be, a man whom she had never met. In the hours between her arrival in England and her marriage, the Princess Sophie-Charlotte of Mecklenburg-Strelitz was dressed in a gown of silver tissue embroidered with silver thread. She had fastened to her neck a velvet mantle laced with gold and lined with ermine. Diamond earrings bobbed from her ears, and sprigs of diamond flowers bloomed on her sleeves.[6] The most striking accessory of all, however, was a diamond stomacher, a kind of lapidary bib that covered the princess's chest and stomach. We do not know exactly what Charlotte was thinking as she stood under the weight of silver, ermine, velvet, and jewels. But we know what many who saw her thought about her stomacher. "The Fond [ground] is a Network as fine as Cat Gut of Small Diamonds & the rest is a large pattern of Natural Flowers, composed of very large Diamonds, one of which is 18, another 16 & a third 10 Thousands pounds price," a lady of the bedchamber noted in her journal. The almost-queen was additionally augmented by "an amazing number of Pearls of a most beautiful Colour & prodigious Size."[7] Charlotte trembled under the weight of her diamond ballast as she took the duke of York's hand and, trailed by ten bridesmaids "all adorn'd with a great number of Jewells," walked to the canopy where she would be joined with the king in marriage.[8]

"As if diamonds were empire," Horace Walpole wrote of the queen, "she was never allowed to appear in public without them."[9] It must here be acknowledged that Charlotte was not a particularly attractive princess. Her own chamberlain once waspishly complimented the queen by saying that "the *bloom* of her ugliness is going off."[10] The king's scouts in Germany had sent word that Charlotte was a fine dancer, and that her face had not been marked by smallpox, weak endorsements that skirted the issue of beauty.[11] But through the accumulation of jewelry, the plain princess became a dazzling queen. A Quaker linen merchant's daughter who eyed her at a Lord Mayor's Day entertainment noted that the stomacher's vast profusion of diamonds produced an "inconceivable" luster.[12] The king was pleased with Charlotte's performance as queen. "Every hour more & more convinces Me of the Treasure I have got," he confided in a letter to his friend Lord Bute soon after the wedding.[13]

The embellishment of Charlotte immediately upon her arrival in England dramatizes the way in which her queenly demeanor was the direct result of the piling on of jewels. Another vestige of the royal courtship, a lock of Charlotte's hair that was delivered to George in advance of his bride's arrival, also marks her transformation from princess to queen. "Pale-brown, more than Cendré," is how Colonel David Graeme described the hair at the time. According to Charlotte's biographer, the king "could not accurately judge its color," but he admired "how soft and fine it felt as it lay in his hand."[14]

The lock of Charlotte's hair was originally intended to fan the king's ardor for his never-seen bride, yet once Charlotte became queen, the severed hair became more than just a sentimental gift. One of the queen's subjects enthused about her majesty's willingness to bestow such keepsakes: "She was told I had wished for a lock of her hair; and she sent me one with her own royal fingers."[15] Charlotte became a queen through the acquisition of luxurious belongings, and by this process she was transformed into a collectible object herself.[16] What had been ordinary hair was now a precious relic; the lock of pale brown hair eventually assumed museum status in the royal collections. "Among memorials of Queen Charlotte," the queen's biographer solemnly avows, "there is none more precious than the long tress of hair reposing in a black box, the lid of which bears a silver plate inscribed with the words 'Queen Charlotte's Hair.' "[17]

The stockpiling of material possessions is such a standard feature of royal existence that Charlotte hardly stands out in a regal crowd. When her son George IV died, his closets and dresser drawers were discovered to be stuffed with "trinkets and trash," including five hundred pocket books, heaps of gloves, and a "prodigious quantity" of women's hair, "some locks with the powder and pomatum still sticking to them."[18] This magpie accumulation suggests a promiscuity at odds with accounts of the collector that emphasize an obsession with orderliness, system, control. Susan Stewart distinguishes between the "proper" collection and the insane collection, which is "a collection for its own sake."[19] The impulse to classify stands as a necessary attribute of the true collector, as opposed to the scattershot accumulator of undifferentiated stuff.

A classificatory impulse is also often cited as the distinguishing feature of the Victorian museum, in contrast with the unruly randomness of the Renaissance cabinet, which Steven Mullaney describes as "a sanctuary for ambiguous things." Mullaney challenges conventional accounts of wonder cabinets as urmuseums by highlighting their lack of systemization. He writes of cabinet treasures: "These are things on holiday, randomly juxtaposed and displaced from any proper context; the room they inhabit acts as a liberty or sanctuary for ambiguous things, a kind of half-way house for transitional objects, some new but not yet fully assimilated, others old and headed for cultural oblivion, but not yet forgotten or cast off." Mullaney identifies the museum so entirely with processes of classification, analysis, and order that he sees the wonder cabinet as the polar opposite of such an endeavor, the final stage of a historical dynamic unique to the Renaissance rather than, in his words, "the proleptic beginning of a civilizing process."[20]

Mullaney is not alone in seeing a disciplinary and classificatory impulse as marking the beginning of a new epoch in collecting history.[21] Tony Bennett argues that the museum evolved in contradistinction to more unruly exhibitions such as the fair, and he strongly aligns museum development with social management. Bennett examines how "the public museum exemplified the development of a new 'governmental' relation to culture in which works of high culture were treated as instruments that could be enlisted in new ways for new tasks of social management." This Foucauldian analysis relies for evidence on the point in museum history when governments became fully engaged in the operation of public exhibitions. For Bennett, the "birth of the museum" really occurs late in the nineteenth century, which explains why, by process of conflation, romantic era collections and exhibitions tend to drop out of his discussion. He writes:

"The public museum, as is well known, acquired its modern form during the late eighteenth and early nineteenth centuries. The process of its formation was as complex as it was protracted, involving, most obviously and immediately, a transformation of the practices of earlier collecting institutions and the creative adaptation of aspects of other new institutions—the international exhibition and the department store, for example—which developed alongside the museum."[22] International exhibitions and department stores, it should be remembered, were mid- to late-nineteenth-century developments.

The hodgepodge of collections and exhibitions accessible to the eighteenth- and early-nineteenth-century collector or museum-goer belie any clean dividing line separating disorderly wondrousness and carefully managed order. One sees instead the exercise of classification in oddly unsystematic ways that seem to undercut the very notion of achieving control through sorting and labeling. This is true of Queen Charlotte's collecting, especially if we look beyond the spoils of her official collections, the jewels and other luxury goods, and turn instead to the remains of her more humble and personal collections: her herbarium, her library, her catalogue of theater prints. These comparatively modest collections distinguish the queen from the more famous male collectors in her family, her husband and eldest son.

Charlotte's diary entries for three days in October 1794 document the king and queen's separate occupations:

Fryday 17th.
After breakfast The Kg went a Hunting . . . myself Elyzabeth
Augusta went to Frogmore, found Mr Price & Mr Digby there.
de Luc read to me till 4
Miss Bab Planta read

Saturday 18th
king hunting.
I went to Frogmore with all the Princesses & returned by one. Dressed, then read
   till 3 after Caffe we worked & read till 8

Tuesday 21st

The Kg went a Hunting. I went to Frogmore with Augusta Elyza and ldy Mary
  Howe. Ernest came just as I was going away which was 12 a Clock. I wrote till
  one, then Dressed. de Luc read till 4.[23]

As the king pursued his sporting adventures, the queen and princesses retreated
to her house at Frogmore, an estate and acreage near Windsor Castle, where,
starting in the early 1790s, and with the assistance of architects, gardeners, and
daughters, Charlotte created a lovely alternative to palace life, an otherworldly
realm in which she oversaw botanical specimens, a book collection, and a printing press.[24] The queen called Frogmore her "little Paradise." She wrote of her
designs for the estate: "My little cottage & garden at Windsor begins to improve. The walk around the fields is cut, planted, & the gravel ordered to be laid;
my plants from Kew beginning to cut a figour in the green house, & a small plan
made for a smart little cottage. The latter is not determined upon, for I go slow
to work in order to make the pleasure last the longer."[25]

Charlotte had pressing reasons for wanting to immerse herself in the preservation and organization of her collected objects, but curating royal possessions
seems to be the general demesne of queens. Faced with his dead brother's 300
whips, his 500 pocketbooks, his 785 pictures, King William IV explained that
George IV had been very fond of "knicknackery," and then divested himself of
George's pets, paintings, and handkerchiefs. William's niece Queen Victoria, by
contrast, grew more and more adamant that not one royal possession be thrown
away or even moved, and so, as Lytton Strachey writes, "mementoes of the past
surrounded her in serried accumulations."[26] These objects were photographed
from several angles, the photos were arranged in albums, and Victoria "with a
gigantic volume or two of the endless catalogue always beside her . . . could feel,
with a double contentment, that the transitoriness of this world had been arrested by the amplitude of her might."[27] Queen Mary, who felt a particular affinity for her great-grandmother Queen Charlotte, and who tried to reassemble
her lost objects, chronicled her own vast holdings in a *Catalogue of Bibelots,
Miniatures and Other Valuables*. Writes Mary's biographer, "To collect, to pre-

serve, to docket, to tidy, and to put in order were primary objectives all through her life."[28]

Long before Charlotte purchased her Frogmore estate, on August 12, 1778, the king and queen, their children, several footmen, two grooms, a dozen servants, a riding master, and the bishop of Litchfield pulled into the courtyard at Bulstrode, the estate of Margaret Cavendish, the duchess of Portland—in all, "33 servants, and 56 personages," counted Mary Delany, a companion to the duchess, who was pleased to be called upstairs by the queen. When Delany met with the royal family, they were wandering in a train to the duchess of Portland's china closet, where "with wondering and enquiring eyes [they] admired all her magnificent curiosities."[29]

Whatever held the royal family members rapt before the duchess's china cabinet kept them coming back to Bulstrode for more. The duchess was unusual in being a female collector who knew no bounds. It is hard to say whether it was the limitlessness of her collecting, or the mere fact of a woman collecting on such an ambitious scale, that caused Horace Walpole, an avid collector himself, to describe her sniffily as a woman who "bought at any price." He went on to note that, late in her life, the duchess "went deeply into natural history, & her Collection in that Walk was supposed to have cost her fifteen thousand pounds."[30] After a visit in 1781, the king's equerry reported, "There are many good Pictures at Bulstrode—Some rare Birds, much Choice old China, & some fine Specimens of Minerals, &c—."[31] When these collections were sold off after the duchess's death, the auction catalogue stated that she had tried to have every unknown species of shell she owned "published to the world," but what she left behind, the catalogue also makes clear, was a clutter of shells in a jumble of unsorted boxes. The auction cataloguer acknowledged that some persons might object to the "Promiscuous Assemblage" of the objects on sale, but most people, he continued, "are not *Methodists*. They love Variety more than Order, and would rather purchase Twenty different Species of *Cones* or *Turbos* in One Lot, than the same Number of *High Admirals* or *Wentletraps*."[32]

On the days when the royal family rode into the courtyard at Bulstrode, the duchess's companions were busily engaged in organizing her collections. On one occasion, for example, the queen found Mrs. Delany hard at work ("in my working dress, and all my papers littered about me") on cut-paper models of the duchess's plants, while the duchess's mother was "*very intent* at another table, making a catalogue to a huge folio of portrait prints."[33] These curatorial efforts eventually collapsed under the weight of the duchess's ever-proliferating objects, but they provided hours of entertainment. "I have undertaken to set the Duchess of Portland's miniatures in order," Delany wrote on another occasion. "You may believe the employment is not unpleasant: this, with going to see places and assisting the Duchess to sort her papers in an evening after our walks, employs almost every hour of the day."[34]

The Bulstrode visits were happy interludes in the royal marriage. On the morning in 1778 that saw the family standing awed before the duchess's china cabinet, the queen discussed chenille work with Mrs. Delany, and the king insisted on bringing that woman a chair. "The King was all spirits and good humour, extreamly pleased, as well as the Queen, with the place and entertainment," Delany wrote. To tell all that passed that morning at Bulstrode, she avowed, "would take a quire of paper."[35]

According to Walpole, the duchess of Portland engaged Dr. Solander "to range & catalogue her Shells, fossils, Insects &c."[36] Daniel Solander was a botanist who had been contracted by Joseph Banks to set sail on Captain Cook's second voyage. If he had gone on this voyage, one of his sailing companions would have been Johann Zoffany.

Zoffany was enlisted by Banks to serve as an artist on Cook's voyage so that, as Banks put it, "the learned World in general might reap as much benefit as possible" from the explorers' discoveries of exotic flora and fauna. Unfortunately for both Zoffany and Solander, Banks decided that the cabins on Cook's ship were too small to meet the needs of his party. The collapse of Banks's plans must have come as an especially bitter blow for Zoffany, who had gathered his own collection of artifacts from the Pacific and the Orient. Banks had apparently promised him a thousand pounds for the voyage, but also a third share of all curiosities.[37] Just when Zoffany was at loose ends, Queen Charlotte intervened, offering him travel money and a commission to paint the finest art collection in Europe. Horace Walpole considered Zoffany a lucky man: "This . . . is better than his going to draw naked savages and be scalped, with that wild man Banks, who is poaching in every ocean for the fry of little islands that escaped the dragnet of Spain."[38]

In painting the duke of Tuscany's art collection, Zoffany made it his own, shuffling the paintings on the gallery walls and adding paintings that did not hang there at all. Zoffany peopled the Uffizi Gallery with traveling Englishmen, "a flock of travelling boys" that Walpole declared "as impertinent as the names of churchwardens stuck up in parishes, whenever a country church is repaired and whitewashed."[39] The "impropriety of crowding in so many unknown figures" was an affront to the wishes of Zoffany's royal patron. When she ordered its painted replication, Queen Charlotte hoped to annex the Florentine collection, that is, to add Zoffany's small reproductions of its artworks to her own. She did not anticipate having Old Master paintings upstaged by a flock of English tourists.

"I should think," Horace Mann wrote to Walpole, "the naked Venus which is the principal figure will not please her Majesty so much as it did the young men to whom it was showed."[40] Zoffany, who had been given special dispensation to have any painting in the gallery or palace taken down so that he could observe it more closely, depicted Titian's *Venus of Urbino* at his painting's front center, tipped before a cluster of connoisseurial Englishmen. Madonna and Child paintings figure prominently in *The Tribuna*, too, but the images that really pop out from the crowd of canvases and statues are Raphael's naked *St. John;* a languorous nude bacchante; the famed *Venus de' Medici*, who, in Zoffany's depiction, is having her backside scrutinized by several gallery visitors; and *The Venus of Urbino*, a figure widely viewed in the nineteenth century as a courtesan. Zoffany's Madonna paintings recede behind the fleshy eroticism of the Venus in particular. *The Tribuna of the Uffizi* positions men as connoisseurs and women as objects of their connoisseurial gaze. Zoffany turned Charlotte's commission into an opportunity to foreground women's status as sexual spectacle.

Zoffany painted himself into the gallery, peering from behind a Raphael, and surrounded by a knot of spectators who are admiring or debating the finer points of this Madonna and Child. (You can see him on the far left side of figure 6; his head is just to the left of the infant in the painting that is being held aloft.) Zoffany's tiny imp face is at the center of their argument, but he seems intent on catching any eye that flutters across the painting's surface. If Queen Charlotte had insisted on insinuating herself into the painting, Zoffany might have hung her on the gallery's wall, a solution he had already hit upon in *The Academicians of the Royal Academy*, which depicts two honorary female members of the academy in portrait busts that hang above the male academicians' casual poses (see fig. 8). Below the busts of their female peers, the male members of the academy cock their heads to one side as they inspect the nude body of a male artist's model who is there for all but the female members to sketch.

The Academicians of the Royal Academy is, like *The Tribuna of the Uffizi*, a sly depiction of the sexism inherent in connoisseurship. The most striking Zoffany connoisseur is the Royal Academy member who jabs his stick into a legless female torso near his feet. This heedless bon vivant exemplifies an enduring stereotype of the collector as lecherous misanthrope. In Thomas Rowlandson's 1799 caricature of connoisseurs, for example, four older men gawk at a painted

Fig. 8. Johann Zoffany, *The Academicians of the Royal Academy* (1771–72). The Royal Collection © 2001, Her Majesty Queen Elizabeth II.

nude on an easel(see fig. 9). One man holds a monocle to his eye, his nose a few inches from the naked woman's knee.

Zoffany's Uffizi Gallery painting was displayed at the Royal Academy in 1780. An engraving of George III and his family attending a Royal Academy show eight years later presents the gendering of connoisseurship in a way that closely matches the Uffizi portrayal. In this picture of the royal family in the exhibition gallery, an accordion of children stretches out on either side of the king and queen—girls on one side, boys on the other (see fig. 10). The princesses are—by positioning and demeanor—distinctly separate from their brothers. They clutch their exhibition catalogues and bunch together in the left of the frame, as if overawed at being in an art gallery. On the other side of the picture, the male

Fig. 9. Thomas Rowlandson,
"Connoisseurs" (1799). Copyright ©
The Trustees of the British Museum.

family members strike confident poses, distinct from one another and from their
sisters. "As male spectators they exist autonomously within the public space defined by the Great Room," writes one commentator, who notes a similarity to
Grand Tour portraiture.[41] The princes, that is, look almost exactly like the English connoisseurs in Zoffany's *Tribuna*.

Fig. 10. Pietro Martini after Johan Heinrich Ramberg, *Portraits of Their Majestys and the Royal Family Viewing the Exhibition of the Royal Academy, 1788.* By courtesy of the National Galleries of Scotland.

In the introduction to the nine-volume set of botanical tables that he dedicated to the queen, the king's mentor and adviser Lord Bute described the kind of aristocratic doldrums that fueled the queen's collecting pursuits. "Short as our existence is, how many find the day too long, how many tedious hours are past in absolute idleness, where even thought is banished," wrote Lord Bute. Reading, he believed, was no cure for this miserable disorder. "After a length of years, employed in reading, tracing every discovery, sucking every flower, we shall meet with little worthy our attention," he lamented, "for although the Press groans with fresh publications, & libraries are continually augmenting, original works seldom appear." The Book of Nature was the "amazing volume" he recommended to stave off the encroachment of dullness, and he singled out botany as being "peculiarly suited to the attention of the Fair Sex."[42]

At Kew Gardens one can find the remains of Queen Charlotte's botanical collection, hundreds of paper folders containing dried specimens of carefully labeled plants. The skeletal fronds are attached to pages with small slips of paper and stored in the partitions of a large wardrobe which stands at the top of a staircase.[43] The brittle plant bits are interesting chiefly because they once belonged to Queen Charlotte. They are labeled in a neat cursive which seems to be Charlotte's own handwriting, but which could also be the handwriting of John Lightfoot, whose herbarium George purchased for £100 so that he could give it to his queen.

When the queen acquired her herbarium in 1788 it was in bad repair, and so an expert was called in to advise on how it should be set right. James Edward Smith had distinguished himself in scientific circles by his purchase of Linnaeus's books, plants, minerals, insects, letters, and manuscripts. He arranged the herbarium in twenty-four mahogany cases, and he visited frequently in order to converse on botany and zoology with the queen and princesses. The royal pupils, according to Smith, talked all at once, and he was concerned about lapsing into botanical impropriety. "I cannot be very full on the various structure of *vesiculae seminales* or on the *vulva hians* of the viola," he wrote.[44] Smith credited the queen with the good sense to furnish her daughters with the means to pass their time in a worthy occupation.

Whatever charms her botanical activities held for the queen, however, they insufficiently riveted the attentions of the trailing princesses. Elizabeth, the aspiring artist of the group, threw herself into the role of impresario. Once, after a dinner of "every delicacy of the season," she conducted her parents and their visitors to a Frogmore grotto, where vocal performers entertained them with glees and songs. Next, the company crossed the lawn to another part of the gardens, where they were met by a group of performers impersonating gypsies. The queen of the gypsies sang a gypsy song and delivered "poetical destinies of good fortune to the several members of the royal family" before retreating into a thicket. The royal entourage then proceeded to a stage erected near a space of ground called the "Hermit's Cell," where the Flemish Hercules, a man named Du Crow, balanced three large coach wheels on his chin, along with a ladder and two chairs in which children sat. Six Hungarian hussars performed "the peculiar dances of their country" on the lawn in front of the grotto, and the interior of a thatched barn "was decorated with flowers, and lighted up with chandeliers in the form of a bee-hive, the upper part suspended by a tassel resembling ears of corn."[45]

Writing of the contrast between female accomplishment and the culture of connoisseurship in the late eighteenth century, Ann Bermingham describes how women were encouraged to develop specific artistic skills—sketching, painting, playing music—that put them on display as performers. Their virtuosity in these limited areas placed them on the opposite side of the spectrum from the connoisseur; they were meant to be looked at rather than to cast their own gaze over others' artistic productions.[46] Queen Charlotte and the princesses could not tour the Uffizi Gallery in the assured, proprietary manner of Zoffany's connoisseurs, but they could make chandeliers look like beehives, and devise ingenious tableaux through which they could picturesquely float.

The princesses and a team of local women worked for days at full tilt in preparation for the party. Lucy Kennedy, who was called into service, recalled: "She [the Princess Royal] Said they were in great Want of Leaves, which I thought I could undertake to do, She gave me A Pattern, and I Came Home and sat down to *Tye up* Rose Leaves, I finished them Next day." Kennedy went on to say, "All the Ladys in Windsor has offered their Services, and are Busy making Flowers, of all Sorts" for a Frogmore ball. She also noted, "[Princess Elizabeth] sais She will want one thousand yards of Garland; the whole Houss is to be Decorated."[47]

The queen's keeper of the wardrobe, a Mrs. Papendiek, kept a journal that was published under the title *Court and Private Life in the Time of Queen Charlotte*. In an illustration titled "Mrs. Papendiek and Child," the author sits half-smiling under a towering hat and mantilla (see fig. 11). Despite Mrs. Papendiek's millinery excess, her journal is full of interesting insider accounts of the queen. It tells, for example, how the royal family, longing for the beautiful gardens of Kew and Richmond, sought out a private garden near Windsor where Charlotte could walk with her daughters. What they found, according to Mrs. Papendiek, was the keeper's house in the Home Park at Windsor: "The Queen was so pleased with it that she with the Princesses and her ladies often passed their mornings there, taking new milk, an egg, and a rasher of home-cured bacon for their lunch, and their cup of coffee after, which Mrs. Gascoigne [the keeper's wife] made excellently."[48]

The theatricality of Charlotte's recourse to a humbler life was as obvious to her contemporaries as it is to us, and she was mocked accordingly. In one typical print caricature, the queen is shown toasting sprats over a fire while her patched pocket bulges with coins (see fig. 12). Another drawing, published in the same year of 1791 and depicting "Summer Amusement at Farmer G——'s Near Windsor," portrays King George operating a butter churn, while the queen hag-

Fig. 11. "Mrs. Papendiek and Child" from a sketch by Thomas Lawrence. Mrs. [Charlotte Louisa Henrietta] Papendiek, *Court and Private Life in the Time of Queen Charlotte* (1887).

Fig. 12. James Gillray, "Frying Sprats" (1791). Copyright © The Trustees of the British Museum.

gles over the price of eggs (see fig. 13). "Good Heavens is it possible that people can be so unreasonable these plentiful times to expect six eggs for a groat," the queen's speech balloon reads. Her hands rest over a table spread with coins.

The caricatures link Queen Charlotte with miserliness, an association that gets reaffirmed in Mrs. Papendiek's gossipy account of Zoffany's dealings with his royal patrons. When completed, *The Tribuna of the Uffizi* was placed in a room at Kew House for inspection by Royal Academicians, who were "unanimous in their opinion of its superlative excellence."[49] But when the subject of how much to pay Zoffany arose, objections were raised to the work. "What in

Fig. 13. "Summer Amusement at Farmer G——'s near Windsor" (1791). Copyright © The Trustees of the British Museum.

the end Zoffany received," Mrs. Papendiek wrote, "I cannot assert, but I am certain that it was under 1,000 £."

According to Mrs. Papendiek, "The picture was put out of sight, and it was not till it was exhibited in the collection of George IV. that it was again even recollected."[50] This account must not be entirely reliable, since we know that it was the talk of the 1780 Royal Academy exhibition, but, except for that airing, the painting seems to have stayed at Kew, where the deranged George was lured in 1788 by a promise that he would be reunited with his queen.[51] The king's doctor recorded that the "Scene when the Queen came to the King was very affecting—he kiss'd her hand passionately & said he held then what was dearest to him in the world." The Lord Chancellor reported the next day that the king was raging afterwards, and so was confined all night in a straitjacket.[52] Nine days later, he removed Zoffany's *Tribuna of the Uffizi* from his wall.[53]

In 1808, a year when the king suffered another bout of mental illness, the queen's use of Frogmore as a collecting retreat became more urgent, or so it seems in the July 13th account of Cornelia Knight, a companion to Princess Charlotte: "I went every evening this week (except this) to Frogmore with the Queen and the Princesses Elizabeth and Mary. The King has been very ill the whole week and continues so."[54] As Knight's account continues, the news of the king vacillates from being cautiously optimistic (July 16: "The King took three jellies, and had a little sleep this morning") to hopelessly dire (July 29: "The King has been as ill as ever, and takes so little nourishment that it is scarcely possible he can recover any strength—his mind as much deranged as ever"). As the king's health disintegrated, and the palace minions grew more distraught, the queen began a course of idyllic reading. On August 5, Knight writes: "I went several evenings with the Queen and Princesses Mary and Elizabeth to Frogmore. The Queen read Thomson's 'Seasons'; but on Thursday the Queen's Council came unexpectedly to propose calling in more physicians, or, at least, that a consultation might be held." On that same day, she reported, "the King had another paroxysm, and is still in a dreadful state of mind, and will take nothing now but water and biscuit." A week later, the king's condition had grown so bad that his lack of will had become a topic of concern ("but it is thought he has made two or three memorandums"). Meanwhile, the queen continued her Frogmore routines. "I went almost every morning to Frogmore with the Queen and Princesses Elizabeth and Mary," Knight reports. "The

Queen read Rogers's 'Pleasures of Memory' and Cowper's 'Task,' and planted little oaks and geraniums."[55]

The turn to pastoral literature, and, in particular, to William Cowper's verse, as an escape from the king's malady is especially poignant, since Cowper himself succumbed to madness. While training for the legal profession in 1763, he collapsed in a nervous panic, attempted suicide, and was checked in to a St. Albans asylum. He later adopted the role of country gentleman, but was still vulnerable to debilitating depression; his mental health deteriorated rapidly before his death in 1800. We don't know which passages of *The Task* Queen Charlotte was reading before she set to work planting little oaks and geraniums, or throughout the rest of the week as she continued to read the poem. But there are many passages in *The Task* that might seem to be addressing Charlotte directly, most notably Cowper's excursus on "the wearisomeness of what is sometimes called a life of pleasure." He writes:

> It is the constant revolution stale
> And tasteless, of the same repeated joys,
> That palls and satiates, and makes languid life
> A pedlar's pack, that bows the bearer down.
> Health suffers, and the spirits ebb; the heart
> Recoils from its own choice—at the full feast
> Is famish'd—finds no music in the song,
> No smartness in the jest, and wonders why.[56]

Cowper's many passages on the pleasures of gardening or of other cozy rural occupations, if they did not inspire, certainly legitimized the queen's retreat to Frogmore and her forays into landscape design and botanical study. If she read as far as the fifth book of *The Task*, with its critique of monarchs, she might have found a further endorsement of her Frogmore sojourns as the antithesis of the dangerous amusements Cowper ascribes to male rulers. He writes:

> Great princes have great play-things. Some have played
> At hewing mountains into men, and some

At building human wonders mountain-high.
 Some have amused the dull sad years of life,
Life spent in indolence, and therefore sad,
With schemes of monumental fame, and sought
By pyramids and mausolaean pomp,
Short-lived themselves, t'immortalize their bones.
Some seek diversion in the tented field,
And make the sorrows of mankind their sport.
 But war's a game, which were their subjects wise,
Kings should not play at.[57]

Frogmore provided an escape from indolence, but Charlotte and her daughters sought there no monumental fame, only a means of diverting themselves from the king's descent into madness. Toward the end of the same month in which Knight first remarked upon the queen's reading of Cowper, she noted, "The Queen read Cowper and Cicero's 'Letters,' and took me with her in the little carriage, drawn by a pony."[58] That diminutive carriage and pony epitomize the faux workaday world of Frogmore. Collecting activities and elaborate decorating schemes served to fill time that stretched before the female members of the royal family like a pathless meadow.

Among the most interesting surviving remnants of Queen Charlotte's collections is her index of theatrical prints. In perfectly legible copperplate cursive, Charlotte wrote the following title on the first page:

A
Catalogue
of Theatrical Prints
Collected
by me
In the Years of 1808–1809
Charlotte R.[59]

There is something unregal, even childlike (Collected by me—Hurray!) about this laboriously inscribed list with its star-struck recording of the queen's engraved prints of actors ranging from Mrs. Abington to La Signora Zamperini. The catalogue title makes clear that the queen, by 1808, saw herself as a collector, but given Charlotte's accumulation of porcelain, ivory furniture, silver plate, oriental curiosities, and coins, such a declaration hardly seems necessary.

In 1808 the king was having paroxysms and the queen was reading Cowper and riding behind a pony. It may seem an odd moment for her to have started collecting theater portraits, but then again, the need for the kind of compelling distraction that a collection could provide would never be stronger. The queen had little control over her immediate destiny, but she could organize her two hundred prints of actors, and then chronicle that organization in a catalogue.

Cultural critics like to link the collector's organizing efforts to grandiose and pernicious attempts at mastery. Thomas Richards, for instance, argues that the British Empire was created through the accumulation of systems of knowledge—lists, statistics, classifications—that afforded an illusion of control. The most compelling part of Richards's argument, however, is his account of the potential unruliness of those records, of how they "required keeping track, and keeping track of keeping track" because of their tendency to run off "in many different directions like the hedgehogs in Alice's game of croquet."[60] Queen Charlotte prided herself on her capacity for tedious tasks. Once, when the queen expressed an interest in copying a James II manuscript her son had recently acquired, she was offered assistance with this "laborious undertaking." She replied, "I am accustomed to such work; I have 400 pages of extracts which I have [made] from various works."[61] The possibility of copying the James II manuscript arose in 1812, the year before the regency bill stamped the king as permanently mad. That is, this task became available at a moment when Queen Charlotte may have had a pressing desire for the diversion that chasing her own hedgehogs could afford.

Royal collections inevitably evince a kind of power, and many of Charlotte's collections served to advertise her exalted status as queen and thus to help consolidate her husband's role as national leader. These collections were the ones that tended to elicit curatorial concern in the aftermath of the queen's death. When Charlotte died on November 17, 1818, after suffering from dropsy of the chest and gangrenous legs, the most pressing matter was the determination of who owned the queen's jewels. The king's secretary was charged with determining whether items on a detailed jewelry inventory were the property of the king and to be set aside, or could be sold as the late queen's property for the benefit of the princesses. The queen had been attended in her final days by her daughters, and by the "good & valuable Mrs Beckedorff," all of whom provided testimonials to the status of Charlotte's jewels. Princess Sophia's affidavit declared, "The Queen has remarked frequently, that She considered The Jewels presented to Her by the Nabob of Arcot, as Her own, & whatever Presents The King had made Her since Her Marriage, as Her own, and at Her own Disposal." Charlotte Beckedorff testified: "Besides the large Pearl Drop, I can speak positively only to a Brilliant Cluster Ring, as, according to Her late Majesty's own Acount of them, belonging to Mecklenburg.—I have some Recollection that

Her Majesty spoke of the large brilliant Cluster Buttons as belonging to Mecklenburg but would not swear to it, nor to the number."[62]

The status of the queen's diamond stomacher was not in dispute. Her will bequeathed it to the king "if it shall please the Almighty to relieve Him from the dreadful Malady," and to the House of Hanover if the Almighty turned out to not be so pleased.[63] The king was not aware of his wife's death. Quarantined in the suite at Windsor Castle where he would spend the remaining fourteen months of his life, he stayed mostly cheerful as he played the harpsichord, conversed with the dead, and complained of not being served enough cherry tart.[64]

The queen's less valuable belongings were dispersed in a more haphazard manner. On February 22, 1819, *The Times* noted that Mrs. Beckedorff had commenced "disposing of the silks, late the property of the Queen, to various ladies who have called at the Queen's-Palace."[65] Demand for material fragments of the dead queen ran high, and likely crested in May of that year, when most of Charlotte's possessions were auctioned off in a series of sales conducted over thirty-five days and realizing £51,598 profit to benefit the princesses.

In a print caricature dating from the day before the first sale, two princesses stand next to the auction podium in beseeching poses. They look grasping and overfed; one of them spills out of the front of her dress (see fig. 14). George IV, depicted as an auctioneer, exhorts, "Pray *my good people* Bid Liberally or the Children will be destitute!!" as he shills his mother's shawl. The caricature emphasizes the unseemliness of the public sale. On the walls of the auction room, and labeled with lot numbers, Charlotte's possessions dangle from hooks.

Perhaps some of the same ladies who sought out Mrs. Beckedorff for swatches of Charlotte's ball gowns also showed up at the auction or hired intermediaries to bid in their names. From a marked-up copy of the sale catalogue, we know that Lady Grenville purchased a pair of square bottles, and Mrs. Brande, Mrs. Cockrant, and Mrs. Wilcox each made off with decorated fans after the first day's sale on May 7, 1819. On another day, and for what seems like a bargain price, Mrs. Anstey purchased a trinket lot comprising "a large girdle and tassel of garnets, two garnet link necklaces, one necklace of large garnets, two of smaller ditto, and two long necklaces of small garnets, a pair of ditto

Fig. 14. "Sales by Auction!—Or Provident Children Disposing of Their Deceased Mother's Effects for the Benefit of the Creditors!!—" (1819). Copyright © The Trustees of the British Museum.

bracelets, eight broaches, three pair of ear-rings and a pair of broaches shaped as bunches of grapes"—all for £14, 14 shillings.[66] The auction catalogue is overwhelming in its weight of stuff: gemstones, books, gimcrackery, stuffed birds.[67] All the things that made Queen Charlotte a collector were assembled for one final time, and this assemblage inspired her acquaintances and subjects to collect what was left of the queen.

Two years after Charlotte's death, the king's secretary set about destroying the queen's letters at the request of her daughters. Pondering, years after the event, a list of the destroyed documents, a curator at the Royal Archives conjured up the scene of an execution: "With each sentence of [this] dismal recital we can almost hear the recurrent thud of the guillotine."[68] The actual moment of destruction, however, was probably far less dramatic: a royal functionary bundled the letters for the palace rubbish, or shoved them into the fire, then went on with the other business of the day.

The collections of kings—except in the extreme case of George IV's hair and glove collections—tend to be preserved intact and entire, enshrined like George III's library, which fills the transparent central column of the new British Library. Today, coffee drinkers in the library cafe gaze across a moat of air to admire the handsome bindings on George's books. Charlotte's books, by contrast, were sold at auction, her papers were destroyed, and her possessions were mostly scattered. When Queen Mary decided that she wanted to reassemble her great-grandmother's lost objects, she took to snatching family heirlooms from lesser royals and from the descendants of Charlotte's acquaintances, there being very little to find. Apart from what Mary managed to recuperate, the remains of Queen Charlotte in the royal holdings tend to be those objects that had a ceremonial or monetary value—her stomacher rather than her copy of Cowper.[69] Her surviving collectibles make it easier to reconstruct the imperial queen than the woman who used curatorial busywork to escape her queenly burdens.

Zoffany's *Tribuna of the Uffizi* was neither auctioned off nor destroyed. You can still view it in a gallery at Buckingham Palace, if you are able to convince the Keeper of the Queen's Paintings that you have a good reason for wanting to do so. Zoffany's painting was a "most curious and laborious undertaking" in its effort to mimic minutely the wondrous profusion of the duke of Tuscany's museum. Zoffany meticulously captured the gallery's dazzling architectural details—the gold and mother-of-pearl arabesques on the blue lapis lazuli of the cupola; the skirting board frieze of birds, fish, and shells; the shelf of drawers which ran around the room on carved and gilded consoles.[70] But he depicted paintings that never hung there, and he rearranged those that did.

Zoffany's painting stands as an enigmatic reminder of the king's mental illness and of the queen's escapist collecting. "This accurate picture has the same effect on the spectator which the gallery itself has on first entering it," a newspaper review of Zoffany's painting noted. The gallery's effect was described by an English visitor to Florence: "The imagination is bewildered, and a stranger of a visionary turn, would be apt to fancy himself in a palace of fairies, raised and adorned by the power of inchantment."[71] Zoffany's painting invoked the same dazed response. The newspaper review went on to declare that "the multitude of excellencies . . . dissipate our ideas, and it requires some time to arrange them before we can cooly examine the merit of any individual piece."[72] This description provides one possible explanation for why the painting so disturbed George III. A man who is going mad may not enjoy having his imagination bewildered or his ideas cast into further disarray.

We cannot determine, at this late date, why George's disaffection for his wife manifested itself in an impatience with Zoffany's painting. We know only that the queen commissioned Zoffany's painting of a collection, that the queen had many collections of her own, and that, despite ordering a picture of a collection and keeping collections of her own, she was, in many ways, boxed out of the connoisseurial world that Zoffany portrays. The painting says nothing about the alternative collecting realm Charlotte created at Frogmore. But as a fanciful catalogue, a make-believe "copy" of the Uffizi Gallery, Zoffany's *Tribuna* mirrors the way in which Queen Charlotte used collecting and cataloguing in the service of escapist fantasy.

CHAPTER THREE

Travels with Napoleon's Carriage

After Napoleon's defeat at the battle of Waterloo, people rushed to the scene of his final engagement, gathering cast-aside weaponry, the ephemera of dead soldiers, and handfuls of soil from what had immediately become sacred ground.[1] Of all the battle relics left behind, however, none inspired as much interest as the carriage Napoleon abandoned when he fled on horseback from enemy combatants. Dark blue with vermilion wheels "heightened in gold," and an undercarriage made of "swan-neck iron cranes," the vehicle was built in the chariot style, and with a state-of-the-art suspension system that minimized jolting over hard surfaces. The lamps at each corner of the carriage's square roof had lit Napoleon's path as he traveled over the steppes of Russia and around the island of Elba and back to Paris in triumph before its final capture at the town of Genappe. The carriage's presence at scenes of both Napoleonic triumph and Napoleonic ruin made it an association object *nonpareil*, one of the most alluring relics of the period's most alluring reprobate.[2]

Romantic era carriages inspired extravagant spending. King George III paid nearly £8,000 in 1762 for a state coach, a behemoth of a conveyance—twenty-four feet long and twelve feet high—busily embellished with tritons, cherubs, lions' heads, a dolphin's head, the figure of Victory, and a footboard made to look like a scallop. The spurned mistress of George's eldest son paraded around London in a carriage decorated with a facsimile of the royal insignia, in this way showcasing her relationship with the prince.[3] Even literary figures we might assume to have had loftier concerns let their vehicular aspirations outstrip their means. Percy Shelley, perpetually behind in his carriage payments, was the bane of the coach maker Thomas Charters, who was still trying to collect on a £532 bill twenty-two years after the poet's death.[4]

Napoleon, at the height of his power, had advertised his roving ambition with his splendid carriage. After his capture, it took on an added glamour because of the glimpse it afforded of his private life. The carriage presented Napoleon's world in miniature, a ruthless conqueror's empire shrunk to the size of a settee. Its intimate contents included the small canteen that held Napoleon's tumbler and china egg cup, as well as his salt box and mustard pot, both with their contents "as left by the Emperor at his last breakfast before the battle of Waterloo still in them."[5] The vehicle was a self-contained and portable museum, replete with Napoleon's most personal possessions. It contained Napoleon's toilette box, his toothbrush, his gold tongue scraper, his shaving brush, and his "Flesh-brush." It counted among its holdings the emperor's personal wardrobe, including a pair of silk stockings with imperial crest, a shirt of very fine cambric, a "pair of Cashimeer small-clothes," a pair of the imperial postillion's boots, as well as spurs, buckles, and silver helmet. For lulls in battle, there was a "Set of Chessmen in a round wooden box, used by the Emperor in the Russian campaign" and a "Set of Markers, for the game of Loto; also from the Russian campaign." In addition, the Napoleon voyeur could imagine the emperor at table, using his "Beautiful small Tea-pot, finely embossed with the arms, crest, and cipher of Napoleon"; his "very handsome Coffee-cup and Saucer"; his silver breakfast plate; his chocolate pot; and his tea caddy, which had been packed, perhaps hastily, with Napoleon's Cross of the Legion of Honor.[6]

The carriage was presented to the Prince Regent by Marshal Blücher after its capture. The prince (who later succeeded to the throne as George IV) refused the opportunity to meet Bonaparte in person, but he cultivated a lively line of fantasy in which he had been personally responsible for the emperor's defeat. Obsessed with Waterloo, George particularly prized a copy of a report the duke of Wellington dispatched after the battle, and he visited the battle site with that national hero. "[George's] descriptions of battles he had never fought were as real as if he had been there," writes one historian, recalling an occasion when George called on Wellington to verify his recollection of a charge down a perpendicular hill. ("Very steep, Sir, very steep," the obliging duke responded.)[7] The Prince Regent liked to see himself as Napoleon's English counterpart. He redesigned Regent Street out of a desire for a processional route that would match the grand boulevards of imperial Paris, and one explanation for his magpie accumulation of bronzes, furniture, china, prints, and medals is that he was trying to create for England an art collection comparable to that of the Louvre, which had been enriched by Napoleon's despoliation of Italy.[8]

George's imaginary engagement with Napoleon draws our attention to the ways in which Napoleonic objects enabled self-aggrandizing fantasies, and thus points forward in time to the appropriation of the carriage by William Bullock (who purchased the vehicle and made it part of a touring exhibition), and by George Gordon, Lord Byron (who used a replica of the vehicle to tour Europe). I set out in this chapter to examine the romantic era traffic in Napoleonic relics, and, more generally, to explore the rise of the association object in this period. Napoleon's carriage came to serve as a means of literal and imaginative transport, and also as proof of the sometimes dubious authenticity of other Napoleonic objects. By revisiting Bullock's display of Napoleon's actual carriage, and by surveying Byron's travels in its similacrum, we can see how these vehicles operated in a relic market founded on literary embellishment and speculative half-truth.

When he left England on April 23, 1816, in the carriage designed to look like Napoleon's own, Byron, like Bonaparte before him, was bailing out of a losing battle. Days before he left England, with tales of his incestuous involvement with his half-sister swirling, he signed a deed of separation from his wife, who suspected that he was insane. When the Napoleonic carriage pulled away from Byron's house in London, a crowd gathered at the door, lured in equal parts by the poet's celebrity, the rumors' salaciousness, and the carriage's curb appeal.

As Byron rumbled across Europe in that summer of 1816, he traced the path of Napoleon's carriage wheels. Byron did so partly because Napoleon had swept across so much of the landscape and left so many marks behind, never leaving untouched the towns and villages through which he passed. "B[uonaparte]'s name is everywhere," Byron's companion John William Polidori wrote. "Who did this? N[apoleon] B[uonaparte].—Who that?—He. There is an inscription to record this."[9]

A Byron family friend, Pryse Lockhart Gordon, who met up with the poet at Brussels in August 1816, was impressed by the carriage's amenities. "Besides a *lit de repos*," he wrote, "it contained a library, a plate-chest, and every apparatus for dining."[10] But Gordon also called Byron's vehicle a "crazy machine," and the carriage fairly immediately proved its impracticality. By the time Byron reached Brussels, it had broken down several times and proved insufficiently capacious for his baggage. "The carriage, the new carriage, has had three stoppages," wrote Polidori as they paused to have it repaired.[11] During the delay Byron borrowed a Cossack horse so he could gallop across the field of Waterloo. The ground there had already been sifted by relic seekers. "If it were not for the importunity of boys, and the glitter of buttons in their hands, there would be no sign of war," wrote Polidori of the souvenir hawkers who sought out pilgrims to the site. Byron was not immune to Waterloo wares; before the day was over, he had purchased a brass cuirass, a helmet with plume, and a sword.[12]

"I am not a collector or admirer of collections," Byron declared as part of a scathing commentary on the plundering of the Parthenon's friezes by Thomas Bruce (Lord Elgin).[13] Byron loathed Elgin for what he saw as the latter's grasping acquisitiveness. "While he and his patrons confine themselves to tasting medals, appreciating cameos, sketching columns, and cheapening gems, their little absurdities are as harmless as insect or fox-hunting, maiden-speechifying, barouche-driving, or any such pastime," Byron wrote. "But when they carry away three or four shiploads of the most valuable and massy relics that time and barbarism have left to the most injured and most celebrated of cities," he continued, "I know no motive which can excuse, no name which can designate, the perpetrators of this dastardly devastation."[14]

For Byron, Elgin's crime of carrying off the Parthenon's friezes (and losing great chunks of them in a shipping disaster) was compounded many times by the crime of turning his home into a "stone shop" and exhibiting the marbles before an unsophisticated audience. In *The Curse of Minerva*, a poetic diatribe on Elgin's mercenary opportunism, Byron exudes venomous disdain for the spectators of the marbles, an audience he derides for both its naïveté and its prurient preoccupations:

> While brawny brutes in stupid wonder stare,
> And marvel at his Lordship's "stone shop" there.
> Round the throng'd gate shall sauntering coxcombs creep,
> To lounge and lucubrate, to prate and peep;
> While many a languid maid, with longing sigh,
> On giant statues casts the curious eye:
> The room with transient glance appears to skim,
> Yet marks the mighty back and length of limb;
> Mourns o'er the difference of *now* and *then*,
> Exclaims, "these Greeks indeed were proper men!"
> Draws sly comparisons of *these* with *those*,
> And envies Lais all her Attic beaux.[15]

Byron faulted Elgin's onlookers for having too sensual an attachment to the marble fragments. The female spectators in his poem mourn the distance between now and then not because of some heightened awareness of an illustrious Greek past, but because of the salacious opportunity the marbles afford them for sizing up the Greek male physique. The "stupid wonder" of the brutish male spectator conjures up its alternative—some more judicious, less slack-jawed response.

Supporters of Elgin's actions claimed he had saved the marbles from certain destruction. Benjamin Robert Haydon chastised those who lamented Elgin's stripping Athens of its antique remains, arguing that "we should rather lament he was not there to strip it sooner, and then perhaps the most beautiful productions in the World would not have been pounded into mortar."[16] Haydon celebrated Elgin as a hero. "Where is the individual that would have had energy enough to persevere through so many obstacles?" he asked. Answering his own question, Haydon conjured up the reputation of Bonaparte. "He that could order the Gladiator to be brought over the Alps, tho it took three months crossing St. Cenis, when he was fighting [the] battle of Austerlitz—would feel a little interested I think for the ruins of Athens." If Elgin had neglected to seize the marbles "from a squeamish fear of offending pedantic Antiquaries," Haydon insisted, "Bonaparte would have had them the moment he had the power."[17]

Byron had no sympathy for Elgin, but he invoked a similar argument when he made off with historical remains. He mailed his Waterloo relics back to his publisher in England, and later supplemented his luggage with the bones of Burgundian soldiers which he had carried away from a chapel at Morat. "Of these relics I ventured to bring away as much as may have made the quarter of a hero," he wrote flippantly. He justified his plunder by comparing his "careful preservation" of these objects to the "less justifiable larcenies of the Swiss postillions, who carried them off to sell for knife-handles."[18] Byron made a distinction, that is, between his gathering of relics as private keepsakes, and others' appropriation of them for commercial purposes, the sale of knife handles, or, in Elgin's case, the creation of a makeshift museum.

Surely Byron visited Bullock's carriage exhibition, but it is unlikely that he saw any parallel between that enterprise and his own genteel crisscrossing of Europe in a look-alike carriage.[19] Bullock purchased Napoleon's carriage for the sum of 2,500 guineas from the Prince Regent and put it on display in his London museum from January until August 1816, afterward touring with it to Bristol, Dublin, and Edinburgh.[20] Byron's low opinion of the behavior of visitors to the Elgin marbles is borne out by the tokens that remain of Bullock's exhibition, contemporary caricatures that depict a chaotic free-for-all, with men and women clambering over the carriage's roof and couples kissing or flirting inside its cabin (see figs. 15 and 16). In his catalogue for the exhibition, Bullock tried to steer the carriage to higher ground, emphasizing its edifying capacity to forge an immediate connection between the spectator and "the greatest events and persons, that the world ever beheld."[21] But in one caricature, three women inspect a chamber pot, and in another, a woman plants a foot on the chest of a prostrate fop.[22] Bullock insisted that "those feelings that must be involved in regarding this object [the carriage], surpass those which could be excited by almost any other upon earth."[23] The feelings on display in the caricatures are mostly those we associate with sex and violence: a crowd at the back of the exhibition brandishes sticks and fists; two men gawk at a print of the Hottentot Venus, who is nude and smoking a pipe.

The caricatures, one drawn by Thomas Rowlandson, the other by George Cruikshank, are remarkably similar in their emphasis on physicality, not just in the form of sexual desire, enacted by the flirtatious and promiscuous visitors to the exhibition, but also in the clutter of physical objects, the stuffed birds encased in the upper-left corner of Rowlandson's drawing, the litter of Napoleonic relics—slippers, nightcap, boots, pistol—strewn on the floor in the foreground. Whatever numinous glamour the carriage possessed, these drawings insist, it was always in danger of deteriorating from divine relic to tawdry clutter.

Still, even as Cruikshank and Rowlandson mock the public fascination with all things Napoleon, they hint at the way Napoleonic objects acted upon (even temporary) possessors. The spectators in the drawings seem excited and energized by their mingling with the emperor's belongings. Their feverish engagement with

Fig. 15. George Cruikshank, "A Scene at the London Museum Piccadilly" (1816). Copyright © The Trustees of the British Museum.

Fig. 16. Thomas Rowlandson, "Exhibition at Bullock's Museum of Boneparte's Carriage Taken at Waterloo" (1816). Copyright © The Trustees of the British Museum.

the relics bestows on these objects the magical power of a fetish, in the word's original anthropological sense. Bullock attributed a similar enchantment to Napoleonic relics when he recalled how his ownership of them had shaped his life. It was "the accidental possession" of a Napoleon medal that had laid the foundation of the London Museum, he maintained. Bullock had "all his life entertained an opinion that his destiny was, in some mysterious way, linked with that of Buonaparte, and that they would somehow proceed and culminate together."[24]

Bullock and Bonaparte did not, of course, culminate together. Napoleon was confined to St. Helena, where he died in 1821, the same year that Bullock, ever the showman, put a family of Laplanders on display in his London exhibition hall. Bullock went on to plan a retirement community in Cincinnati, to sojourn

in Venezuela, to visit Berlin, and to die an unheralded death in Chelsea. Before
he did all of these things, however, he cannily realized eight times his initial in-
vestment in the carriage by charging people for the privilege of examining
Napoleon's equipage at close range. His Napoleonic exhibition "was more ad-
vantageous in a pecuniary point of view" than the entire labors of [his] life.[25]
Even if Bullock's principal interest in the carriage was mercenary, he, like the
Prince Regent before him, imagined himself as Napoleon's alter ego and rival.
Recalling the carriage's contents, years after the exhibition, Bullock enthused:

> These (like Elijah's mantle) gave me the power of accomplishing, in a few months,
> what, with all his talents, riches, and armies, [Napoleon] could never succeed in doing;
> for in that short period I over-ran England, Ireland, and Scotland, levying a willing
> contribution on upwards of 800,000 of his Majesty's subjects; for old and young; rich
> and poor, clergy and laity, all ages, sexes, and conditions, flocked to pay their poll-tax,
> and gratify their curiosity by an examination of the spoils of the dead lion.[26]

In Cruikshank's drawing of Bullock's exhibition, one of the spectators has
donned Napoleon's traveling coat, and he poses as if wielding a whip and holding
imaginary reins.[27] Napoleon's cloak helped Bullock's visitor imagine himself as
the impresario of extraordinary acts, as Napoleon en route to his next conquest.

Relic collecting predates the romantic period, but the fascination with the
physical remains of noteworthy people increased exponentially in the late
eighteenth century. Susan Pearce remarks on the anachronistic quality of the

collecting habit, "its ability to carry on quite happily into a new generation modes of operation which belong to the previous generation, or generations."[28] She links the persistence into the romantic period of relic collecting to an appetite for sensationalism that had never lost (and, one might add, never loses) its hold.[29] But a particular constellation of forces linked to consumerism and historicism made the ongoing appetite for sensationalism especially powerful in the romantic period. One factor was the desire for novelty that suffused romantic literary culture and that also advanced the forms of modern consumerism developing in that era. The increased appetite for sensationalism was a manifestation of this larger pursuit of the not-yet-experienced. And the striving after novelty, ironically, accelerated the pursuit of the old, the fervent effort to recover vestiges of a newly resonant past.

Consider, for example, the romantic era's exaltation and exhumation of Shakespeare. Shakespeare's plays were regularly performed before the late eighteenth century, but at that moment he became the fetishized playwright we know today; his plays were annotated, his life story written and rewritten, and his belongings sought out and preserved.[30] The dawn of bardolatry arrived with the felling of a mulberry tree that stood in the garden of Shakespeare's final home ("New Place") in 1756. When a canny local businessman purchased wood from the tree and turned it into cases for weights and scales, as well as other souvenir objects and toys, a new memorabilia industry took off. By 1765, a walnut tree in front of Shakespeare's birthplace had gone missing, adding to the supply of Shakespearean lumber from which association tea chests and tobacco stoppers could claim to have been fashioned.[31]

After Napoleon's death at St. Helena, the trees that lined his grave site were stripped of their branches, the wood carried away and slivered into souvenirs. A "Piece of Napoleon's Willow" is a standard item of Napoleana; a catalogue of one collection describes its "fragment of the trunk of the willow-tree in whose shade Napoleon was wont to sit during the years of his exile, and under which he was buried."[32] In June 1830, a Mr. Childers bought the tree against which Wellington stood at Waterloo, and cut it up for timber out of which to make presents. "He gave the Duke of Rutland enough for a chair," Haydon reported, going on to lament, "You can't admit the English into your gardens, but they will strip your trees, cut their names on your statues, eat your fruit, & stuff their pockets with bits for their musaeums."[33]

Collecting Napoleonic relics could become such a popular pastime because Napoleon himself was a product of the era's avid consumer culture and heightened sense of historicity. Napoleon had associated himself with so many physical objects that the supply of Napoleonic possessions was bottomless. Even after his final capture, he continued to be ringed by material goods; the Prince Regent made sure that Napoleon would be supplied with suitable accoutrements even as he was being cast into exile. Around the same time William Bullock was preparing to put Napoleon's carriage and its contents on display, his brother George, a furniture maker, won a commission to outfit Napoleon's home at St. Helena. While William Bullock was taking Napoleon's carriage furnishings on tour, George Bullock was gathering furniture, curtains, and floor coverings for twenty-six rooms at New Longwood House. He supplied silver, glass, china, and earthenware services, "a vast *batterie de cuisine*" which, after Napoleon's death, became nearly as sought after as the ephemera of the emperor's last battle.[34]

The continent was for Byron a literary as well as a military memorial ground. He visited Petrarch's house and grave. He traversed "all Rousseau's ground—with the Heloise before me" and was struck by the force and accuracy of Rousseau's descriptions. Byron wrote, "Meillerie—Clarens—&Vevey—& the Chateau de Chillon are places of which I shall say little—because all I could say must fall short of the impressions they stamp."[35] He visited the summer house where Gibbon finished his *History*, and he snipped acacia leaves from Gibbon's garden. Byron sneered at collectors such as Elgin, but he cherished his own modest gathering of literary souvenirs.

Six years before Byron replicated Napoleon's carriage, William Godwin credited association objects like the ones to which the poet was drawn with the power to transform their possessors. In his 1809 *Essay on Sepulchres*, Godwin wrote of his attachment to the physical aspects of a dead friend: "Though I should adopt the creed of bishop Berkeley, and believe that the body of my friend . . . was nothing, yet I can never separate my idea of his peculiarities and his actions, from my idea of his person." Godwin insisted that everything associated with his friend—"his ring, his watch, his books, and his habitation"—acquired a value that was "not merely fictitious." "They have an empire over my mind," he wrote. "They can make me happy or unhappy; they can torture, and they can tranquillise; they can purify my sentiments, and make me similar to the man I love."[36]

Godwin anticipates in reverse Jean Baudrillard's view of collected objects as "mental precincts over which [the collector] holds sway."[37] In Godwin's meditation on association objects, artifacts of the dead hold sway over the living; the usual linkage of empire with the conscription of captured objects is turned upside down as the objects come to dominate their possessor. Godwin is willing to grant power to the supposed physical remains of even the fictional dead. He writes of his attachment to the physical traces of dead authors: "I am not content to visit the house in Bread-Street where Milton was born, or that in Bunhill-Row where he died, I want to repair to the place where *he now dwells*" (*Sepulchres*, 77). But then, curiously, he expresses a willingness to mark not only the graves of writers but also the fictional graves of their creations. He writes: "Yet to an imaginary person I do not refuse the semblance of a tomb. . . . [P]oetical scenes affect us in somewhat the same manner as historical: I should be delighted to visit the spot where Cervantes imagined Don Quixote to be buried, or the fabulous tomb of Clarissa Harlowe" (*Sepulchres*, 85).

One can read Godwin's odd assertion in two ways: either actual markers of human experience are so crucial that he is willing to fabricate them so that those touched by Clarissa can further commune with her invented physical remains;

or, alternatively, objects are so embellished by sentimental narratives that the actual objects are less important than the stories that accrue around them. Whatever the case, Godwin's plans for the marking of (real and imagined) graves grows complex. He suggests a map, to be called "the Atlas of those who have Lived, for the Use of Men Hereafter to be Born," and prescribes that it should be "plentifully marked with meridian lines and circles of latitude, 'with centric and eccentric scribbled o'er,' so as to ascertain with incredible minuteness where the monuments of eminent men had been, and where their ashes continue to repose" (*Sepulchres*, 112). He further recommends that a catalogue be compiled in order to exhibit "in a brief compass the places of sepulture of the Illustrious Departed." He ends his *Essay* by calling this imagined catalogue a "precious relic" to the man of sentiment, and a "Traveller's Guide, of a very different measure of utility, from the 'Catalogue of Gentleman's Seats,' which is now appended to the 'Book of Post-Roads through Every Part of Great Britain" (*Sepulchres*, 114 and 115).

Godwin's elaborate apparatus—a configuration of grave markers, maps, catalogues—in support of literary grave sites, both actual and imagined, anticipates the way in which the legitimating narratives connected to Napoleonic objects took on lives of their own.

While fleeing at Genappe, Napoleon's coach driver, a Dutchman named Jean Hornn, had two fingers lopped off and several shots fired into his legs. Months later, Hornn suffered the further indignity of being recruited by

Bullock to stand sentinel over the carriage display. Like the carriage's battle scars, which Bullock highlighted in his exhibition catalogue—"there are two sabre cuts, which were aimed at the coachman when the carriage was taken"— Hornn's body attested to Napoleon's travels and travails. Bullock emphasized the coachman's impeccable credentials in an address to the public. "The authenticity of the man, as coachman of Bonaparte, Mr. Bullock feels himself perfectly competent to assert," he wrote, insisting that the means he had used to "prevent the possibility of imposture" were "far more than sufficient to dismiss scepticism." These statements prefaced Bullock's publication of *The Narrative of Jean Hornn, Military Coachman to Napoleon Bonaparte*, which tells the story that Napoleon's carriage might have told if it could have spoken for itself.[38]

During the romantic period, object narratives—tales of sofas, thimbles, old shoes, and pincushions—multiplied into a distinct genre that seems to have stemmed from a communal desire to know what physical things had to say.[39] *The Narrative of Jean Hornn, Military Coachman to Napoleon Bonaparte* does not literally let Napoleon's carriage speak for itself, but it is so preoccupied with carriages in general that it might rightly be placed in a subcategory of the object narrative genre. When Hornn recalls his time spent traveling to the frontiers of Spain, the *Narrative* notes that Napoleon's "suite consisted of ten or twelve carriages, which moved in three divisions" (*Narrative*, 19). When Napoleon attended the marriage of Maria Louisa, the daughter of the emperor of Austria, Hornn's recollection specifies that "the cavalcade included forty-four carriages; of which number eight belonged to the Imperial household" (*Narrative*, 29). When Hornn conjures up the "extraordinary appearance" of the French army's retreat from Moscow, the image he recalls is that of "files of carriages, three or four abreast, extended for several leagues" (*Narrative*, 39). One gets the distinct sense from Hornn's narrative that if his fingers had not been cut off in the vicinity of Waterloo, he would have been using them to count battle vehicles.[40] His blinkered perspective conjures up a history composed of carriages, a narrative in which Napoleon amounts to the sum of his vehicles. Hornn's narrative testifies to the authenticity of Bullock's carriage, but, just as important, it also links that carriage to a series of exciting stories. These stories enhanced the carriage's allure, and increased the vehicle's ability to legitimate other putative Napoleon possessions, many of them linked to that man and his exploits by only the most tenuous of narrative threads.

Where there is a Napoleonic teapot or tongue scraper there is an authenticating narrative ready to lash itself to history. As the moment of acquisition of a particular object recedes further and further into the distant past, the conscientious collector or curator strives ever harder to tease out the bits of corroborating evidence that will definitively confirm the object's unique status. Take the piece of Napoleon's intestine once part of the holdings of the Museum of the Royal College of Surgeons of England, acquired in 1841 from the museum of Sir Astley Cooper. The authenticity of the specimen's origin was called into question by Sir James Paget in 1883, when he wrote in a footnote to a catalogue entry, "The truth of the statement that these portions of intestine were taken from the body of the Emperor Napoleon I is open to grave doubt."[41] He then marshaled the postmortem account of Napoleon's personal physician to contrast Cooper's description of a cancerous growth on the piece of small intestine to the sound state of Napoleon's tissue. But that did not put the case to rest; the authenticity of the specimen was debated at length in a 1960 article on the object— nineteen years after it had been destroyed by bombing during a World War II air raid.

The authenticating story, with its mixture of hard fact and innuendo, exponentially enhances its correlative object—especially in the case of the missing intestine, which exists as a smudge on a wrinkled backdrop in grainy photographs. Body parts are the most intimate of association objects, and they inspire the most elaborate corroborating stories, the most strident quasi-scientific testimony. The bookseller A. S. W. Rosenbach purchased a collection of Napoleonic relics that once belonged to Napoleon's priest; these included a fine holland shirt, a handkerchief marked with his cipher, and, more startlingly, "a mummified tendon taken from Napoleon's body during the post-mortem."[42] The word "tendon" is a polite euphemism for a body part that Rosenbach's biographer refuses to identify by accurate name. "Few so intimate portions of a man's anatomy have ever been displayed to so many," the biographer writes, noting also that Rosenbach took "Rabelaisian delight" in talking about his relics, and put them on exhibition at the Museum of French Art, where the "tendon" garnered the most attention. The body part's materiality, however, was so pressing that it threatened to dissolve the swirl of narratives and leave only a queasy visceral response. Visitors to Rosenbach's relic exhibition peered into a glass case to find something that looked "like a maltreated strip of buckskin shoelace or shriveled eel."[43]

Perhaps because it was such an ostentatious conveyance, perhaps because it had carried Napoleon so far, perhaps because it was associated with his ultimate downfall, the carriage came to play a particularly important role in the authentication of putative Napoleonic objects, such as the pen box and pistols belonging to Sir Walter Scott. A female descendant who compiled a catalogue of Scott's "personal relics and antiquarian treasures" describes a Napoleonic blotting book in his possession: "It is tied with three pairs of greenish-blue ribbons, fringed with gold beads, and passing through a hollow ball of gold filigree so as to form a sort of tassel." She then documents the "tradition" that linked the "portfolio" to Napoleon's carriage. "There are various interesting references to the Emperor's carriage and its contents in the annals of Waterloo; and, although the portfolio is not mentioned, we venture to quote from them," she writes.[44] Scott's relative then quotes at length from Colonel Charras's account of the seizure of the carriage, and from Blücher's thrilling description of Napoleon caught unaware as he was about to retreat: "He jumped out, threw himself on horseback without his sword, when his hat tumbled off."[45] So alluring was the carriage that even though there was no actual evidence to link Scott's portfolio to this conveyance, its history served to enliven the unrelated object by encouraging the reader to imagine Napoleon blotting a freshly inked page, just before Blücher's men closed in.

By April 1817, Byron and his carriage had reached Rome. Like Bullock's exhibition, Byron's appearances were announced by newspapers, but it would have been difficult to miss his entourage even without the attendant publicity. Reports of Byron's reputation preceded him to every destination, and the carriage was driven by a "dreadful smacker of his whip" who wore thigh boots, a blue and red coat, and a leather hat with a broad brim.[46] When the poet encountered a party of English sightseers on the roof of St. Peter's, one matron stood as if her feet were rooted to the ground, so alarmed at the "terrible reprobate" that she ordered her daughter to avert her eyes: "Don't look at him, he is dangerous to look at."[47]

Byron enjoyed his ability to strike fear in the hearts of English mothers, to inspire the same thrill of terror that caused the English Princess Augusta, caught up in reading a book about Bonaparte, to startle her maid by crying out, "O! *you Devil*," as if the emperor himself had invaded her boudoir.[48] He actively cultivated an identification with Napoleon, and not just by traveling in a replica of his carriage. The narrator of *Don Juan* boasts that he "was reckoned, a considerable time, / The grand Napoleon of the realms of rhyme."[49] And Byron took "childish delight" in adopting his estranged wife's family name of Noel because of the opportunity it provided for him to make Napoleon's initials his own— N. B. for Noel Byron.[50]

While Byron was rumbling around in a replica carriage, he wrote most of his best poems. He worked on the third canto of *Childe Harold's Pilgrimage* while driving through Belgium and up the Rhine Valley in April and May 1816; he finished the canto in Switzerland at the beginning of July. He began *Manfred* in Switzerland in August of that same year, completing it in Venice the following January. In 1817 he traveled from Venice to Ferrara, Bologna, and Florence, then back to Venice, on to La Mira, and back to Venice again in November. By early January 1818, he had completed work on the fourth canto of *Childe Harold*. In July 1818, Byron began "virtually at the same time *and* together" *Don Juan* and his *Memoirs*, John Clubbe notes, linking these two undertakings to Byron's "hawk-like" following of Napoleon's fortunes in exile.[51] By mid-1818, Byron had accumulated a Napoleonic library of books and journal articles, many of which reported that the emperor had begun his memoirs. Emulating Napoleon's example as an autobiographer, Byron "began his own two-pronged assault on posterity."[52]

In what was perhaps Byron's most impressive feat of peripatetic poetry writing, he composed twenty-six stanzas of *Childe Harold* on the day he rode from Brussels to Waterloo and back. The next day he was asked by Pryse Lockhart Gordon's wife to write a few lines in her scrapbook. Byron's two-stanza contribution remarked on the appropriate way to commemorate the field of Waterloo:

> Is the spot mark'd with no colossal bust?
> Nor column trophied for triumphal show?
>
> None; but the moral's truth tells simpler so,
> As the ground was before, thus let it be;—[53]

The lines obliquely suggest the futility of commemorating history and its heroes with physical objects. By scrawling in Mrs. Gordon's scrapbook, however, Byron turned these lines from what would become *Childe Harold's Pilgrimage* into an especially valued association object, something she could use to commemorate her close encounter with the poet Byron.[54]

Gloating over his own poetic brilliance in an 1819 letter to a friend, Byron wrote: "As to 'Don Juan'—confess—confess—you dog—and be candid— . . . Could any man have written it—who has not lived in the world?—and tooled in a post-chaise? in a hackney coach? in a Gondola? against a wall? in a court carriage? in a vis-a-vis?—on a table?—and under it?"[55] The word "tool" was a slang term for driving—that is, one could "tool" a coach. But Byron here also seems to be drawing on the long-standing use of the word to refer to a penis. He associates the writing of *Don Juan* to driving about in all manner of vehicles, and also to the sexual activity consummated in those conveyances. Tooling around in a vehicle modeled to look like Napoleon's own increased Byron's creative potency, or at least helped him to believe in this kind of literary enhancement.[56]

At his 1819 auction, Bullock sold Napoleon's carriage to a coach builder named Hopkinson for £168. Hopkinson then sold the carriage, in part payment of a bad debt, to another coach builder, Robert Jeffreys, whose address was on Gray's Inn Road. There, as far as we know, Napoleon's carriage quietly spent the next twenty-five years.

"Nothing is too trivial for the Napoleon enthusiast," wrote A. M. Broadley in his *Napoleon in Caricature*.[57] This statement can be found in any edition of Broadley's book, but it stands out most forcefully in the extra-illustrated edition compiled between 1911 and 1913 by a Napoleon collector named Alfred Brewis from Newcastle–upon Tyne. Brewis turned the two-volume *Napoleon in Caricature* into a multivolume work by embellishing it with Napoleon ephemera: playbills, notices, portraits.

Brewis's grangerized Broadley presents a reversal of the usual system of authentication, in which stories—actual and invented—testify to the value of association objects. Brewis preserved what is probably the sole surviving copy of *The Coach That Napoleon Ran From*, a piece of advertising frivolity pitched at a child audience. The tract tells the carriage's story in the familiar cadence of "the house that Jack built":

> The wonderful COACH, from which NAPPY flew,
> At BULLOCK'S Museum is open to view;
> And if you will please, to take a walk in,
> The whole will be shown, as neat as a pin;
> His Watch, Knives and Forks, and Cup you will see,
> Besides his Gold Pot, for making his tea;
> His Plates, Spoons, and Bedstead, and, to be short,
> His Silver Utensils, of every sort;
> And if you wish you, may have a step through,
> The CARRIAGE so famous, from fam'd WATERLOO![58]

Attached to Brewis's copy of the tract is a ticket that announces it will admit the bearer to the exhibition of Bonaparte's military carriage at the London Museum "or in whatever part of the United Kingdom it may happen to be exhibited" (see fig. 17). Long separated from any small hand, this scrap of paper nonetheless invites us to imagine a curious child viewer poised to visit Bullock's museum. The ticket animates the verse—and vice versa.

Susan Pearce suggests that a capacity to become rubbish is an inherent fea-

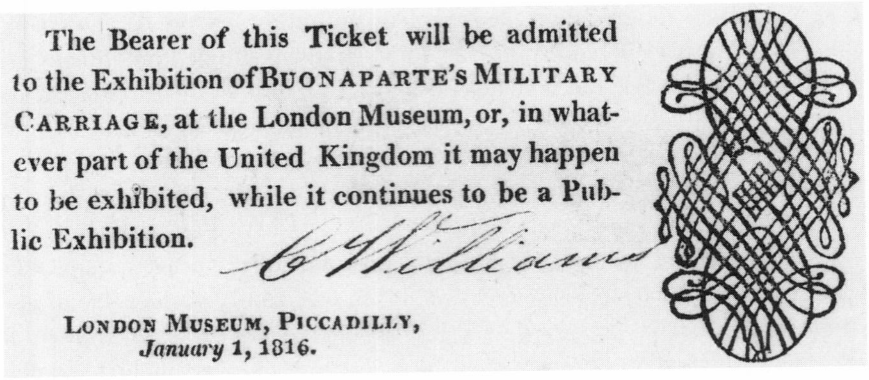

The Bearer of this Ticket will be admitted to the Exhibition of BUONAPARTE'S MILITARY CARRIAGE, at the London Museum, or, in whatever part of the United Kingdom it may happen to be exhibited, while it continues to be a Public Exhibition.

C. Williams

LONDON MUSEUM, PICCADILLY,
January 1, 1816.

Fig. 17. Ticket to Bullock's exhibition of Napoleon's carriage from Curzon b.2, fol. 128. By kind permission of the Bodleian Library, University of Oxford.

ture of all collections because "although all collections are a part of the function of knowledge and have their niche in intellectual history, some do this much more powerfully than others, and some so feebly as to make a negligible statement."[59] But no Napoleonic vestige is so slight that it will not balloon in importance when coupled with an authenticating story. Brewis's objects enliven Broadley's narrative, but Broadley's narrative motivated Brewis to rescue and protect items that, storyless, would turn into rubbish.

Napoleon's carriage, too, survived as long as it did because of the symbiotic relationship of object and narrative, but it was always in danger of retreating permanently into darkness, of rotting away unnoticed in a carriage house on Gray's Inn Road.

The penultimate sighting of Byron's Napoleonic carriage was at the cremation of Shelley's body on a beach near Viareggio in 1822. Shelley's "corpse fell open and the heart was laid bare," wrote Edward Trelawny, who orchestrated the event.[60] Leigh Hunt, arriving on the scene with Byron, took refuge from the horrors of the funeral pyre. "I remained inside the carriage," he wrote, "now looking on, now drawing back with feelings that were not to be witnessed."[61] Later that night, as Hunt and Byron rode in Byron's carriage through the forest of Pisa, they drank too much and broke into song. "What the coachman thought of us, God knows," Hunt wrote, "but he helped to make up a ghastly trio."[62]

A year later, as he was leaving Italy for Greece, Byron asked Charles Barry to sell some of the possessions he was leaving behind and to take care of others. He wrote, "I particularly recommend to your Care my own travelling Chariot—which I would not part with for any consideration." This missive inspired Byron's biographer to ask, "Was he dreaming of a triumphal return to England in his Napoleonic carriage?"[63]

The carriage resurfaced one final time in Australia. It had come into the possession of Charlotte Harley, who as a girl had inspired Byron's dedication "To Ianthe" in *Childe Harold's Pilgrimage*. The dedication and preface to Byron's poem draw attention to the peripatetic circumstances of the poet. "The following poem was written for the most part, amidst the scenes which it attempts to describe," Byron begins his preface, before going on to write, "It was begun in Albania; and the parts relative to Spain and Portugal were composed from the author's observations in those countries." The first line of Byron's dedication "To Ianthe" asserts the impossibility of finding a presence like hers even in those climes, where, Byron writes, "I have late been straying."[64] His actual Ianthe married a Waterloo veteran, Major General Anthony Bacon, and moved to Australia, where she apparently left the carriage upon her return to England. Years later the carriage was discovered by a traveler at Lake Wangary, near Port Lincoln. According to the historian Ernestine Hill: "It was in a fair state of preservation, though dilapidated, with the aura of old romance in the scrolled crest, *Crede Biron*. Alas, in the outside of a wayside inn, the fowls were roosting in it. In the grooved leather cushions where genius had brooded lay an egg. So the chariot of Apollo, the most glorious, most notorious coach of London in its day, was left at world's end to ruin and neglect."[65] Hill depicts the carriage as the seat of genius, as the source of both Byron's notoriety and his creative power, and thus affirms the poet's own sense of the vehicle's numinous capacity.

The Byron family motto, with its second-person imperative form of the verb *credere*, directs the observer to "Trust Byron." The scrolled crest, happened upon in Australia, stood as certification of the carriage's Byron association.[66] Trust that this carriage actually belonged to Byron, it had now come to say. Or perhaps: it is only necessary to believe that this carriage is authentic in order to make it so. In any event, Byron's souvenir of Napoleon had been transformed into a souvenir of Byron himself.

Napoleon's actual carriage was eventually purchased by Madame Tussaud and displayed as part of her Napoleon Gallery, where it lost none of its associative luster. One Tussaud visitor recalled gazing at it for several awestruck seconds: "It looked black, shapeless and funereal, though it was dark blue, expertly designed and full of use for the living." The same visitor, conjuring up Napoleon's peripatetic lifestyle, noted that the carriage had "fixtures for maps, telescope, soap, surgical supplies, wines, spirits, sword, pistols and other articles that can be left to a humdrum imagination," but what he remembered most was "the little apparatus of three folding steps which seemed to me to have been made for a small girl."[67]

Tussaud's descendants had the carriage glazed so as to protect it from ruthless souvenir hunters, whose "mutilations" made it necessary for the Tussaud operatives to keep in stock rolls of cloth "to renew the lining from time to time." Marie Tussaud's great-grandson wondered "how many people in different parts of the world now show their friends strips of cloth purporting to be taken from the original lining of the Napoleon carriage, whereas the 'souvenirs' are really 'relics' of the looms of Yorkshire?"[68] In this way, the interior of Napoleon's actual carriage, over time, became a palimpsest of replacement fabric.

Napoleon's carriage was destroyed by a fire at Tussaud's gallery in 1925. Of one thing we can be certain. The upholstery scraps that were torn from the vehicle's interior and secreted away by Tussaud ticket holders have grown their own stories by now, whether these remnants ever made contact with Napoleon or not.

CHAPTER FOUR

BELZONI IN RUINS

When Giovanni Belzoni came across the tomb of the pharaoh Ay, the successor to Tutankhamen, on the bank of the Nile, he took out his chisel and carved "DIS-COVERED BY BELZONI—1816" over the gateway. A year later, on breaching the temple of Ramesses II at Abu Simbel, he left his name, the names of his fellow adventurers, and the date on the north wall of the sanctuary near the statues of deities. When he broke into the pyramid of Khephren at Giza, he inscribed his name and the date in the burial chamber.[1] A seated colossus in the British Museum has Belzoni's name written near its left foot, and the sarcophagus of Seti I stationed in the basement of Sir John Soane's Museum in London has "BELZONI" printed near its rim, the lone Roman letters amidst the rows of hieroglyphs.

Competition was fierce among collectors of Egyptian artifacts in the early nineteenth century, and it was customary to mark ownership in this way. In his *Narrative of the Operations and Recent Discoveries within the Pyramids, Temples, Tombs, and Excavations in Egypt and Nubia,* Belzoni recalls taking possession of sixteen large blocks of stone on the island of Philoe, only to find them later "mutilated and written upon in the French language,'*operation manquée.*' "[2] A proprietary impulse fueled the practice of leaving a signature behind, but also a desire to lend permanence to one's fleeting presence. When William Turner ascended the pyramids of Giza with Belzoni in 1819, he found the accumulated graffiti of past English Kilroys. "On the stones scattered about were the names of several of my countrymen, (some as old as the beginning of the last century,) and I could not resist putting mine in such good company."[3] Flaubert, touring Egypt in 1850, was infuriated to discover that a certain Thompson had carved his name in huge letters on Pompey's column. "It can be read a quarter of a league away," Flaubert complained. "There is no way to see the column without seeing the name 'Thompson' and consequently without thinking of 'Thompson.' "[4]

Belzoni, a native of Padua, was an enormous man who stood six and a half feet tall in his stocking feet. He made a name for himself in London as a performing strongman and pantomime giant before traveling to Egypt in 1815 as a hydraulics expert. After improving the irrigation system in Mohammed Aly's garden near Cairo, he allied himself with the British consul general Henry Salt, who helped finance his tomb-raiding operations. Belzoni excavated the temple of Ramesses II at Abu Simbel, he opened the grotto sepulchre of Seti I, and he penetrated the second pyramid of Giza, before returning to Europe. In 1821 he used William Bullock's Piccadilly museum building as the venue for his staging of a re-created Egyptian tomb, and there he displayed sundry Egyptian artifacts he had gathered on his travels.

Belzoni's archaeological pursuits rode the crest of a wave of enthusiasm for all things Egyptian, a fascination that had been fueled by Nelson's 1798 victory over Napoleon at the Battle of the Nile. In the aftermath of the battle, Nelson's mistress, Emma Hamilton, described how his name was celebrated in street signs and grand illuminations, as well as in women's fashion. "My dress from head to foot is alla Nelson," she wrote. "My earrings are Nelson's anchors; in short, we are be-Nelsoned all over."[5] A month later she sent Nelson triumphal congratulations. "If I was King of England," she wrote, "I would make you the most noble puissant DUKE NELSON, MARQUIS NILE, EARL ALEXANDRIA, VISCOUNT PYRA-

MID, BARON CROCODILE, AND PRINCE VICTORY, that posterity might have you in all forms."[6]

"Every thing now must be Egyptian: the ladies wear crocodile ornaments, and you sit upon a sphinx in a room hung round with mummies," wrote Robert Southey in 1807, in advance of the publication by Napoleon's Egyptian monument commission of the twenty-one-volume *Description de l'Égypte* (1809–1828), a magisterial opus which heightened interest in Egyptian motifs. Southey continued: "The very shopboards must be metamorphosed into the mode, and painted in Egyptian letters, which, as the Egyptians had no letters, you will doubtless conceive must be curious. They are simply the common characters, deprived of all beauty and all proportion by having all the strokes of equal thickness, so that those which should be thin look as if they had the elephantiasis."[7]

Southey was not the only one to note the lack of proportion in British representations of Egyptian design. The architect John Soane, who objected to the "Egyptian mania," wondered "what can be more puerile and unsuccessful than the paltry attempt to imitate the character and form of [Egyptian] works in small and confined spaces." The essential qualities of Egyptian buildings and monuments were, for Soane, a "prodigious solidity and wonderful magnitude."[8] The same features may have inspired another architect who set out to erect a pyramid in the vicinity of Primrose Hill.[9]

William Bullock's Egyptian Hall, where Belzoni staged his Egyptian tomb exhibition in 1821, further underscored the association between Egyptian design and giant dimensions. The building's 1812 renovation, based on plates in the *Description de l'Égypte*, incorporated two colossal Egyptian figures in its façade. Exotic architectural details—cavetto cornices, torus moldings, corbel-arched windows—made the building stand out among the more somber-faced edifices of Piccadilly, and caused Leigh Hunt to grumble about the inappropriateness of its placement (see fig. 18).[10] "Egyptian architecture will do nowhere but in Egypt," Hunt wrote in *A Saunter Through the West End*. "There, its cold and gloomy ponderosity ('weight' is too petty a word) befits the hot, burning atmosphere and shifting sands. But in such a climate as this, it is nothing but an uncouth

Fig. 18. Thomas H. Shepherd, "Egyptian Hall, Piccadilly." Copyright © The Trustees of the British Museum.

anomaly."[11] The new building was designed to stop saunterers like Hunt in their tracks, and on that count it was wildly successful. "The absurdity . . . renders it a good advertisement," Hunt conceded. "There is no missing its great lumpish face as you go along."[12]

The collector, it is often noted, shores himself up through his association with rare and valuable objects, turning the collected object, torn from its original context, into a projection of the self. "Its absolute singularity," Jean Baudrillard writes, "allows me . . . to recognize myself in the object as an absolutely singular being."[13] The larger the collected object, it logically follows, the larger the potential for self-aggrandizement. Giovanni Belzoni, in associating himself with Egyptian objects, linked his name to artifacts known first of all for their enormous scale. In this way he attempted to make a name for himself, but also to make people forget his prior claim to theatrical fame.

Belzoni gathered his archaeological finds at a time when Thomas Bruce (Lord Elgin), William Hamilton, and Charles Towneley had become associated with gatherings of antique objects that were ultimately immortalized in British Museum collections bearing their names.[14] But Belzoni's ambiguous social status as a foreigner and a former stage giant made his effort to distinguish himself by association with collected objects a more complicated affair than it was for these affluent men. What is more, regardless of how he tried to set his name in stone, the objects Belzoni uprooted ultimately resisted his appropriation. Many of Belzoni's finds came to reside in the British Museum, but the name he made for himself through the collecting of Egyptian objects was a perishable entity that kept threatening to crumble or get carried away. These days, it is entirely possible to stumble across the name Belzoni without thinking of Belzoni at all.

Belzoni's collecting career coincided with and dramatizes the romantic literary affection for large objects, and should be viewed in the context of a general romantic preoccupation with gigantic ambition. Romantic poets are most celebrated for their short lyrics, but they nearly all took Milton as their model and aspired to writing large poems. Keats's *Endymion* is one such exercise, an attempt to "make 4000 lines of one bare circumstance and fill them with poetry." Keats characterized the long poem as "a test of Invention which I take to be the Polar Star of Poetry," and went on to ask, "Did our great Poets ever write short Pieces?"[15] Wordsworth, too, was bent on creating a gigantic work of art. He saw

The Prelude as the "ante-chapel" to the grand cathedral of his planned magnum opus.[16]

These forms of literary ambition are directly related to the romantic preoccupation with posthumous acclaim. As Andrew Bennett suggests, "one of the key motivations of the literary as it was conceived and defined in the Romantic period is the possibility of future, posthumous recognition or canonisation."[17] Wordsworth's *Prelude* was his attempt to construct a poetic monument to himself. It manifests the same desire for immortality that we see in the last passage of "Lines composed a few miles above Tintern Abbey," where the narrator portrays his female companion as a potential museum for his posthumous self. He looks forward to "after years," when her mind "shall be a mansion for all lovely forms," her memory "a dwelling-place / For all sweet sounds and harmonies," and—especially—for thoughts of him. "Oh! then, / If solitude, or fear, or pain, or grief, / Should be thy portion," the narrator advises his companion, "with what healing thoughts / Of tender joy wilt thou remember me."[18]

The belief that immortality could best be achieved through the creation of large works of art was not cherished solely by poets; the painter Benjamin Robert Haydon stands as the most ardent advocate of this line of thinking. In the year before Belzoni mounted his exhibition, Haydon used Bullock's venue to display his gigantic painting *Christ's Triumphal Entry into Jerusalem*. The frame of this work weighed six hundred pounds, and the first attempt to hang it resulted in the snapping of a massive iron ring. By the time Belzoni's exhibition opened, Haydon had ordered a canvas nineteen feet long and fifteen feet high, on which he began to paint a depiction of the raising of Lazarus that featured a nine-foot-tall Christ. According to Haydon's biographer, "if he had had any success he certainly would never have stopped till he had painted the largest picture in the world."[19] Haydon was egged on by William Hazlitt, who championed his very large paintings. "[Haydon's] genius is gigantic. He is of the race of Brobdignag, and not of Lilliput. . . . He bestrides his art like a Colossus," wrote Hazlitt. Lamenting artistic under-reaching in *The Spirit of the Age*, Hazlitt faulted those artists who, confronted with some noble monument of art, were "content to admire without thinking of rivalling it."[20]

We discover a link between large material objects of the kind Belzoni excavated and grandiose artistic projects of the kind promoted by Keats and Haydon in eighteenth-century commentary on sublime experience, a state of wonderment elicited by encounters with the very large.[21] Edmund Burke, in his *Philosophical Enquiry into the Origin of Our Ideas of the Sublime and Beautiful* (1757), writes, "Greatness of dimension, is a powerful cause of the sublime," going on to specify that height and depth are more conducive to sublime experience than length. "An hundred yards of even ground will never work such an effect as a tower an hundred yards high, or a rock or mountain of that altitude."[22] Burke is echoed by Kant, who, in his *Observations on the Feeling of the Beautiful and Sublime* (1763), maintains, "The sublime must always be great," and similarly discriminates between the sublime effects produced by largeness projected in different dimensions. "A great height is just as sublime as a great depth," Kant writes, "except that the latter is accompanied with the sensation of shuddering, the former with one of wonder. Hence the latter feeling can be the terrifying sublime, and the former the noble." As a particular instance of the great height that is associated with the wonder-inducing noble manifestation of the sublime, Kant conjures up an Egyptian pyramid, the sight of which "moves one far more than one can imagine from all the descriptions."[23] He continues to dwell on the magnitude of pyramids in the *Critique of the Power of Judgment* (1790), where he specifies the optimal conditions for achieving full satisfaction from encounters with these immense structures. One must come neither too close nor be too far away, Kant maintains, for, in the latter case, parts of the pyramids will be obscured by distance, but in the former case, the eye will be too slow to register the pyramid as a whole. He writes, "[T]he eye requires some time to complete its apprehension from the base level to the apex, but during this time the former always partly fades before the imagination takes in the latter."[24]

Kant's comments on the sight of an Egyptian pyramid suggest the imagination's key role in the creation of a state of wonder. Here and elsewhere Kant locates sublime experience in the mind of the viewer. "True sublimity," he writes, "must be sought only in the mind of the one who judges, not in the object in nature, the judging of which occasions this disposition in it." He goes on, "Who would want to call sublime shapeless mountain masses towering above one another in wild disorder with their pyramids of ice, or the dark and raging sea, etc.? But the mind feels itself elevated in its own judging if, in the consideration of such things, without regard to their form, abandoning itself to the imagination and to a reason which, although it is associated with it entirely without any determinate end, merely extends it, it nevertheless finds the entire power of the imagination inadequate to its ideas." For Kant, the imagination's effort to come to grips with objects so large as to be impossible to entirely comprehend—even with the assistance of reason—ennobles the mind of the imaginer. The sublime experience results from the imagination's failure to comprehend an object's seeming infinity. This semblance of infinity is made possible "through the inadequacy of even the greatest effort of our imagination in the estimation of the magnitude of an object."[25] Even as the imagination is stymied in its efforts, the imaginer is enlarged.

When romantic artists sought to aggrandize themselves or solidify their reputations through creating poems and paintings on the largest possible scale, they did so in the context of an understanding of the sublime that encouraged this kind of pursuit. Burke notes that whatever raises a man in his own opinion "produces a sort of swelling and triumph that is extremely grateful to the human mind," and he suggests that this swelling is never more perceived than when we are confronted with awe-inspiring objects, "the mind always claiming to itself some part of the dignity and importance of the things which it contemplates."[26] The artist trying to capture the world in all its enormity is made, by this process, more enormous himself. He is enlarged by his association with large objects.

If Belzoni encountered the views of sublime experience set forth by Burke and Kant, he likely did so at second or third hand, as they were diffused into the culture at large. Nevertheless, in his self-representations he masterfully capitalized upon the association between large objects and sublime experience. The arc of Belzoni's career, however, demonstrates both the fragility of sublime experience and the risks of overreaching for enormity as a means of achieving permanence.

It is a curious fact of literary history that Wordsworth was transfixed by Belzoni's strongman act. Belzoni performed for spectators who had grown used to seeing giants and who were not easily impressed by feats of strength. "We have often witnessed a man by the assistance of a table, balance with his hands and feet, a number of persons," wrote one witness, who was jolted out of strongman ennui by Belzoni's impressive technique, his refusal of "machines and various tackle" to assist his undertaking. Belzoni lifted as many as ten men from a base attached to his belt. When he was finished, he had one on each of his shoulders, and one on his back, with "the whole forming a kind of Pyramid." He then moved across the stage "as easy and graceful as if about to walk a minuet," and displayed a flag "in as flippant a manner as a dancer on the rope."[27]

Belzoni, who performed under the billing of "The Patagonian Sampson," underscored his exoticism by costuming himself in animal skins or vaguely Eastern trappings which befitted the haziness of his advertised provenance (see fig. 19). Patagonia was portrayed as a legendary land of giants in unreliable travel narratives of his day. "The gorgeous splendour of his Oriental dress was rendered more conspicuous by an immense plume of white feathers," wrote one member of his audience, who admired how the feathers, "like the noddings of an undertaker's horse, increased in their wavy and graceful motion by the movements of the wearer's head."[28] A dignified man, Belzoni acquitted himself seriously even while wearing seven men and an undulating plume. One spectator recalled "his youthful, pleasing, and even genteel appearance, which caused much speculation . . . how such a person could be a mere *conjurer* and *showman*."[29]

Wordsworth witnessed Belzoni performing in *Jack the Giant Killer* at Sadler's Wells, and marked the experience in a passage of book seven of *The Prelude*. There, he describes the "ample recompense" he received from witnessing "singers, rope-dancers, giants and dwarfs, / Clowns, conjurors, posture-masters, harlequins / Amid the uproar of the rabblement, / Perform their feats."[30] Wordsworth catalogues the range of entertainment possibilities on display at Sadler's Wells, and, indirectly, the rivals with whom Belzoni vied in trying to capture the public's attention. By 1804, Belzoni's status as tallest biped was under siege. In a print caricature vaunting the "Wonderful Irish Giant," Patrick Cotter, who claimed to be eight feet seven inches tall, rests his hand on Belzoni's

GIOVANI BAPTISTA BELZONI.

Fig. 19. Engraving by A. B.
Van Assen from a drawing by
James Parry, "The Patagonian
Sampson" (1804). The Harvard
Theatre Collection, Houghton
Library, Harvard University.

head.[31] Walter Scott called Belzoni "the handsomest man (for a giant) I ever saw or could suppose to myself," but it is clear that the émigré strongman was facing stiff competition on the giant circuit, and was in danger of being supplanted by the "Infant Hercules," a four-year-old who could hoist 140 pounds.[32]

"If you are celebrated for writing verses or for slicing cucumbers for being two feet taller or two feet less than any other biped," wrote Scott, "your notoriety becomes a talisman, an 'Open Sesamum' before which everything gives way, till you are voted a bore & discarded for a new plaything."[33] Scott's comment on the fickle nature of celebrity sheds light on Wordsworth's fascination with Belzoni. The poet and the sideshow giant were, to Scott's chagrin, equally vulnerable to the vagaries of public taste. Wordsworth may have admired Belzoni merely as an impressive human specimen, but he may also have felt some solidarity with and sympathy for a performer who was operating under the same market forces that the poet despaired of in his Preface to the *Lyrical Ballads*. There Wordsworth writes of the public's "degrading thirst after outrageous stimulation," a desire for novelty that Burke conjures up in his treatise on the sublime and beautiful so as to position sublime feeling in opposition to "an appetite which is very sharp, but very easily satisfied," and which "has always an appearance of giddiness, restlessness and anxiety."[34]

Thomas De Quincey was shocked "beyond expression" by Wordsworth's confession that "whereas he would not walk for a quarter of a mile to see the man whom all the world should agree to crown as its foremost *intellectual* champion, willingly he would go three days' journey through a wilderness to see Belzoni!" For De Quincey, Wordsworth's confession was "inhuman in its degradation."[35] He thought that Wordsworth entertained a "beggarly idea of renown" by "regarding as nothing all the intellect and worth of England as compared with a man seven feet high, who could walk about with a living pyramid on his shoulders."[36] As Susan Stewart notes, "the giant, from Leviathan to the sideshow freak, is a mixed category; a violator of boundary and rule; an overabundance of the natural and hence an affront to cultural systems."[37] Although largeness can inspire awe, it can also elicit revulsion in its strong invocation of the gross physicality of the body. "It is impossible to suppose a giant the object of love," Burke writes in the *Enquiry* before going on to state, "I do not remember in all that multitude of deaths with which the Iliad is filled, that the fall of any man remarkable for his great stature and strength touches us with pity; nor does it appear that the author, so well read in human nature, ever intended it should."[38] Belzoni's large body trundled across the stage under a bevy of other bodies, and inevitably drew attention to the power—but also the gross materiality—of the human form.

Belzoni was, according to one acquaintance, "very sedulous to sink the posture-master in the traveler," but when he became a collector of Egyptian artifacts, he was still vulnerable to the vagaries of celebrity.[39] His new reputation as a traveling adventurer could not protect him from less flattering associations. Walking down the street with Cyrus Redding in the summer of 1820, Belzoni was mistaken for Bartolomeo Pergami (sometimes called Bergami), the Italian courtier whose purported affair with Queen Caroline was the focal point of the royal divorce proceedings being adjudicated in the House of Lords at that time.[40] The two men were chased down the street by a London mob intent on collaring the queen's companion. The confusion of Belzoni and Pergami was grounded in physical similarities. Pergami was a "startlingly handsome man, well over six feet tall, with black curling hair, dark eyes and handsome physique," and was credited with "nigh superhuman powers" of strength.[41] The excited mob was unable to distinguish between one large foreigner and another: "Bergami and Belzoni were all one with the multitude." According to Redding, "both names were foreign, and if foreign they must needs be identical."[42]

Belzoni chronicled his Egyptian exploits in his *Narrative of the Operations and Recent Discoveries within the Pyramids, Temples, Tombs, and Excavations, in*

Egypt and Nubia; and of a Journey to the Coast of the Red Sea, in Search of the Ancient Berenice; and Another to the Oasis of Jupiter Ammon. The elongated name highlighted the scope of his travels and the size of the objects he collected on his way. So, too, did the series of lithograph drawings of tombs that Belzoni published to accompany the *Narrative.*[43] In one of these drawings, the colossal head of Memnon dominates the frame, and a multitude of workers engaged in the statue's transport become a blur of tiny turbans. Behind the central image of the Memnon head and its movers, another group of small human figures are dwarfed by ruined pillars that tower over their heads. Such images underscore the disparity in scale between Belzoni and the artifacts he unseated.

Belzoni signaled his awareness of the cultural currency of the sublime through literary tableaux in which he dramatized the experience of that moment of astonishment when, according to Burke, "the mind is so entirely filled with its object, that it cannot entertain any other, nor by consequence reason on that object which employs it."[44] Belzoni repeatedly evokes the hugeness of his finds in an attempt to conjure in his readers a similarly awed response. Writing of the ruins of Thebes, he notes, "I had to pass before the two colossal figures in the plain. I need not say, that I was struck with wonder. They are mutilated indeed, but their enormous size strikes the mind with admiration" (38). Recalling his approach to the avenue of sphinxes at Karnak, he describes how these monuments' size strikes the visitor with wonder. On entering the temple there, he was "lost in a mass of colossal objects, every one of which was more than sufficient of itself alone to attract [his] whole attention" (152–53). He describes a "forest of enormous columns, adorned all round with beautiful figures," and declares himself located at the seat of holiness. Writing of the view of temple ruins in the distance, he enthuses, "These altogether had such an effect upon my soul, as to separate me in imagination from the rest of mortals, exalt me on high over all, and cause me to forget entirely the trifles and follies of life" (153).

The experience of the sublime that Belzoni tries to replicate in his writing, however, is a highly tenuous constellation of feelings, always in danger of being disrupted. Belzoni's description of being lost in a temple's mass of colossal objects is quickly followed by a rude jolt that causes all high feeling to dissipate. Belzoni writes, "I was happy for a whole day, which escaped like a flash of lightning; but the obscurity of the night caused me to stumble over one large block of stone, and to break my nose against another, which, dissolving the enchantment, brought me to my senses again" (153).

The conflicting forces of sublime feeling and brute physicality collide most dramatically in Belzoni's account of his removal of an obelisk at Philoe. His effort to transport a granite obelisk "twenty-two feet in length, and two in breadth at the basis," one that was "not smaller in height than that in St. George's Fields, but of a stone of a much heavier quality," was stalled by an unanticipated impediment he met at the dock:

> The pier appeared quite strong enough to bear at least forty times the weight it had to support; but, alas! when the obelisk came gradually on from the sloping bank, and all the weight rested on it, the pier, with the obelisk, and some of the men, took a slow movement, and majestically descended into the river, wishing us better success. I was not three yards off when this happened, and for some minutes, I must confess, I remained as stiff as a post. The first thing that came into my head, was the loss of such a piece of antiquity; the second was, the exultation of our opponents, after so much questioning to what party it belonged; and, lastly, the blame of all the antiquarian republic in the world. (358, 357)

The obelisk loses something of its majesty as it is gradually submerged in water, and Belzoni, at the same moment, becomes more like an obelisk himself—"stiff as a post"—just as the obelisk is losing its fixed purchase on the landscape. Despite Belzoni's efforts to invest his objects with a sublime aura, their obdurate bulkiness gets in the way of this ambition.

The obelisk episode is reproduced in Sarah Atkins's hagiographic tribute to Belzoni's determination, *The Fruits of Enterprize* (1821), which rewrites Belzoni's *Narrative* for a juvenile audience. Belzoni, the Italian émigré, becomes in Atkins's account, and perversely, a paragon of English determination. After the pedantic mother-narrator of the text recounts one of Belzoni's adventures, her son enthusiastically responds: "Right! right! I like Belzoni, because he possessed real courage. . . . When I am a man, mother, I mean to be a traveller, and to possess as much perseverance as *our Belzoni!*" For Atkins, Belzoni's *Narrative* becomes proof of the chauvinistic sentiments espoused in Anna Letitia Barbauld's *Hymns for Infant Minds,* the most famous of the moralizing children's tracts of the day. Atkins's narrator concludes her account of Belzoni's adventures with the reminder that "we ought to be very grateful that we live in better times [than did the ancient Egyptians]," a sentiment that reminds her son Bernard of the Barbauld verse:

> I thank the goodness and the grace
> 　　Which on my birth have smil'd,
> And made me, in these Christian days,
> 　　A happy English child.

> I was not born, as thousands are,
> 　　Where God was never known,
> And taught to pray a useless prayer
> 　　To blocks of wood and stone.[45]

The Egyptian objects that Belzoni excavated are transformed into meaningless bric-a-brac in this passage. And even as the *Fruits of Enterprize* fawns over Belzoni's heroism, it, too, conveys the inadvertently slapstick nature of the obelisk episode. The illustration of this incident in Atkins's volume departs from the book's other images, which emphasize Belzoni's grandeur and heroism. In the plate captioned "Belzoni's Distress in observing a part of the Obelisk in the Water" (see fig. 20), a distraught Belzoni gestures wildly as the obelisk tips out of his control.

Given that a too close association with the objects he excavated could made him look ridiculous, and given his desire to erase his former theatrical career, it is striking that Belzoni so often conflates himself in the Narrative with the objects he claims to be rescuing. Describing how he endured the persecution of French agents competing for archaeological treasures, Belzoni writes, "Had I

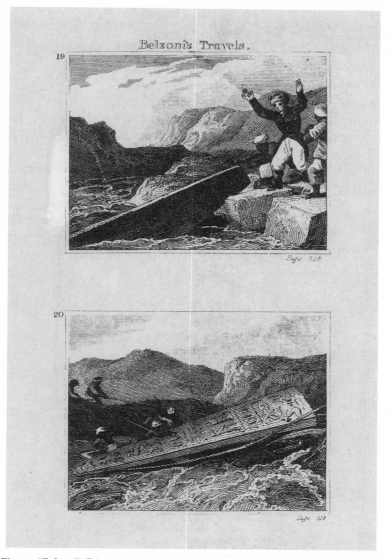

Fig. 20. "Belzoni's Distress in observing a part of the Obelisk in the Water." Sarah Atkins, *The Fruits of Enterprize Exhibited in the Travels of Belzoni in Egypt and Nubia* (1821).

not determined to stand, like a pyramid defying the wind, against all their nu-
merous attacks, which poured on me like a torrent, I should not have been able
to proceed, even from the commencement" (113). Portraying himself as a pyramid among pyramids and a giant among giants, Belzoni seeks to exalt himself by
association with huge artifacts, but he also risks reminding the reader of the
meaner aspect of the gigantic, its association with rude physicality rather than
awe-inspiring sublimity.

The unstable valence of the gigantic—its capacity to seem either noble and
heroic or gross and crude—is perhaps what elicits the fear of narrative incom-
mensurability that haunts Belzoni's accounts. Writing of the ruins of Thebes, he
worries about the transmittability of sublime experience, referring often to the
disparity between his original experience and his attempt to describe it. "It is absolutely impossible to imagine the scene displayed, without seeing it," he writes.
"The most sublime ideas, that can be formed from the most magnificent specimens of our present architecture, would give a very incorrect picture of these
ruins; for such is the difference, not only in magnitude, but in form, proportion,
and construction, that even the pencil can convey but a faint idea of the
whole"(37). "I wish that I had been a poet," Belzoni writes on another occasion,
"that I might sing in verse the beautiful ideas and sensations I felt"(382).

The most famous poetic treatment of sublime failure occurs in book six of
Wordsworth's *Prelude*. In his depiction of crossing Simplon Pass,
Wordsworth portrays himself being cast into temporary dejection when, after

losing sight of some of his companions and wandering without a confident sense
of where he is headed, he learns from a passing peasant that he has successfully
passed over the Alps without being aware that he has done so. "*We had crossed the
Alps*," Wordsworth writes in italicized disbelief, denied the triumphal sense of
gazing from a clearly identified highest peak. He immediately turns to the imagination—"That awful Power rose from the mind's abyss"—as a means of talking
himself out of his disappointment, of dispelling the "melancholy slackening"
that ensued upon the peasant's tidings. In Wordsworth's account, the sublime
experience is anticipated but never arrives, and so must be replaced by the
vaguely described machinations of the imagination, producer of "something
evermore about to be."[46]

"Something evermore about to be," "effort," "expectation," and "desire," are
the confusing antecedents for what Wordsworth refers to as "banners militant"
at the beginning of a passage in which he conjures up ancient Egypt as a means
of conveying the power of the imagination:

> Under such banners militant, the soul
> Seeks for no trophies, struggles for no spoils
> That may attest her prowess, blest in thoughts
> That are their own perfection and reward,
> Strong in herself and in beatitude
> That hides her, like the mighty flood of Nile
> Poured from his fount of Abyssinian clouds
> To fertilise the whole Egyptian plain.[47]

As many have noted, Wordsworth internalizes the experience of the sublime so
it is not dependent on the vicissitudes of external objects. In so doing, he curiously enlists the association between Egyptian objects and great magnitude to
aggrandize the imagination by association.[48] Wordsworth wrote these lines years
before Belzoni embarked on his career as an Egyptologist, but the passage allows
us to draw parallels between the poet's and the collector's avocations.

In an essay that pursues this line of thought, John Whale sees Elgin's graffito'd signature on his purloined marbles (and by extension Belzoni's many similar acts of inscription) as evidence that the collector might be read as a poet/artist manqué as well as proprietor. Whale writes, "The ambivalence of his act of artistic stewardship sounds the paradigmatic problem of certain kinds of Romantic creativity and their relationship to egotistical assertion and incipient colonialism in the construction of art."[49] The poet, like the collector, gathers objects from the world around him and uses them to suit his own purposes. The objects, however, are not entirely compliant; Wordsworth's depiction of being denied a peak experience in the Alps dramatizes the obdurateness of the physical world. One might describe the experience of the Wordsworthian sublime as a state of being self-consciously wonder-struck, stunned by some marvelous thing, but simultaneously worried about the origins or durability of this sensation. Wordsworth's compensatory swerve from the missed mountain peak to his own imagination underscores the unreliability of large objects as instigators of sublime events.

Is it possible to manufacture a sublime experience? That was the task Belzoni set himself when he organized the interior of Bullock's Egyptian Hall in a fashion that attempted to replicate the experience of entering an Egyptian tomb. Bullock reproduced the two most impressive chambers from the tomb of Seti I using wax impressions he had made there.[50] Visitors to the exhibition would first enter the "Room of Beauties," twenty feet long and fourteen feet wide, with a low ceiling and dim lighting, before passing into the "Entrance Hall," an even larger room which included depictions of "twelve gods carrying a snake with human heads projecting from it; more snakes intricately coiled in patterned loops and whorls; ibis-headed gods and demons without arms; mummies end-lessly stretched upon a serpent-headed couch."[51]

In a surviving picture of the exhibition, a young man stretches out on a bench, and none of the spectators seems visibly awed by gods or demons or mummies (see fig. 21). According to Marguerite Gardiner, the countess of Blessington, who left an account of the visitors to Belzoni's display, schoolboys entertained themselves "by discovering likenesses to each other, in the monstrous deities displayed on the wall." The boys' governess responded to their questions by "sententiously reading extracts from Belzoni's Description, not a word of which the little innocents could understand." An old lady, setting aside her copy of the *Description*, resorted to a more personal store of wisdom for her reply to a child's query about pyramids: "Why, a pyramid, my dear, is a pretty ornament for the centre of a table, such as papa sometimes has instead of an epergne." A younger woman complained that "as to looking at a set of Egyptian frights, it never entered into my head. I have not heard of Egypt since my governess used to bore me about it when I was learning geography; and as to tombs and pyramids, I have a perfect horror of them."[52]

If these blasé visitors had ventured upstairs, they would have encountered a scale model of the entire tomb, one that Belzoni claimed would "convey an idea of the astonishment we must have felt at every step." The guidebook to the exhibition states, "This model gives an exact view of the pyramid in the reduced proportion of one foot to one hundred and twenty feet. . . . and . . . every stone of the length of one inch, is in the proportion of ten feet long." The guidebook also, in a description of a pyramid model, reminds the reader of the "enormous magnitude of this astonishing monument."[53] Belzoni's exacting reminders of scale were meant to encourage the reader to imagine how big the objects repre-sented by the models actually were, but this required acts of mental arithmetic and extrapolation that may have been too much to ask of visitors who were pre-occupied with comparing pyramids to table ornaments, and who did not seem to register the sublime effect Belzoni had in mind.

The centerpiece of Belzoni's exhibition should have been a sarcophagus from the sepulchre of Seti I which was made "of oriental alabaster," and which was "minutely sculptured within and without, with several hundred figures."[54] In his *Narrative*, Belzoni marvels at the sarcophagus's splendor. "I cannot give an ade-

Fig. 21. "Mr. Belzoni's Exhibition of an ancient Egyptian Tomb." By kind permission of the British Library (Crach 1. Tab. 4. B4, vol. 14, pl. 262).

quate idea of this beautiful and invaluable piece of antiquity," he writes, "and can only say, that nothing has been brought into Europe from Egypt that can be compared with it."[55] Because of a dispute over ownership, the sarcophagus did not appear in the exhibition, which presented instead a one-sixth scale model of the saloon in which it had been discovered.

Belzoni carried out a delicate social dance with the trustees of the British Museum as he tried to assert his pecuniary right to the sarcophagus in letters that survive in the museum's archive. He wrote of his "infinite satisfaction" at having the sarcophagus "reserved for the British Museum," where it was always his "ardent desire to see it destined, if not finally deposited—as a Monument unique of its kind and unrivalled among all the Museums in Europe." After making his request to exhibit the sarcophagus, he concluded: "Such a concession, even did no pecuniary claim exist on my part, might perhaps be considered not unfavourably by the enlightened and liberal Institution to which I am addressing myself and towards an individual who has been mainly instrumental in enlarging the *National Collection* of Antiquities, placed in your charge."[56]

The trustees' leisurely response to Belzoni's letter suggests that his projection of himself as a fellow arbiter of "Taste & Art" did not supersede other less flattering representations. They did not reply to Belzoni's letter until December 12, three months after he made his request, and then only to let him know that his letter would be brought before the committee again when they had heard from Henry Salt, the British consul general who had helped finance Belzoni's excavations.[57] The curt response did nothing to encourage Belzoni's view of himself as a fellow antiquarian; the trustees focused solely on the question of ownership and gave Salt's claims priority over those of Belzoni by refusing even to consider Belzoni's request until the consul general had placed a value on the Egyptian objects under consideration for purchase by the museum.

Salt tried to distance himself from his former associate. Frustrated by the fact that his negotiator, Bingham Richards, had used Belzoni's valuation of the sarcophagus as the basis for a demand to the trustees, Salt wrote to Richards: "Nothing vexes me so much as the circumstance that you should have, by this line of acting, given the Trustees reason to suppose that I have been in collusion all the time with that prince of ungrateful adventurers—God knows, on the contrary, that I always believed his offer to be a fictitious one, and that I have but one wish, never to have my name coupled with his."[58]

If Wordsworth and Belzoni ever met—and there is no direct evidence that they did—the meeting most likely took place through the auspices of Benjamin

Robert Haydon. Haydon noted in his diary the illustrious company that dined in proximity to his painting of Lazarus: "Sir Walter Scott breakfasted with Lazarus before him, Belzoni dined, and so did Wordsworth."[59] In another entry, Haydon peopled his workroom with a similarly distinguished company, writing: "What pleasures have I enjoyed in that study! In it have talked & walked Scott, Wordsworth, Keats, Procter, Belzoni, Campbell, Cuvier, Lamb, Knowles, Hazlitt, Wilkie, and other Spirits of the Time. I offered them the comforts not the luxuries of life. They all were pleased to come, and as they sat at table, the entry into Jerusalem or Lazarus formed the back ground to their heads" (2:442) Haydon wanted to believe that he was one with that eminent retinue, but he particularly identified with Belzoni. "Belzoni felt my character and I felt his!" he wrote after the traveler's death (2:477).

Haydon identified with Belzoni because of their similarly large ambitions, but also because of what he perceived as a shared history of persecution. "In every sense Belzoni is a grand fellow," he wrote. "He suffered in his progress, as all suffer who dash at once on great undertakings which thousands have feared to touch" (2:321). Haydon also sympathized with the fraught nature of Belzoni's celebrity. "Strange it is that the very people who make a man celebrated by talking of his name, which they cannot avoid," the painter wrote of Belzoni, "revenge themselves by attaching every thing to it that can lower & bring him down to their own or an inferior level" (2:322).

"Belzoni, Byron!—within a week!" Haydon lamented upon hearing news of both men's deaths in May 1824 (2:485). The two died five months apart—Belzoni on December 3, 1823, during an expedition to discover the Niger River, and Byron on April 19, 1824, while working to advance the Greek struggle for independence at Missolonghi—but the news reached Haydon in distressing juxtaposition. Their similarly ignominious deaths—Belzoni by dysentery, Byron from malaria—in the midst of orientalist exploits joined their fates, but Haydon did not make this connection, choosing instead to emphasize their epic status. "Belzoni is dead!" he wrote: "An ancient Hero in modern flesh"(2:477).

The sole comment Byron left behind in reference to Belzoni was a belittling allusion to his foreignness: "Belzoni *is* a grand traveller and his English is very prettily broken."[60]

Belzoni's sarcophagus, ultimately turned down by the British Museum, was purchased by the architect John Soane in his "greatest coup as a collector."[61] "In making an empty tomb the centre-piece of his domestic museum," one commentator has noted, "Soane was creating what would inevitably be seen as a monument to himself."[62] Soane, who had to tear down a wall of his house in order to get the sarcophagus into his basement, celebrated his acquisition with a series of receptions at which the sarcophagus was lit by lamplight. He kept newspaper accounts of these parties in a clippings scrapbook, allowing himself to recall his collecting coup and social triumph through the favorable press coverage the receptions garnered.

Haydon described Soane's house as a "perfect labyrinth," and depicted visitors to the reception coming upon the library "after wandering about below, amidst tombs and capitals, and shafts, and noseless heads, with a sort of expression of delighted relief at finding themselves again among the living, and with coffee and cake!"[63] It is unclear whether these dazed visitors, when faced with the sarcophagus, called to mind Belzoni or Soane or no collector at all.

Haydon ran into a silver-haired Samuel Taylor Coleridge amidst the "mad fritter of antiquities" in Soane's gallery, their first meeting in seventeen years.[64] Coleridge was, according to Haydon, "half-poetical, half-inspired, half-idiotic," and he epitomized unrealized ambition; his notebooks provide a lexicon of grandiose literary projects that were either never begun or left incomplete. In his essay on Coleridge in *The Spirit of the Age*, Hazlitt writes: "Persons of the greatest capacity are often those, who for this reason do the least; for surveying themselves from the highest point of view, amidst the infinite variety of the universe, their own share in it seems trifling, and scarce worth a thought, and they prefer the contemplation of all that is, or has been, or can be, to the making a coil about doing what, when done, is no better than vanity."[65] Coleridge, standing in Soane's gallery, tried to convince Haydon that a man of genius should "put forth no more power than was sufficient for the purposes of the age in which he lived." Haydon was not impressed. Coleridge spoke, Haydon wrote, as if "genius was a power one could fold up like a parasol!"[66]

Even as Soane was using the sarcophagus as the highlight of a monument to himself, Belzoni's widow was hoping to use it to glorify her husband's name. Sarah Belzoni believed that Soane had purchased the sarcophagus with the understanding that she had the right to buy it back from him. As Soane was hosting his receptions, Mrs. Belzoni was making demands through an emissary for the sarcophagus's return, so that she could display it in a remounting of the Egyptian tomb exhibition in Leicester Square.[67]

It was a bad idea to cross Belzoni's wife—Sarah Belzoni nursed grievances and anticipated revenge.[68] A typical entry in the commonplace book she kept over many years: "Lady [H] is very cunning sly, shallow headed and shallow hearted—she does everything for *effect* and her peculiar method is to *conceal* what she wishes to hide."[69] When Edward J. Cooper dared to suggest, in his *Views in Egypt and Nubia*, that one of Belzoni's drawings was "not quite so accurate as is desirable," Sarah Belzoni fumed in the margins. Addressing the author directly, she claimed to have no knowledge of which Belzoni designs he could possibly be referring to, and suggested indignantly that Cooper had mentioned Belzoni "merely to observe and give an hint that Belzoni could make a mistake." Had her husband had the time and money of others, she concluded, the likes of Cooper would not have dared to attempt anything after him.[70]

Soane did not relinquish his claim on the sarcophagus, but he managed to make peace with Belzoni's widow, perhaps by letting his receptions serve to advertise her planned spectacle.[71] But Sarah Belzoni's Egyptian exhibition in Leicester Square was ultimately thwarted by the public's hunger for novelty. "Her attempt to revive an exhibition that had already run out its day, was not likely to be successful, especially as it was of a nature to demand some little knowledge of history and geography," Cyrus Redding recalled. The remounted exhibition "could not possess the attraction for the multitude, either visibly or intellectually, that we have seen lavished to prodigality upon an abortive brat, christened Tom Thumb."[72] Even if Tom Thumb had not been drawing public attention elsewhere, the failure of the exhibition may have been preordained by the death of Belzoni. The Egyptian artifacts needed to be tethered to their charismatic collector in order to retain restless audience members who were not necessarily interested in Egyptian culture for its own sake. Egyptian artifacts, first separated from their original sacred settings, had now begun to float free of Belzoni as well. Even though Sarah Belzoni tried to reinvigorate the exhibition by adding new mummies, the artifacts on display were growing inert.

Years after the exhibition closed, the novelist Jane Porter, soliciting funds on behalf of "the forlorn Widow of the singularly persevering Traveller poor Giovanni Belzoni," described her as existing in "a state of the humblest poverty at Brussels (whither she retired, in the first instance for the sake of cheapness)."[73] Sarah Belzoni's "museum and dormitory" was populated by a mummy, an African macaw, and an Angola cat. "She has not thrown off her weeds, and seldom stirs beyond her threshold," wrote another visitor to Mrs. Belzoni's abode. "Fragments of skulls, skeletons of rare animals, and various other articles of great interest to her, are carefully preserved, because they were collected by her dear departed friend."[74] Belzoni's wife later made her way from Brussels to the Channel Islands, apparently traipsing back across the channel with scale drawings of Seti I's tomb, the last ramshackle vestiges of Belzoni's museum.[75]

Belzoni's name did not entirely disappear after his death, but it surfaced more sporadically. A year after Soane put the Belzoni sarcophagus on display, Wordsworth wrote a letter of reference for a Mr. James Houtson, a man who was seeking a job in the Colonial Office. The renowned poet established Houtson's credentials in a roundabout way. "His late Brother," Wordsworth wrote, "was the person who buried Belzoni."[76]

In a final effort to immortalize her husband, Sarah Belzoni commissioned a strategic memorial engraving (see fig. 22). In this posthumous depiction, a half-length portrait of Belzoni floats in the sky over a hodgepodge array of his Egyptian artifacts: a pharaoh's head and arm, the sarcophagus of Seti I, the Philoe obelisk, and a statue of the young Memnon.[77] As Belzoni looms over the Egyptiana beneath him, he is joined with these wayward and broken objects. His bust is exalted by its position in the clouds, but only temporarily so. One expects it will eventually fall to earth and collide with the shards of statuesque figures down below.

The engraving calls to mind Wordsworth's most enigmatic poem. In the second stanza of the eight-line "A slumber did my spirit seal," Wordsworth characterizes the posthumous fate of the mysterious Lucy:

> No motion has she now, no force;
>   She neither hears nor sees,
> Rolled round in earth's diurnal course,
>   With rocks, and stones, and trees.[78]

Fig. 22. Fabroni portrait of Belzoni. By kind permission of the British Library (Crach T. Tab. 5B, vol. 14, f. 264).

Just as Belzoni becomes yoked to his objects in the engraving, so Lucy becomes encircled by the physical objects of the natural world. In both portrait and poem, the juxtapositioning of remembered person and solid objects seems more brutal than ennobling. Both memorialized figures are in danger of being battered by the large entities that surround them.

Belzoni underscored the sublimity of the giant Egyptian objects he collected and displayed so as to invest himself with a grandeur to which he could not otherwise lay claim. He believed that he could win for himself a measure of immortality by acting as a purveyor of sublime experience. The reputation he gained as an adventurer and collector, however, proved no more lasting than the celebrity he earned by carrying a pyramid of men across a stage.

Wordsworth, too, tried to "grasp the most stupendous objects," by embarking on the writing of *The Prelude*, which was designed to give monumental status to his story of poetic development. But "A slumber," one of his smallest poems, challenges the romantic assumption that large objects—monuments, poems, paintings—best serve to invoke sublime experience. "A slumber did my spirit seal" has been called an uninterpretable poem, and, perhaps for this very reason, it has inspired a very large body of scholarly speculation.[79] The poem's inscrutability leaves the critic stymied as she tries to wrest interpretive control, relegated to a state of unresolved wonder. One of Wordsworth's tiniest poems has best served his desire to become a giant among poets.

There is a Belzoni mummy thumb in the Peabody Essex Museum in Salem, Massachusetts, that no one knows quite how to place; it is catalogued under the grim heading of "human remains." An exiled Belzoni obelisk in Dorset has, according to a visiting Egyptologist, "never struck roots," seeming "slightly dismal and unreal as a pastiche or a counterfeit."[80] The two caryatids of Isis and Osiris that once supported a broken architrave on the façade of the Egyptian Hall now flank the entrance to the Museum of London.[81]

The Belzoni sarcophagus, by contrast, has stayed put. It is still beached on the rubble of its lid in the basement of Sir John Soane's house, now a museum, where a recent visitor, in search of Belzoni's engraved signature, was confidently assured by a guard that no such name could be found.

CHAPTER FIVE

MARY ANNING RECOLLECTED

One surviving vestige of Mary Anning's fossil collecting activities is an aquatic reptile with tapering paddles attached to a barrel-shaped body, and the kind of long neck and small head we associate with cartoon dinosaurs. Anning discovered this, the first articulated plesiosaur skeleton ever found, in 1823. Another still-extant Anning remain is a fossil celebrated as "one of the largest and most complete Lower Jurassic ichthyosaurs known," a dolphin-shaped "fish-lizard" nearly seven meters long, whose crocodile snout and large eye socket suggest predatory habits.[1] These marvelously exotic creatures speak most directly of Anning's prowess as a fossil collector. Yet another, more enigmatic vestige of Anning's collecting is a small, nondescript volume of poetry, quotations, and prayers carefully transcribed in neat cursive. The handwritten book would not, at first glance, seem to have much to do with fossil collecting at all.

Mary Anning (1799–1847) gained a reputation in the early decades of the nineteenth century as a fossil collector extraordinaire whose finds served as the building blocks of the nascent geological sciences. The fossil record in its earliest realization led directly to the development of evolutionary theory, but at the moment when Anning was gathering them, fossils were romanticized as vestiges of ancient history and compared to other wonders of earlier times. Gideon Mantell titled his seminal work on geology "Medals of Creation," and Maria Hack, in her *Geological Sketches and Glimpses of the Ancient Earth*, a children's guide to geology, compared a naturalist's endeavors to those of an antiquary digging among the ruins of Herculaneum. Thomas Hawkins, an avid collector who purchased some of Anning's finds, described the remains of the great "sea-dragons" as being "wrapt in the Grave-clothes of many Ages," and inscribed "like the mummies of old Aegyptus, in a language abandoned evermore."[2]

Mary Anning learned how to find fossils from her father, a carpenter who supplemented his income by hunting "curiosities" from the fossil-rich coastline of Lyme in southeast England. After his death in 1810, the Anning family was plunged into poverty. When Anning was twelve, her brother Joseph found what looked like a lizard's skull embedded in a fallen rock. He left her to discover the creature's seventeen-foot-long torso high above the shore. This giant ichthyosaur fossil, purchased by a local aristocrat for £23, eventually found its way into William Bullock's London museum.[3] Anning thus embarked on a career as a fossil hunter.

Anning's commonplace book, part of the holdings of the Dorset County Museum, does not mention fossils, which explains why it has been referred to mostly in passing, even by historians of science who, in recent years, have sought to depict Anning as the Rosalind Franklin of paleontology. Just as Franklin's crystallographic portraits enabled James Watson and Francis Crick to deduce the double helical structure of DNA, so Anning's fossil finds advanced the work of male scientists such as Louis Agassiz and Gideon Mantell. And just as Franklin's work went uncelebrated when her male colleagues went on to win the Nobel Prize, so Anning's contributions were, if not completely overlooked, only glancingly acknowledged.

The commonplace book, however, can help us to understand aspects of Anning's collecting practice that a strict attention to science, as we understand it, will not. The poetic gleanings that are preserved in Anning's commonplace book draw our attention to the literary aspects of early-nineteenth-century natural history writing, the ways in which poetry was enlisted to help make sense of inscrutable and terrifying fossil remains.[4] Anning's literary compilation helps us to keep in mind that a clear division between fact and fiction, science and mythology, had not yet come to exist in the first part of the nineteenth century.

Anning's commonplace book begins with a poem by George Gordon, Lord Byron, then ricochets back and forth between feminist writings and notes on celestial bodies before lingering over the poetry of Henry Kirke White and, finally, offering transcripts of prayers by Thomas Wilson, Bishop of Sodor and Man.[5] Anning copied out a poem sympathizing with the plight of "The Magdalene" and opening with the lines: "Oh turn not such a with-ring look / On one who still can feel, / Nor, by a cold and harsh rebuke,/ An outcast's mis'ry seal!" She transcribed a brief passage from Tobias Smollett's "Ode to Independence" that portrays Independence as the "guardian genius" who teaches youth to despise "Pomp's tinsel livery." And she wrote out four lines from Hannah More's long poem "Florio: A Tale." The More passage she singled out is part of a description of a model daughter, Celia, who "Led by Simplicity divine, / . . . pleas'd and never tried to shine."

A separate passage of More's poem comments on the editorial practice implicit in the gathering of literary snippets in a commonplace book. The poem's protagonist Florio is characterized by his preference for reading selections from books rather than the entire volumes. More writes, "He read *Compendiums, Extracts, Beauties, / Abrégés, Dictionnaires, Recueils, / Mercures, Journaux, Extraits, and Feuilles*." He risks, acccording to More, missing the "plan, detail, arrangement, system" of any book by skimming "the cream of others' books" and "plucking bon-mots from their places." More suggests that Florio reads only to give himself topics for fashionable conversation. She emphasizes the insubstantiality of the literary excerpt, its disassociation from larger realms of knowledge and belief.[6]

Reading Anning's commonplace book, we are similarly removed from the systems of belief that may have impelled her to single out particular passages. We can only intuit how these excerpts may have served her, and we are predisposed to dwell on the feminist implications of the early selections in the volume—the Magdalene poem, a passage from Anna Seward's letters that states,

"Nothing but an independent fortune can enable an amiable female to look down, without misery, upon the censures of the many, and even in that situation their arrows have power to wound"—and to lose interest when we get to the pious offerings of Bishop Wilson with which the volume concludes. If you were reading the volume for insight into Anning's psyche, you would suspect that she had followed an emotional trajectory from reckless passion to spiritual control. If you were reading the commonplace book to understand her collecting career, you might, like one Natural History Museum curator, find it "scarcely appropriate" for preservation alongside Anning's fossil finds.[7] Even W. D. Lang, who wrote a series of articles documenting Anning's contributions to the development of paleontology, and whose dedication to Anning ensured that the volume was ultimately preserved in the Dorset County Museum, was oddly dismissive of its pages: "If they do not tell us much, at least these fragments point to the simplicity and piety of this remarkable and good-hearted woman."[8]

The commonplace book counters Lang's representation of Anning. The poems she preserved there hint at an Anning who was interested in the self-mythologizing of Byron, who saw her collecting practice as a means of exalting herself and of pushing the boundaries of female experience.

In Anning's time, Lyme Regis was already a popular tourist venue, "a sort of Brighton in miniature, all bustle and confusion, assembly-rooms, donkey-riding, raffling &c. &c.," with plenty of furnished lodgings to let.[9] Jane Austen described the remarkable situation of Lyme's principal street "almost hurrying into the water," and the "very beautiful line of cliffs stretching out to the east of town."[10] In the summer of 1999, the donkeys were gone, and the principal street was populated chiefly by sunburnt parents who, loaded with beach chairs and recalcitrant inflatable toys, herded children from the beach to bed-and-breakfast inns. Although the sunbathers were oblivious to this fact, the town was poised for the invasion of the Anning aficionados.

These Anning specialists were arriving to take part in a symposium, sponsored by the Lyme Regis Philpot Museum, and billed as a "bicentennial celebration in honour of the first woman geologist." The museum's name honors a notable Lyme Regis family; three Philpot sisters were Anning's contemporaries and also her companions in fossil collecting.[11] Lyme Regis's most famous living resident at the time of the bicentennial, however, was the writer John Fowles, who, as the former curator of the museum, and longtime champion of Anning, was the *éminence grise* of the conference. In his 1969 novel *The French Lieutenant's Woman*, Fowles declared it "one of the meanest disgraces of British palaeontology" that scientists used Anning's finds to make their reputations, but that "not one native type bears the specific *anningii*."[12] In the informational material for the conference, Fowles was touted as "one of the greatest living writers," and also as the kind benefactor who had "offered his splendid garden for a Strawberry Tea." It seemed faintly ironic that a man who had created the creepy protagonist of *The Collector* in order to express his hatred of the "lethal perversion" of collecting would preside over a gathering of people joined together by a specific interest in the greatest fossil collector of all time.[13] The protagonist of Fowles's novel is a butterfly collector who kidnaps and imprisons a young woman artist, and who, by novel's end, has set out in pursuit of his next female specimen. Naomi Schor calls Fowles's character the perfect enactment of the sexist Baudrillardean characterization of the collector as "a man whose extreme castration anxiety leads him to a pathological need to sequester the love-object."[14] It was odd that the writer who had created a devastating fictional exemplar of the sexually deviant male collector was reigning benevolently over a conference that celebrated a woman collector. Given his status as a novelist, it was also noteworthy that Fowles was so firmly allied with those who rallied against fictionalizers of Anning's story.

The official convener of the 1999 Anning symposium was Sir Crispin Tickell, patron of the museum, former warden of Green College, Oxford, British permanent representative to the United Nations, president of the Royal Geographical Society, and a great-great-great-nephew of Mary Anning. It was the last of these credentials that established Tickell's claim to convener status, and although he served in this capacity in a benevolent manner, delivering a genial introductory paper in which he reviewed the salient features of Anning's story (all too familiar to the Anning enthusiasts in the lecture hall), the listing of his credentials in the conference program became, in retrospect, the first sally in a repressed dispute over who had the right to speak for Mary Anning and what kind of story they should tell.

Sir Crispin was not the person who had typed up the program, or organized the group photograph, or arranged the geological walks, or seen to it that a video recording would be made of the entire proceedings. He was not the person who apologized in the printed conference information that arrangements to serve tea and coffee during the morning break had "come unstitched at the last moment," and so recommended that conference-goers "disperse rapidly to cafes, pubs, etc., in the town." These were the responsibilities of the Lyme Regis Philpot Museum curator, a conscientious woman who hovered in the side aisle of the Marine Theatre, and who precipitously resigned before the symposium was over in a development that went unheralded and that hinted of subterranean schisms.

Tickell convened, and the museum curator fretted about coffee, but it was really Hugh Torrens's symposium. Torrens, a geology historian at Keele University and the author of the most detailed account of Anning's life and practice, a published address to the British Society for the History of Science, was scheduled to speak on "Mary Anning's Life and Times: New Perspectives" at the end of the first day of papers.[15] With John Fowles's blessing, Torrens had been working on the definitive study of Anning for over a decade by the time of the symposium. In the 1987–88 curator's report for the Lyme Regis Museum, Fowles noted, "Dr. Torrens hopes to have his book on Mary Anning published in a year or two," going on to mention Torrens's discovery of many "lost" letters, and to voice a hope that the book would "clarify considerably our grossly legend-distorted picture of Mary." Fowles went on to admit that he had been less than helpful as curator to many who wanted to write about Anning. "That was because I already knew the right person was tackling the problem, and that we did not need one more error-perpetuating account just to fill a space in the grockle market," he wrote, using a derogatory local term for tourists.[16] So keen was Torrens on absolute accuracy that he could not stop himself from correcting Fowles's statement in *The French Lieutenant's Woman* that not one native type bears the specific *anningii*. In a footnote to his address to the British Society for the History of Science, Torrens provided three exceptions to Fowles's observation: the bivalve genus *Anningia* (later renamed *Anningella*), the liassic coral genus and species *Tricycloseris anningi*, and the ostracod species *Cytherelloidea anningi*.[17]

Many different kinds of people were newly interested in Mary Anning—historians of science, local historians, fossil collectors, geologists, paleontologists, children's book writers, museum curators, fossil preservationists, as well as Stephen Jay Gould, the keynote speaker, who embodied several of these roles in the person of one man. And so the symposium had more than the standard potential for developing the rifts that shiver through every academic conference. The fault lines in this instance separated United Kingdom participants from North American participants, and, in an even more geographically specific winnowing process, Locals from Outsiders. The fault lines also, and more tellingly, divided scientists from storytellers and artists. Hugh Torrens could not claim Mary Anning as kin, but his symposium status was assured by his reputation as a scholar bent on ferreting out nonscientific nonsense and squashing dubious legends, particularly those promulgated by children's book writers who focused on the child Anning. "A cavalier attitude to facts stands as the hallmark of the wholly *child-centred* view of Anning," Torrens wrote, going on to specify, "Most of these child-centred views now come from abroad."[18]

The legends that remained of Anning's childhood by the time of the symposium had been worn as smooth as marbles by retelling. There was the Anning who survived being struck by lightning as a fifteen-month-old child. Anning's nurse had her "hair cap and handkerchief much burnt and the flesh wounded," according to the sobering report of her widower. John Haskings recalled, "The Child was taken from my wifes arms and carried to its parents in appearance dead but they was advised to put it in warm water and by so doing it soon recovered."[19] Anning "had been a dull child before but after this accident she became lively and intelligent and grew up so," according to her nephew.[20] The lightning episode served as the ur-story for the ichthyosaur-discovering twelve-year-old-girl of the myriad juvenile biographies that went about making up details when facts were lacking. Lawrence Anholt's *Stone Girl, Bone Girl*, which was published in the year before the Anning symposium, and which circulated among participants as the latest example of a problematic genre, begins: "When Mary Anning was a baby, she was struck by lightning. It split a huge elm tree and threw Mary right out of her nurse's arms." The storyteller then begins elaborating on the known details for sentimental effect. Anholt describes the infant Anning opening her eyes, reaching a hand to her father's face, and moving him to realize: "Mary Anning was no ordinary child."[21]

The stories helped sustain a small Anning tourist industry. Anning was not the only famous past resident of Lyme Regis. The hummingbird obsessive John Gould was born there, and so was Thomas Coram, founder of an orphanage whose vestigial remains—a playground and a display case of foundling tokens—survive in London. Anning, however, was the only former denizen around whom a modern tourist business could revolve, albeit in the stately manner of an antique carousel, and fueled mostly by postcards and informational brochures.

Anning was painted in the 1840s by William Gray, and this portrait was repainted by B. J. M. Donne, an Anning acquaintance, soon after her death. In both versions of the portrait, Anning resembles a hummock with a head and holds a pickaxe against her body with the same arm from which a collection basket hangs like a pocketbook (see fig. 23). A small black and white dog presses its muzzle to the ground near her feet. Anning's actual dog fell victim to the hazards

Fig. 23. B. J. M. Donne, copy of a portrait of Mary Anning by William Gray (1850). Copyright © The Natural History Museum, London.

of his owner's occupation. "The Cliff fell upon him and killed him in a moment before my eyes," Anning wrote in a letter to a friend, going on to say, "It was but a moment between me and the same fate."[22]

Speaking in tones as "oracular as those of a Pythoness," Anning once warned a fellow collector that a desirable ichthyosaur fossil could not be successfuly extracted "because the marl, full of pyrites, falls to pieces as soon as dry."[23] The particular fossil in question was not visible at high tide; the same tidal forces that wore down coastal rock formations, allowing 190-million-year-old fossils to surface like the pentimento of an old painting, made fossil collecting a particularly dangerous business. Anning described coming across part of a plesiosaur and losing track of time. "I so intent in getting it out that I had like to have been drownded and the man I had employed to assist me," she wrote, adding, "After we got home I asked the man why he had [not] cautioned me about the tide flowing so rapidly [and] he said I was ashamed to say I was frightened when you didn't regard it."[24]

Anning braved the dangers of unstable shorelines, but she also had to steel herself against a fear of the uncertain beings that might be paddling around off shore. Since the principle of extinction was not convincingly demonstrated until 1812—as part of the "Observations préliminaires" of Georges Cuvier's *Recherches sur les ossemens fossiles*—Anning first scrambled around the cliffs of Lyme in search of fossil remains without complete confidence that a fully fleshed plesiosaur might not advance on an incoming tide. If she believed contemporary speculation about this creature, she would not have been entirely surprised if a lizard head with crocodile teeth had arisen from the waves, followed by a neck "of enormous length" attached to a trunk with the ribs of a huge chameleon and the paddles of a whale.[25] According to Cuvier, the creature's structure was "the most heteroclite, and its characters altogether the most monstrous, that have been yet found amid the ruins of a former world."[26]

Many of Anning's most spectacular fossil finds are mounted in display cabinets at the London Natural History Museum, but her commonplace book only temporarily found a home there. The provenance of the volume underscores its anomalous status as an Anning remain. The volume was given by one of Anning's friends to Richard Owen, the superintendent of the natural history department of the British Museum.[27] The British Museum's natural history collections were eventually moved to the Natural History Museum in South Kensington, which opened in 1881. Owen's colleague there, Charles Davies Sherburn, offered the volume to the British Museum in 1935. Even though many of Anning's fossils were housed at the South Kensington museum, Sherburn apparently saw no use for her commonplace book, and neither did the curators of the British Museum, where it was politely rejected by Idris Bell, who described the volume as consisting of "just the sort of extracts or jotting which a young lady of the period might be expected to make," but as having "no permanent value."[28]

Bell was essentially correct in his assessment of the book's typicality. It *does* consist of just the sort of extracts a young lady of the period might be expected to copy, and so it is unsurprising that it begins with a poem by Byron. Byron poems were staple elements of women's commonplace books in the romantic era, as William St. Clair has noted. St. Clair's personal collection of these idiosyncratic volumes establishes Byron as a favorite of commonplace book anthologizers, as the poet of "long-suffering constant tragic love."[29] An affection for Byron poems was so clear a marker of a certain kind of rarefied sensibility that Austen uses it in *Persuasion* to characterize the mournful Captain Benwick, a widower with a literary bent who is possessed of "a tolerable collection of well-bound volumes." *Persuasion* is partly set in Lyme, and Austen lingers over the view from the Cobb, "its old wonders and new improvement," in the moments before Louisa Musgrove falls from that elevated walkway onto the pavement of the Lower Cobb. Just before Louisa's fall, Captain Benwick is quoting Byron to Anne Elliot: "Lord Byron's 'dark blue seas' could not fail of being brought forward by their present view." Benwick has already proven himself intimately acquainted with the "impassioned descriptions of hopeless agony" penned by Byron. He regularly repeats with "tremulous feeling, the various lines which imaged a broken heart, or a mind destroyed by wretchedness," and his Byron quoting is cause for concern. Anne Elliot feels compelled to steer him away from Byron and toward "our best moralists," to encourage him to read works better "calculated to rouse and fortify the mind by the highest precepts."[30]

By the time Mary Anning transcribed the poem, Byron's reputation as a poet of lost love and of swashbuckling romance was well established. To inaugurate her commonplace book Anning selected a poem Byron wrote in the last months of his life, when he had dismissed poetry as a poor alternative to heroic action and traveled to Greece to help in that country's battle for independence. She copied it into the volume under the title "On this Day I complete my thirty-sixth year," a line Byron used only as a subtitle; he titled the poem with the date and place where it was written: "January 22nd 1824. Messalonghi." No matter what title is given to it, the poem presents a Byron who wanted to be known for heroic action rather than tremulous feeling. Anning, too, had a penchant for bold endeavors, and she, too, was interested in her public reputation. She may have felt a particular affinity for Byron's poetry as she fashioned herself as a death-defying adventurer.

The scientists and historians of science who had gathered for the Mary Anning symposium wanted Anning to be portrayed as a scientific collector like themselves, fact accumulators who felt obliged to track down every last clavicle or rib that could be used to reconstruct Mary Anning's collecting career. And Anning did fit this model, with her marvelous discoveries and her intelligent discernment of anatomical detail. Announcing the discovery of a new plesiosaur fossil to William Buckland in December 1830, Anning wrote:

> It is without exception the most beautiful fossil I have ever seen. The tail and paddle is wanting (which I hope to get at the first rough sea) every bone is in place, in short if it had been made of wax it could not be more beautiful, but I should remark that the head is twice as large in proportion as those I have hitherto found. The neck has a most graceful curve and what makes it still more interesting is that resting on the bones of the pelvis is, its Coprolite finely illustrated.[31]

One can see in this letter Anning's appreciation of both the fossil's scientific usefulness and its aesthetic appeal. She promises to try to achieve an intact specimen, one that would be of most use to the student of anatomy, and she compares the size of the plesiosaur's head to those of others she has found. She also, however, highlights the graceful curve of its neck, as well as its most interesting feature: coprolites clearly visible on the bones of the pelvis. Coprolites are the fossilized remains of waste products, in this case, plesisaur feces. As Anning surely appreciated, they have the pleasing appearance of a spray of beads.

Anning's artful description of the plesiosaur fossil is just one example of the insistent literariness that permeated natural history writing in her day.[32] "A serpent threaded through the shell of a turtle" is how William Buckland characterized a plesiosaur, demonstrating the imaginative bent of early writers on geology.[33] "Their works, although devoted to science, are also an ornament to literature," wrote the author of the "Remarks Introductory" to Gideon Mantell's *Wonders of Geology*.[34] Mantell himself drew on romantic poetry to make his scientific points, conjuring up Shelley's depiction in *Queen Mab* of "those viewless beings, / Whose mansion is the smallest particle / Of the impassive atmosphere," while describing beings "so minute as to elude our unassisted vision."[35] Thomas Hawkins, the fossil collector and Anning compatriot, also conjured up the stirrings of a poetic muse. Describing the intricately tessellated bones of a plesiosaur appendage, he exclaimed, "What a multitude of pentameters belong to those ossicular strings every one of them worth a necklace of oriental pearls."[36]

The line separating scientific description and literary embroidering was not yet firmly drawn because the extinct creatures under examination, often extrapolated from a jumble of bones, had the shape-shifting quality of fairy-tale dragons. William Buckland, in his *Bridgewater Treatise* on geology and mineralogy, concluded a section on the fossil saurians by admitting "that they at first seem much more like the dreams of fiction and romance, than the sober results of calm and deliberate investigation." A few pages later, warming to his subject, he described pterodactyls by reference to Milton's fiend, who "O'er bog, or steep, through strait, rough, dense, or rare / With head, hands, wings, or feet, pursues his way, / And swims, or sink, or wades, or creeps, or flies."[37]

Newly discovered anatomical knowledge was communicated through the publication of scientific memoirs, the word "memoir" here connoting an observation or record of a particular species, as in Sir P. M. de Grey Egerton's "Memoir on a peculiarity of structure in the neck of the ichthyosaurus."[38] Buckland wrote approvingly of Roderick Murchison's "excellent memoir on a fossil Fox," and Mantell commended the 1821 "Memoir on the genus Ichthyosaurus," written by William Conybeare and Henry De la Beche, in which "the osteology of the original was so fully elucidated, as to leave but few points undetermined, for the investigation of subsequent observers."[39] But at around the same time that "memoir" was being used to signal "a dissertation on a learned subject on which the writer has made particular observations," a plural form of the word was coming to indicate more personal recollections.[40] Thomas Hawkins's 1834 *Memoirs of Ichthyosauri and Plesiosauri, Extinct Monsters of the Ancient Earth* merges the scientific and the autobiographical meanings of the word. In it, Hawkins fondly records his own history as a collector: "A tyro in collecting at twelve years of age, I then boasted of all the antiques that were come-at-able in my neighbourhood, but finding that every body beat my cabinet of coins and pottery I addressed myself to worm-eaten books and at last to fossils." We might note that here, as usual, fossils get elided with other collectible vestiges of the past—coins, pots, books—as Hawkins documents the trajectory of his collecting career, writing his autobiography as a collector. But he also documents anatomical differences in adherence with the scientific sense of the memoir genre. He provides minutely detailed descriptions of particular fossils, such as the *Ichthyosaurus chiroligostinus* whose six hundred pieces he had fixed in sulfate of lime "in a case that weighed half a ton." Hawkins's *Memoirs* conveys his own crazed enthusiasm for collecting, his willingness to "carry away whole quarries," but it also details the important features of his fossil remains.[41]

The double aspect of Hawkins's memoir in its status as both autobiography and anatomy dramatizes the blending of literary and scientific aspirations in the romantic period. Hawkins's propensity for "perfecting" his fossils by manufacturing missing bits highlights the interplay of imaginative speculation and scientific data gathering that were often interwoven in romantic era collecting practice. Wrote Anning of Hawkins's fossil "completing" endeavors: "He is shuch an enthusiast that he makes things as he imagines the ought to be; and not as they are really found."[42]

Scrupulous Anning historians approved of the Anning who disapproved of Hawkins's fabrications. In order to have her taken seriously as an early paleontologist, Anning's scientific advocates at the conference wanted to separate her from the "sentimental limpets" who latched onto the most romantic aspects of her story—the mostly women writers who had written about Anning with general or child audiences in mind.[43] The Anning who was entangled in popular literature was faintly distasteful to scholars who wanted to advance her scientific credentials. But in their emphasis on fact-checking and myth-squashing, they risked overlooking the ways in which Anning was caught up in some myth-making of her own, and the extent to which she benefited from the proliferating legends.

Anna Maria Pinney, who spent the autumn and winter of 1831 in Lyme, where her brother was campaigning to become the first member of Parliament elected to represent Lyme and Charmouth, provides the most vivid contemporary account of Mary Anning. Pinney wrote of her mother's reluctance to trust her alone with "this extraordinary character," recalling breathlessly a collecting expedition:

> She [Anning] goes out just before the waters begin to ebb, and we climbed down places, which I sd. have thought impossible to have descended had I been alone. The wind was high the ground slippery and the waves beating against the Church Cliff as we went down. Our dangers were by no means over, for when we had clambered to the bottom of the Corporation wall, we had frequently to walk along the blue lias cliffs, where there was just room to stand and no more the sea being behind us. In one place we had to make haste to pass between the dashing of two waves, before I knew what she meant to do, she caught me with one arm round the waist, and carried me for some distance, with the same ease as you would a baby.[44]

Pinney's Anning is a dashing figure who lived a life of close escapes and dangerous schemes, and who rescued young girls in peril with the easy and confident strength of a romance hero.

Pinney describes a Mrs. Stock who played a formative role in Anning's evolution as a fossil collector. It was Mrs. Stock who, according to Pinney, gave Anning her first book of geology and encouraged her scientific pursuits. Pinney compares the role Mrs. Stock played for Mary Anning to the dangerous influence of the most extravagant fictional heroine of the day, Germaine de Staël's Corinne. "It [the book *Corinne*] would have the same weakening effect on the character, as the friendship of Mrs. Stock," Pinney writes. Staël's character, an *improvisatrice* known for spontaneous dramatic performances and impetuous passion, inspired women artists of the period. When Corinne performs at the Capitol in Rome, she arouses "interest and curiosity, astonishment and affection from all who behold her." Staël describes her as "an inspired priestess, joyously devoting herself to the cult of genius."[45] Mrs. Stock seems to have nurtured Anning's sense of grandiose potential; she declared Mary Anning "a being of the Imagination."[46]

Besides describing being swept off her feet by Anning, Pinney recorded another instance of the "wild romance of her character." When the East Indiaman ship the *Alexander* was lost off Portland, Anning discovered the body of a beautiful woman that washed up near Lyme. Pinney writes, "Mary unentangled the sea weeds which had attached itself to her long hair, and performed all other offices due from the living to the dead."[47] The drowned woman was Lady Jackson, who had been returning from India with her children.

Anning was used to patrolling the coastline for vestiges of the long dead, but the newly waterlogged body of Lady Jackson was an unusual find. In contrast to the spare skeletal remains of ancient sea creatures, the corpse of Lady Jackson must have been a complicated mess, the soft flesh wreathed in seaweed and tugged by sodden layers of full-skirted apparel. In Pinney's depiction, Anning resembles a besotted knight carrying out tragic and futile ministrations. Until a friend arrived to claim it, Pinney notes, the body was deposited in the local church, where Anning went daily to bestrew Lady Jackson with flowers.

It is easy to imagine several reasons why the Mary Anning that Anna Maria Pinney describes would have been moved to copy the particular Byron poem that opens her commonplace book. Speaking as a man exhausted by past love affairs, the narrator of Byron's poem writes:

'Tis time this heart should be unmoved
Since others it hath ceased to move,
Yet though I cannot be beloved
Still let me love.

My days are in the yellow leaf
The flowers and fruits of love are gone—
The worm, the canker and the grief
Are mine alone.[48]

Byron presents in this poem a jaded version of his former dashing poetic self. The narrator might be an older version of one of his famous romance heroes, Conrad of *The Corsair*, for example, who thrilled readers with his chivalrous rescue of the slave Gulnare. The narrator of the poem Mary Anning copied out washes his hands of such romantic entanglements, but he conjures them up nonetheless, while going on to suggest that the "yellow leaf" of his waning days might still smolder. The poem continues:

The fire that on my bosom preys
Is lone as some Volcanic Isle,
No torch is kindled at its blaze
A funeral pile!

The stanza hints at a suppressed power, a force that the narrator suggests he will harness for the larger national concerns of Greece. Byron writes:

But 't is not thus—and 't is not here
Such thoughts should shake my soul; nor *now*
When glory seals the hero's bier
Or binds his brow.

The Sword—the Banner—and the Field;
Glory and Greece around us see!

> The Spartan borne upon his shield
> Was not more free!

But even though Byron's narrator distances himself from amorous passion, he encourages the reader to recall the many poetic former versions of his "mad, bad" self. He purports to break clean of his past, to fix his mind solely on Greek military victory, but his old alter-ego haunts his newly invented one. The poem's narrator ultimately turns to death in battle as the best means to "tread reviving passions down," ending with this final admonition:

> If thou regret'st thy youth, why *live?*
> The Land of honourable Death
> Is here—up to the Field and give
> Away thy Breath!

> Seek out—less often sought than found,
> A Soldier's Grave—for thee the best,
> Then look around, and choose thy ground,
> And take thy Rest.[49]

The trajectory from romantic passion to death in battle that the poem portrays was not a career path available to Anning, but she may have identified, nonetheless, with the poem's invocation of both heroic action and chastened aspirations. Certainly Pinney's version of Anning would suggest that she invented for herself a flamboyant persona that ran counter to conventional standards of female behavior. The possibility that she cherished Byron's poem as a model for her own self-fashioning accords with Thomas Goodhue's reading of Anning's religious background as a springboard for strong female self-definition. Goodhue observes that accounts of "triumphant deaths," such as the obituary of a sixteen-year-old Lyme girl written by Anning's pastor for the 1801 *Theological Magazine and Review* (an issue Anning owned), encouraged young women to see themselves as having significant vocations.[50]

Anning also singled out for transcription Henry Kirke White's "Solitude," a poem that shares the despairing tone of Byron's second-to-last poem, and one which anticipates (and possibly inspires) Byron's imagery. In a precursor of Byron's "My days are in the yellow leaf," White writes:

> The autumn leaf is sear and dead,
> It floats upon the water's bed;
> I would not be a leaf, to die
> Without recording sorrow's sigh![51]

Byron was an admirer of White, who died in 1806 at the age of twenty-one, and he penned an elaborate tribute poem that addresses "Unhappy White," and describes him as a genius brought low by his ambitious scholarly pursuits.[52] Byron's "On this day I complete my thirty sixth year" and White's "Solitude" resonated for Anning with their valorization of emotional isolation and amorous despair. And both poets' actual deaths and subsequent intensification of celebrity may have inspired Mary Anning's self-mythologizing tendencies, her construction of herself as a risk-defying adventurer who braved storm and tide in pursuit of fossils.

Then again, Anning may have liked these poems for less personal reasons. Byron's poem becomes in Anning's commonplace book—and, most likely, in many other women's commonplace books—a souvenir of Byron's death, and the very fact of this death may explain why Anning singled out the poem for inclusion. Poems about loss and death were staples of romantic era commonplace books; the practice of compiling poems in private anthologies was seemingly driven by a strain of morbid sensibility.

Anning may have copied the poem from the *Morning Chronicle*, where it appeared in a version very similar to her transcription on October 29, 1824. Or perhaps she copied someone else's copy of the *Morning Chronicle* printing of the poem. Another feature of commonplace book poems is their tendency to be passed from one person's volume to another's, multiplying the poem's souvenir associations. By choosing Byron's poem out of all the poems she might have copied into her commonplace book, Anning made that poem her own, imbuing

it with a significance that was unique to her own circumstances. But the fact that
so many individual commonplace books share an aesthetic of loss makes one
wonder whether the act of compiling a commonplace book somehow caused the
compiler to engage a prefabricated set of aesthetic values.[53] Anning may have
copied Byron's poem to mark her commemoration of his death or, perhaps, to
mark her identification with Byron's vision of heroic action. Or the poem may
record only Anning's dalliance with a certain cultural strain of morbid sensibility,
a strain that manifested itself in commonplace books as a whole. The copied
poem allows us no certainty about its place in Anning's affections. We can only
survey her possible reasons for preserving it, a sheaf of possibilities that refuse to
be transformed into one definitive explanation.

A "hysterical teenager" is how Torrens referred to the diarist Anna Maria
Pinney during the question and answer session that followed his Anning
symposium address. In his disparagement of Pinney, Torrens was following the
lead of William Dickson Lang, who could not attend the Anning symposium because he was long dead, but whose ghost hovered over the proceedings. In fact,
the presenters derived a large part of their information from the series of Anning
papers Lang published from the 1930s through the 1950s, mostly in the *Proceedings of the Dorset Natural History and Archaeological Society*. The Keeper of the
Department of Geology in the British Museum's natural history department and
a specialist in the study of the paleontological succession of the Blue Lias cliffs of
Charmouth (near Lyme Regis), Lang was the first scholarly collector of Anning

documents. In articles with titles such as "Mary Anning and the Pioneering Geologists of Lyme," "More about Mary Anning," "Mary Anning and a Very Small
Boy," and "Mary Anning's Escape from Lightning," he inched Anning's reputation forward, turning up facts relating to her discoveries or her acquaintances
and reporting his finds in a series of respectful articles.

Lang was determined to give Anning her due; he laid out the scope of her ac-
complishments, chronicling the testimonials of her male peers: Gideon Mantell's claim that "all the most valuable fossils" in a collection purchased by the
British Museum "had been obtained by the indefatigable labours of Miss Mary
Anning,"[54] Thomas Allan's observation that Anning was responsible for the
"preservation of some of the finest remains of a former world that are known in
Europe."[55] But Lang, who carried out research on the coast of Dorset, and who
settled there upon his retirement, was also invested in constructing a particular
version of Anning. He wanted her to be known not as "the Mary Anning of legend, something of a village blue-stocking, nor . . . [as] the creature of fancy, a
daintily romantic figure," but rather "as surmised by reading between the lines
of her own recorded remarks (few though they be), a plain practical, honest, and
humble woman: one who rose to her opportunities and put her talents to the
best use."[56] For whatever reason, Lang was compelled to distance Anning from
literary realms, from the female intellectual salons conjured up by his reference
to blue-stockings, as well as from the "daintily romantic" figures that one would
find in popular poems. Lang's Anning is a comparatively bland entity—plain,
practical, honest, humble—who has been stripped of her aggrandizing legends.
By distinguishing between Anning as a literary figure and Anning as a figure of
fact, Lang positioned himself on the fault lines of the symposium he would not
live to attend.

It was Lang who first drew attention to Pinney's diary, but he suppressed her
more fervent outbursts. He transcribed sections of the diary in preparation for
writing "Mary Anning and Anna Maria Pinney," but he left out bits of the original
in this article.[57] In his ongoing effort to construct one kind of Anning (dutiful and
industrious), he erased Pinney's allusion to another kind of Anning (self-aggrandizing and impassioned). "I really love Mary Anning," Pinney wrote in one of

Lang's suppressed passages. "Had she lived in an age of chivalry she might have been a heroine with fearless courage, ardour, and peerless truth and honour."[58]

After Anning's death in 1847, the executor of her sister-in-law's will remarked that "the death of Mary Anning, was a serious loss to the town, as her presence attracted a large number of distinguished visitors, who able to appreciate her genius, were desirous of perambulating with her."[59] Three years before she died, one of the more famous would-be perambulators, the king of Saxony, visited her fossil shop. When asked to record her name in the king's pocket book, Anning obliged, then returned the book with the boast, "I am well known throughout the whole of Europe."[60] Anning's encounter with the king of Saxony allows nearly all Anning commentators to suggest, quite reasonably, that her fossil-collecting expertise gave her an unusual confidence. Anning's assertion of her own celebrity recalls Byron's famous claim that he awoke and found himself famous after the publication of *Childe Harold's Pilgrimage*. This assertion, perhaps more than the *Childe Harold* sale figures, has worked to irrevocably link celebrity with Byron's name. Anning may or may not have been thinking of herself in Byronic terms when she autographed the king of Saxony's pocket book.

There was no tea—that was the disappointing thing about the strawberry tea held in John Fowles's back garden. The Anning symposium participants walked through John Fowles's house, past the living room which was being cordoned off by John Fowles's second wife (who was ostensibly welcoming participants to her home, but who may have been making sure that none of the participants started nosing around in John Fowles's library), and then straggled around the backyard. They walked about balancing dishes of strawberries and navigating around people with whom they had spent too much time in the three days of symposium events.

The field trips that had taken place directly before the strawberry tea had further tended to separate the scientists from the fabulists, since participants had to choose between going on a geological excursion or tracing Mary Anning's footsteps in a walk around Lyme Regis. One could either wear sturdy shoes and scramble over rocks and stare up at the hard edges of dangerously unstable cliffs, or one could wear any kind of shoes and walk around the town, listening to stories about places where Anning once lived or where someone Anning knew once lived, near-historic sites whose Anning-related buildings had been torn down and replaced with tearooms.

As Hugh Torrens made his way around John Fowles's backyard, he did so as the acknowledged sovereign of Mary Anning studies, the man who had worked hardest to ascertain her exact place in scientific history. Torrens had spent years gathering shards of lost information about Mary Anning—the name of her London dealer and the commission he charged, the sum she had been paid for each of her specimens and the whereabouts of those specimens as they changed hands, the type of fossil that had been the object of her last sale and where that starfish was now. And other people—children's book authors, biographers, North Americans—were taking all those shards and arranging them into stories, some of them accurate, some of them not.

There is a history of objects that still waits to be written, Torrens had proclaimed plaintively at the end of his symposium lecture, and "the history of the curation of [geological] collections has been even more ignored than the history of those collections," he had written years before the conference, perhaps anticipating his thankless future status as the chief Anning fact-checker among the strawberry-eating enthusiasts, some quizzing him on his sources as they bunched together like fossil crinoids in John Fowles's backyard.[61]

In his "Hints for Collecting Fossil Bones," Gideon Mantell insists on the value of keeping a faithful record of even an imperfect and unknown fossil. Just as the antiquary preserves shreds of ancient manuscripts in the hope that later discoveries may enable him to interpret these now unintelligible records, "so the geologist should treasure up every fragment of an undetermined organism remain, for the time may arrive when other specimens will explain its nature, and prove it to possess considerable interest."[62]

Part of the most legendary Anning fossil, the ichthyosaur she gouged out of a cliff when she was twelve, is on display in the London Natural History Museum, but only the part that was her brother's find (see fig. 24). The British Museum purchased the whole specimen from William Bullock in 1819, but then either neglected to keep the body, or else lost track of exactly which ichthyosaur torso belonged with the Anning head. The skull has comparatively little scientific value, but it holds a key place in the Anning legend, commemorating by its missing bits Anning's first major find.

The commonplace book which contains the Byron poem Mary Anning transcribed is known as the "Fourth Notebook." No first, second, or third notebook survives. It most likely dates from the decade when Anning was in her forties; she would die of breast cancer at age 47 in 1847.[63] If we had her earlier note-

Fig. 24. Fossil skull found by Joseph Anning in 1811. Copyright © The Natural History Museum, London.

books we might be able to speak with more confidence about her affection for romantic poets, or about her affinity for Byronism, or about the influence literary gleanings had on her fossil collecting endeavors. As it stands, the commonplace book commemorates only Anning's affection, possibly fleeting, for Byron's second-to-last poem.

The tea over and the symposium drawing to a close, the conference participants could look forward to the keynote address that Stephen Jay Gould, the
symposium attender best known outside Anning circles, was poised to deliver.
Gould was accompanied to the conference by the photographer Rosamond Wolff
Purcell, with whom he had collaborated on a gorgeous photo essay on collectors
titled *Finders, Keepers*. The book dwelled particularly on nineteenth-century
artists' renderings of fossils and the role they had played in the advancement of
scientific knowledge. Writing of the drawings in Louis Agassiz's *Poissons fossiles*,
Gould described them as the primary working tools of early paleontologists, "not
some fluff added later for the sake of art and commerce." The drawings were for
Agassiz "both his centrifuge and his computer."[64] Purcell's photographs and
Gould's accompanying essays sought to demonstrate how the division between
science and art was foreign to nineteenth-century science.

Hugh Torrens had taken up the title of Gould's and Purcell's *Finders, Keepers*
in his address to the British Society for the History of Science. " 'Collectors,' "
he wrote, "is much too all-embracing a term in the English language, since it is
used for both those who find and those who keep." Torrens continued, "Gould's
title obscures the obvious point that the finders (the Annings of this world) are
not—for economic reasons in their case—often the keepers."[65] But Gould, in his
symposium address, did not have any particular interest in arguing the fine
points of Anning's status as a collector, or in finding new details of Anning's life
and career. He spoke about the history of brachiopod identification, the way the
organism was once known familiarly as a "hysteriolith" or "wombstone." Gould
had clearly noted the anti-storytelling faction at the symposium, and he began
his talk with a defense of fiction writing as an illuminating force. He noted that
Anning had become the subject of legendary, not vicious, fictions, and then he
proceeded to deliver a paper that had nothing to do with Anning at all, but addressed the interplay between scientific progress and popular mythology in the
naming of fossil snails. Gould's talk, like Gould's previous essay writing on the
natural world and on the history of science, yoked a literary sensibility with a scientist's command of facts. His brief subsequent career came to further dramatize
the way in which scientific and literary concerns are typically set in opposition.

Three years after the Anning symposium, Stephen Jay Gould went the way of the giant plesiosaurs and ichthyosaurs, struck down while still in his scholarly prime. Two months before he died, there arrived in bookstores his final work, a grand epoch-marking volume in the tradition of Darwin's *Origin of Species*. In *The Structure of Evolutionary Theory*, Gould sought to affirm his reputation as a scientist, which had been undermined by his success as a storyteller. Gould the popular essayist was thrust into the shadow of this large and recondite final book, as if he had, at last, succumbed to the notion that science trumped literature, that hard facts counted more than literary flourishings.[66]

The Byron poem, like the fossil head marooned amidst more intact remains, calls attention to missing parts, pieces of a story that may never be entirely recuperable even by Anning completists. Anning is no more reducible to the sum of her surviving parts than the extinct creatures whose remains she prised out of rock. What scholars and storytellers make of her will always be highly dependent on their own proclivities and predispositions.

There may be no more idiosyncratic way of understanding Mary Anning's collecting practice than by means of a stray romantic poem that found its way into her commonplace book. The fragmentary remains of Anning's collecting career, and the tensions that career has incited among those most interested in preserving her reputation, allow me to make observations that are tangential to, but still illuminating of, Anning's collecting history. These remains help me to demonstrate the entanglement of romantic poetry in the realms of early nineteenth-century fossil collecting. They assist me in calling into question the forms of certitude that structure academic writing. Finally, the sequestered Byron lyric and the severed fossil head allow me to suggest one final time the allusiveness and elusiveness of romantic objects, and the mental provinces they shared with romantic poems.

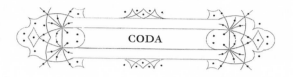

LIGHTS OUT FOR THE ROMANTIC COLLECTORS

Edward Silsbee, the Shelley devotee who purchased the poet's guitar, was one of the second-to-last generation of romantic collectors, though not the most remarkable one. For theatricality, he was surpassed by Fred Holland Day, a Keats enthusiast who photographed himself as Jesus Christ, and who tortured Amy Lowell by withholding access to manuscript letters she needed to complete her biography of Keats. Day's treasures included a copy of Keats's 1817 *Poems* inscribed to Wordsworth, a framed portrait of Keats with a lock of his hair under the glass, and a series of letters the poet wrote to his beloved Fanny Brawne, these last the particular objects of Lowell's pursuit. Another Keats researcher who sought out Day recalled a setting reminiscent of Miss Bordereau's chamber in *The Aspern Papers*. Day was "pinned into his bed with huge blanket pins," pleased to be set apart from those who had to "dash here and there in quest of something."[1] He asked whether his visitor would, if she were allowed to read his Keats letters, "promise never to make any use of the information or any reference to them," at which point the researcher conceded defeat, ate cookies, and went home.[2]

The battle Day waged against scholars who wished to use his Keats collection dramatizes the divide that was developing between amateur and academic collectors even as Silsbee was seeking out Shelley remains. Despite insinuating himself into Claire Clairmont's Florentine household, Silsbee did not ultimately come out the victor in his pursuit of Shelley spoils. He was thwarted in his efforts by Harry Buxton Forman, a Shelley bibliographer who was able to meet the selling price of Clairmont's niece, Paola Clairmont, in cash. Silsbee could only offer "bills at long date," so despite his protestations—"It has been by a great misunderstanding that they have been offered to another," he wrote mournfully—Forman won out.[3] Forman acquired Shelley's letters, "his hair, some pinches of his ashes, his inkstand, diaries, note-books and other papers and relics."[4]

If you believe the version of Silsbee provided by Forman's friend Thomas Wise, this outcome was just. Wise claimed to have known Silsbee well, and in his view, Silsbee was "an amusing chap in his way, but an utter cad in some of his actions." Wise recalled lunching with Silsbee and Forman several years after the Clairmont papers had been dispersed, and hearing Silsbee recount with glee how he had cheated Paola Clairmont out of a manuscript notebook by promising to marry her. "He thought we should admire his 'smartness,'" Wise wrote, "whereas he simply filled us with disgust." As the three men parted, the two scholars shook their heads over the diabolism of Silsbee. "How can God have made such a man?" Forman reportedly exclaimed.[5]

The notebook was a sore topic for Forman, who had expected it to be among the Shelley papers he purchased, and who had, instead, been "left lamenting" over its absence.[6] But Forman and Wise were in no position to cast aspersions on Silsbee's character, since they went on to win notoriety as forgers of literary rarities who contrived elaborate bibliographic "evidence" to legitimize their fakes. Wise's copy of the so-called Reading edition of Elizabeth Barrett Browning's *Sonnets from the Portuguese*, a "matchless association volume," was encased in a crimson morocco binding inset with locks of Elizabeth and Robert Browning's hair. "Extremely bizarre," one commentator has called the elaborate presentation of the Reading *Sonnets*, given the fraudulent nature of the book's contents; even if the Reading *Sonnets* had not been a fake, "the volume would still be distasteful."[7]

Even though Forman and Wise had scholarly motivations for their Shelley collecting, they, like Silsbee, understood the power of association objects and succumbed to their seductions. Forman pasted into his library's holdings a bookplate that depicted him toiling at his desk, holding a feather pen, as if it were necessary for him to carry out his Shelley scholarship with the kind of pen Shelley would have used. In the bookplate drawing, Forman is surrounded by Shelley treasures: portraits, a manuscript scroll, and an imposing bust with "Shelley" engraved across its base, lest there be any confusion about the identity of the sculpted head with the swirl of windswept hair.

When Forman's collections were auctioned off in 1920, there was a toupee's worth of romantic hair on offer. There were locks of Fanny Brawne's hair and hair that had once belonged to William Hazlitt. You could have bought Allegra Byron's hair or hair previously combed by Claire Clairmont. Shelley's ashes were available for purchase mounted under glass ("surrounded with 12 acquamarines") or stowed in a cardboard box.[8] When Thomas Wise catalogued his Shelley library in 1924, he listed a volume of manuscript documents which Forman had acquired from Claire Clairmont. The book was bound in ruby red Levant morocco with gilt frames containing the hair of Mary and Percy Shelley inserted in the front doublure. In the end doublure was an urn-shaped frame containing a fragment of Shelley's skull. Wise wrote, "The tiny heap of Shelley's ashes, including fragments of his skull, inserted in the end cover of the volume, is an object of deep and pathetic attraction, and stands unique as a memorial of one of the greatest English poets."[9]

It is possible to look charitably on Edward Silsbee's attachment to particular Shelley relics, to note the way he used them to vaunt his love of Shelley and to enlist others in this affection. It is harder to read about the Shelley skull fragment that Wise made part of his book binding and not feel squeamish about the practice of collecting, to sense the dust gathering and the library walls closing in.

Walter Benjamin conjures up childhood as the source of a playful mode of collecting, and he suggests that the child collector's passion lingers on, "but with a dimmed and manic glow, in antiquarians, researchers, bibliomanics."[10] There was something a little childlike about Silsbee's enthrallment by particular Shelley items—his worshipful handling of Shelley's notebook, his benefactory involvement with Shelley's guitar—and this distinguishes his collecting from Forman's and Wise's more single-minded approach to Shelley objects. Silsbee cherished particular Shelley relics, but he also dispersed them in a manner that was very different from the bibliographers' efforts to compile complete collections of all Shelley publications and related ephemera. "I have succeeded in accumulating a collection of Shelleyana more nearly approaching completeness than has ever yet been gathered either in this country or in America," wrote Wise in a preface to the 1924 catalogue of his Shelley library.[11] Silsbee was intent on celebrating Shelley (and himself by association); Wise wanted to consign every last piece of the poet to his archive.

There was money to be made in Shelley publications so rare that no one had ever seen them; the manic pursuits of Forman and Wise stem from greed, but also from a classifying compulsion that for many theorists separates the true collector from an enthusiast such as Silsbee. Silsbee wanted to commune with Shelley, whereas Wise and Forman wanted to claim ownership of everything he ever wrote, even if that involved inventing items that could not be found. Their background as collectors furthered their bibliographic forgeries. "By being so intimately involved in collecting, they were able both to conceive new forgeries and then market them among their fellow collectors," writes one historian of their crimes.[12] When James turned the actual Silsbee into a fictional scholar-collector, he transformed him into a collector more like Wise and Forman; he made him aspire to being master of Aspern's remains.

Scholarly practice as a form of striving after completeness and total mastery in the manner of the collectors Wise and Forman can be a deathly undertaking, especially as forms of knowledge proliferate, and the impetus to "cover" a field requires denser and denser citational webs. Everyone has heard of a scholar whose archive grew beyond anyone's ability to shape it, whose files, after his death, were trundled out of a department office on a handcart. Wise and Forman's manufacturing of "rare" books and bibliographic evidence stands as the dark extreme of the painstaking pursuit of factual detail, the insistence that no scholarly stone go unturned. We might imagine another method of deflecting the deathly drive for total mastery: a critical practice that takes seriously the increasingly weighty accumulation of history, theory, criticism, but that also finds inspiriting ways to convey scholarship.

Throughout these pages, I have explored the grip that objects have over their owners and the ways in which romantic structures of feeling—a longing for permanence, a fascination with perfect beauty, a preoccupation with authenticity, a propensity for grandiose endeavors—contribute to this hold. The collecting habits of the romantic era figures discussed here challenge the too-automatic association of collecting with the pursuit of dominance and link collecting instead to self-sustaining fantasies founded on harmless (or ineffectual) forms of control. The beleaguered Queen Charlotte used her collecting activities as a mode of escape from the king's madness and from her own ennui. A replica of Napoleon's carriage allowed Byron to invoke the French emperor's luster as he wrote poetry on the fly. A Byron poem copied by the fossil collector Mary Anning played a part in her construction of herself as a mythic being. Even in those instances in which collectors might seem to be caught up in exercises of control—the pursuit and identification of hummingbirds, for example—they are less invested in the completion of a series or the construction of total order than in the pleasure of the systematizing, however doomed to ultimate failure.

In preparing to write this book, I amassed an archive of material on romantic collectors extensive enough for a volume several times larger than the one you are reading. This book's current size and design stand as my effort to avoid the pretense of total mastery and its resultant scholarly bloatedness. In turning my back on a set of serviceable scholarly conventions (linear structure, authoritative argument, definitive conclusion) and substituting those associated with more literary—especially romantic literary—genres (disjunction, uncertainty, fragmentation), I run the risk of seeming Silsbee-like: unprofessional, dilettantish, and silly. But if Silsbee has become a reigning spirit of this study, as well as an initial impetus, it is because of that collector's unsystematic delight in romantic objects, a pleasure that suffuses as well both Benjamin's writings on collecting and his eccentric advocacy of a criticism consisting entirely of quotations.[13] Benjamin writes of collecting as a process of renewal: "Other processes are the painting of objects, the cutting out of figures, the application of decals—the whole range of childlike modes of acquisition, from touching things to giving them names."[14] There are lively and deathly forms of collecting, collections that are enlisted in the creation of something new, and collections that are focused only on concretizing the dead. I am no Benjamin, nor even a Silsbee, but I sought to take seriously those collectors' enthusiasms when turning the contents of too many overstuffed file folders into this book.

All the romantic relics have been impounded by now, or nearly so. You might still be able to pick up a lock of Shelley's hair at auction, but most such objects were in the hands of their last private owners by the 1920s. In the catalogue

Fig. 25. Shelley relics filmstrip (Roll 307.2). By kind permission of the Bodleian Library, University of Oxford.

of his collection, Thomas Wise writes, "To collect such a Shelley Library again will be impossible," and he was probably right. The last best opportunity to get a good start on a romantic poet collection had been Harry Buxton Forman's auction three years before. Forman's offerings fueled the longings of the last generation of romantic collectors, the likes of Luther Brewer, who had to settle for collecting Leigh Huntiana since he could not afford to collect a poet of Shelley's standing, and Carl Pforzheimer, who came to own Shelley's copy of *Queen Mab* after it passed through Forman's hands. Both men's collections have since become institutionalized; their most cherished relics are in the charge of preservation specialists.

It may not matter that we no longer handle romantic poets' hair or ashes or musical instruments—at least not without gloves and a curator standing by—or that we no longer set eyes on the eyes of someone who once knew them, and believe that something could be transmitted by that person's mere gaze. We are getting further and further away from these objects, speeding into a digitized future that makes the photographs Benjamin feared would strip objects of their auras take on a numinous quality of their own.[15] These days, if you want to see Shelley's guitar, which Silsbee bestowed upon the Bodleian Library, you will be encouraged to purchase a Shelley relic filmstrip in the library gift shop (see fig. 25). This photographic vestige of Shelley's personal belongings vies with souvenir bookmarks and Bodleian T-shirts for the visitor's trade. The filmstrip in the library gift shop attests to the relics' ongoing allure. Both tourists and scholars still long to communicate with physical remains of romantic poets, even through the obsolete tracery of the filmstrip. In so doing, and at this late moment in time, these library visitors reenact the romantic era fascination with collected objects.

NOTES

Introduction

1. See the wonderful collection guides highlighting the Shelley holdings in the Bodleian Library and the Carl H. Pforzheimer Collection: B. C. Barker-Benfield, *Shelley's Guitar* (Oxford: Bodleian Library, 1992); Stephen Wagner and Doucet Devin Fischer, *The Carl H. Pforzheimer Collection of Shelley and His Circle: A History, a Biography, and a Guide* (New York: New York Public Library, 1996).

2. The Victorian Shelley editor W. M. Rossetti wrote to Richard Garnett of his attempt to track down this volume during a proposed visit to Sir Percy Shelley. "One detail that I had wished to look into is that affair of the copy of Keats said to have been burned along with Shelley's corpse: Lady Shelley, herself is (I think) the only authority in print for this story of the burning, tho I find collateral indications that Leigh Hunt affirmed the same thing. Now I dare say I have told you that Trelawny says the book can certainly not have been burned: that no one save himself burned anything, & he did not burn the book. . . . [L]ately, in looking over some old letters, I found one of yours (1870) saying that Mrs Garnett saw the Keats among the Shelley relics, & therefore rejects the story of burning." Letter 392, 5 November 1875, in "Letters about Shelley from the Richard Garnett Papers, University of Texas," ed. William Richard Thurman (Ph.D. diss., University of Texas, 1972), 274–75.

3. E. J. Trelawny, *Recollections of the Last Days of Shelley and Byron* (London: Edward Moxon, 1858), 120. Richard Holmes calls Trelawny an incorrigible myth-maker and notes that he obsessively rewrote his account of Shelley's death, which accumulated "more and more baroque details, like some sinister biographical coral-reef." Richard

Holmes, "Shelley Undrowned," in *Interrupted Lives in Literature*, ed. Andrew Motion (London: National Portrait Gallery, 2004), 24.

4. The institution was chosen, according to Richard Garnett, because it was already the depository of the Shelley manuscripts and relics belonging to Lady Shelley, wife of the poet's son. Richard Garnett, introduction to *Journal of Edward Ellerker Williams* (London: Elkin Mathews, 1902), 11. Lady Shelley, writing to Garnett in May 1894 expressed her pleasure at the Bodleian's reception of her relics: "They have given me a cabinet all to myself with a covered glass top under which are placed the relics I have treasured so dearly for the last forty years of my life—It is a great happiness to have seen them there & to know that they are considered the most valuable collection they have ever received." Thurman, "Letters about Shelley," 206. William St. Clair wryly describes University College's acceptance of another Shelley object, the sentimental Onslow Ford sculpture of the drowned poet, as "part expiation for having expelled the most distinguished man ever to attend the college." William St. Clair, *Trelawny: The Incurable Romancer* (London: John Murray, 1977), 231. Shelley was expelled for advocating atheism.

5. *Times* (London), 22 June 1898.

6. "Lines: When the lamp is shattered," in *The Complete Poetical Works of Percy Bysshe Shelley*, ed. Thomas Hutchinson (London: Oxford University Press, 1923), 661.

7. "With a Guitar. To Jane," in *Shelley's Poetry and Prose*, ed. Donald H. Reiman and Neil Fraistat (New York: W. W. Norton, 2002), 479.

8. On the fetishization of Shelley, see Eric O. Clarke, "Shelley's Heart: Sexual Politics and Cultural Value," *Yale Journal of Criticism* 8 (1995): 187–208. For a discussion of the allure of Shelley's cremation story, see Kim Wheatley, "'Attracted by the Body': Accounts of Shelley's Cremation," *Keats-Shelley Journal* 49 (2000): 162–82.

9. Stephen Gill, *Wordsworth and the Victorians* (Oxford: Clarendon Press, 1998), 15.

10. "Hymn to Intellectual Beauty," in *Shelley's Poetry and Prose*, 93–94. Ted Underwood notes that "Romantic-era representations of history often depend on a special sense that sees or hears historical depth in the inanimate world," most especially in ghosts, another instance of romantic poets' material remove. Ted Underwood, "Romantic Historicism and the Afterlife," *PMLA* 117.2 (2002): 237.

11. This is not true of critical commentary on the verse of those women poets whose work, as Stuart Curran notes, is "occupied continually in discriminating minute objects or assembling a world out of its disjointed particulars." Stuart Curran, "Romantic Poetry: The I Altered," in *Romanticism and Feminism*, ed. Anne K. Mellor (Bloomington: Indiana University Press, 1988), 189.

12. M. H. Abrams, *The Mirror and the Lamp: Romantic Theory and the Critical Tradition* (New York: Oxford University Press, 1953), 52. Abrams quotes Hazlitt's "On Poetry in General," the first lecture in his *Lectures on the English Poets*, vol. 5 of *The Complete*

Works of William Hazlitt, ed. P.·P. Howe (London: J. M. Dent, 1930), 3. Frederick Pottle also, in his 1952 article "The Case of Shelley," writes of that poet, "He seldom takes a gross, palpable, near-at-hand object from the world of ordinary perception and holds it for contemplation: his gaze goes up to the sky, he starts with objects that are just on the verge of becoming invisible or inaudible or intangible and he strains away even from these." Frederick A. Pottle, "The Case of Shelley," *PMLA* 67.5 (1952): 601.

13. Marjorie Levinson, "Insight and oversight: reading 'Tintern Abbey,'" in *Wordsworth's Great Period Poems* (Cambridge: Cambridge University Press, 1986), 14–57.

14. Jerome J. McGann, *The Romantic Ideology: A Critical Investigation* (Chicago: University of Chicago Press, 1983), 1.

15. Mary Poovey, *A History of the Modern Fact: Problems of Knowledge in the Sciences of Wealth and Society* (Chicago: University of Chicago Press, 1998), 327. Alan Liu, by contrast, argues that present-day cultural criticism reenacts a romantic preoccupation with the discrete detail as a portal to immanence. Alan Liu, "Local Transcendence: Cultural Criticism, Postmodernism, and the Romanticism of Detail," *Representations* 32 (1990): 75–113.

16. For a refutation of this critical view, see Onno Oerlemans, *Romanticism and the Materiality of Nature* (Toronto: University of Toronto Press, 2002). Oerlemans argues for the importance of romantic empiricism and an openness to the material, particularly as a component of environmentalism.

17. Preface to *Lyrical Ballads*, in *The Prose Works of William Wordsworth*, ed. W.J.B. Owen and Jane Worthington Smyser, 3 vols. (Oxford: Clarendon Press, 1974), 1:132. "The world is too much with us," in *The Poetical Works of William Wordsworth*, 2nd ed., 5 vols., ed. Ernest de Selincourt and Helen Darbishire (Oxford: Clarendon Press, 1952–59), 3:18.

18. My thanks to Tom Keymer for drawing my attention to this passage of *The Prelude*. William Wordsworth, *The Prelude: 1799, 1805, 1815*, ed. Jonathan Wordsworth, M. H. Abrams, and Stephen Gill (New York: W. W. Norton, 1979), 2.224–25. Hereafter cited in the text by book and line number from the 1805 edition.

19. Stephen Bann, *Romanticism and the Rise of History* (New York: Twayne, 1995), 6–7. Bann argues that "the sense of history generated in the Romantic period was . . . qualitatively as well as quantitatively different from what had gone before" (6). See also Stephen Bann, *The Clothing of Clio* (Cambridge: Cambridge University Press, 1984), and *Under the Sign: John Bargrave as Collector, Traveler, and Witness* (Ann Arbor: University of Michigan Press, 1994). Michel Foucault identifies the period between 1775 and 1825 as the moment when "a profound historicity penetrates into the heart of things, isolates and defines them in their own coherence." Foucault, *The Order of Things: An Archaeology of the Human Sciences* (New York: Pantheon Books, 1970), xxiii. Greg Kucich points out the gender blindness of academic historiography—including

the work of Michel Foucault, Stephen Bann, and Benedict Anderson—which he surveys as a prelude to his discussion of romantic women writers' "massive investment in the field of historical construction." Greg Kucich, "Romanticism and the Reengendering of Historical Memory," in *Memory and Memorials, 1789–1914: Literary and Cultural Perspectives*, ed. Matthew Campbell, Jacqueline M. Labbe, and Sally Shuttleworth (London: Routledge, 2000), esp. 15–19. See also James K. Chandler's study of romantic historicism, *England in 1819: The Politics of Literary Culture and the Case of Romantic Historicism* (Chicago: University of Chicago Press, 1998).

20. The literature on collecting, in our own time, is growing by leaps and bounds. Its claim to being a distinctive field of study has been reinforced by the publication of the excellent *Journal of the History of Collections*, and by the anthologies of critical essays compiled by Oliver Impey and Arthur McGregor (*The Origins of Museums* [Oxford: Clarendon Press, 1985]), by John Elsner and Roger Cardinal (*The Cultures of Collecting* [Cambridge: Harvard University Press, 1994]), and by Leah Dilworth (*Acts of Possession: Collecting in America* [New Brunswick, N.J.: Rutgers University Press, 2003]), as well as by the series of historical documents gathered by Frank Herman in *The English as Collectors: A Documentary Chrestomathy* (New York: W. W. Norton, 1972), and by Susan Pearce and Ken Arnold in *The Collector's Voice: Critical Readings in the Practice of Collecting*, 4 vols. (Burlington, Vt.: Ashgate, 2000–). Our understanding of the avocation of collecting has been enriched by an outpouring of critical studies. See Susan Stewart, *On Longing: Narratives of the Miniature, the Gigantic, the Souvenir, the Collection* (1984; reprint, Durham: Duke University Press, 1994); James Clifford, *The Predicament of Culture: Twentieth-Century Ethnography, Literature, and Art* (Cambridge: Harvard University Press, 1988); Krzysztof Pomian, *Collectors and Curiosities: Paris and Venice, 1500–1800*, trans. Elizabeth Wiles-Portier (Cambridge: Polity Press, 1990); Nicholas Thomas, *Entangled Objects: Exchange, Material Culture, and Colonialism in the Pacific* (Cambridge: Harvard University Press, 1991); Werner Muensterberger, *Collecting: An Unruly Passion* (Princeton: Princeton University Press, 1994); Paul Martin, *Popular Collecting and the Everyday Self* (London: Leicester University Press, 1999); and Susan M. Pearce's impressive and ongoing body of work on the subject: *Museums, Objects, and Collections: A Cultural Study* (Washington, D.C.: Smithsonian Institution Press, 1993), *On Collecting: An Investigation into Collecting in the European Tradition* (New York: Routledge, 1995), and *Collecting in Contemporary Practice* (London: SAGE Publications, 1998). See also *Pictures, Patents, Monkeys, and More . . . On Collecting* (New York: Independent Curators International, 2001), the catalogue to a traveling exhibition, which contains essays by Ingrid Schaffner, Fred Wilson, and Werner Muensterberger.

Related to these studies of the avocation of collecting are the essays gathered by Arjun Appadurai in *The Social Life of Things: Commodities in Cultural Perspective*

(Cambridge: Cambridge University Press, 1986), especially Igor Kopytoff, "The Cultural Biography of Things: Commoditization as Process," 64–91. Also see the special issue of *Critical Inquiry* devoted to "Things," edited by Bill Brown, especially Brown's introduction, "Thing Theory" (*Critical Inquiry* 28 [2001]: 1–22), and his earlier effort to theorize things in "How to Do Things with Things (A Toy Story)," *Critical Inquiry* 24 (1998): 935–64. Lorraine Daston brings together essays on a variety of interesting things in *Things That Talk: Object Lessons from Art and Science* (New York: Zone Books, 2004).

21. For a discussion of the Philadelphia periodical *the Port folio* as a repository of literary artifacts, see Laura Rigal, *The American Manufactory: Art, Labor, and the World of Things in the Early Republic* (Princeton: Princeton University Press, 1998), esp. 123.

22. Lorraine Daston and Katharine Park, *Wonders and the Order of Nature, 1150–1750* (New York: Zone Books, 1998); Stephen Jay Greenblatt, *Marvellous Possessions: The Wonder of the New World* (Oxford: Clarendon Press, 1991); Barbara M. Benedict, *Curiosity: A Cultural History of Early Modern Inquiry* (Chicago: University of Chicago Press, 2001). See also Paula Findlen, *Possessing Nature: Museums, Collecting, and Scientific Culture in Early Modern Italy* (Berkeley: University of California Press, 1994); and Marjorie Swann, *Curiosities and Texts: The Culture of Collecting in Early Modern England* (Philadelphia: University of Pennsylvania Press, 2001).

23. Coombes's study of the role that Victorian and Edwardian museums played in advancing a Eurocentric view of Africa and Africans demonstrates the productivity of this line of investigation. See Annie E. Coombes, *Reinventing Africa: Museums, Material Culture, and Popular Imagination in Late Victorian and Edwardian England* (New Haven: Yale University Press, 1994). On the architecture of Victorian natural history museums, see Carla Yanni, *Nature's Museums: Victorian Science and the Architecture of Display* (Baltimore: Johns Hopkins University Press, 1999). See also Kevin McLaughlin's discussion of Dickens's early novels and collecting in *Writing in Parts: Imitation and Exchange in Nineteenth-Century Literature* (Stanford: Stanford University Press, 1995).

24. Eric Gidal, *Poetic Exhibitions: Romantic Aesthetics and the Pleasures of the British Museum* (Lewisburg, Pa.: Bucknell University Press, 2001); Grant F. Scott, *The Sculpted Word: Keats, Ekphrasis, and the Visual Arts* (Hanover, N.H.: University Press of New England, 1994). See also Philip Fisher's classic essay "A Museum with One Work Inside: Keats and the Finality of Art," *Keats-Shelley Journal* 33 (1984): 85–102; chap. 3 of James A. W. Heffernan, *Museum of Words: The Poetics of Ekphrasis from Homer to Ashbery* (Chicago: University of Chicago Press, 1993); and Bruce Haley, *Living Forms: Romantics and the Monumental Figure* (Albany: State University of New York Press, 2003).

25. *The Diary of Benjamin Robert Haydon*, 5 vols., ed. Willard Bissell Pope (Cambridge: Harvard University Press, 1963), 3:452.

26. See Karen Swann's description of her encounter with an image of Keats's death mask and the resultant "elegiac delusion." She describes "that impossible feeling that 'the poet is not dead'—but merely sleeping, dreaming, wasting, capable of swimming back to us—in the face of the certain knowledge of death." Karen Swann, "The Strange Time of Reading," *European Romantic Review* 9 (1998): 275. See also the articles in the special issue of *South Atlantic Quarterly* devoted to "Afterlives of Romanticism," especially James Chandler's discussion of the ways in which romanticism both haunts and "informs" the fictions of W. G. Sebald. James Chandler, "About Loss: W. G. Sebald's Romantic Art of Memory," *South Atlantic Quarterly* 102.1 (2003): 235–62.

27. Barker-Benfield, *Shelley's Guitar*, 191.

28. For an account of Claire and Pauline Clairmont's interactions with Silsbee, see Marion Kingston Stocking, "Miss Tina and Miss Plin: The Papers Behind *The Aspern Papers*," in *The Evidence of the Imagination: Studies of Interactions between Life and Art in English Romantic Literature*, ed. Donald H. Reiman, Michael C. Jaye, and Betty T. Bennett (New York: New York University Press, 1978), 372–84.

29. *Some Reminiscences of William Michael Rossetti*, 2 vols. (New York: Charles Scribner's Sons, 1906), 2:353.

30. *The Diary of W. M. Rossetti, 1870–1873*, ed. Odette Bornand (Oxford: Oxford University Press, 1977), 267.

31. W. M. Rossetti, "Talks with Trelawny," *Athenaeum*, 5 August 1882, 176.

32. On the critic as anthologist, see Leah Price, *The Anthology and the Rise of the Novel* (Cambridge: Cambridge University Press, 2000), 145.

33. Carolyn Steedman, *Dust* (Manchester: Manchester University Press, 2001), 18.

34. Sylva Norman, *Flight of the Skylark: The Development of Shelley's Reputation* (Norman: University of Oklahoma Press, 1954), 12.

35. John Forrester, "'Mille e tre': Freud and Collecting," in Elsner and Cardinal, *The Cultures of Collecting*, 228. See also Lynn Gamwell and Richard Wells, eds., *Sigmund Freud and Art: His Personal Collection of Antiquities* (New York: Harry N. Abrams, 1989).

36. *The Complete Letters of Sigmund Freud to Wilhelm Fliess, 1887–1904*, trans. and ed. Jeffrey Moussaieff Masson (Cambridge: Belknap Press of Harvard University Press, 1985), 110.

37. Jean Baudrillard, *The System of Objects*, trans. James Benedict (London: Verso, 1996), 87. Susan Stewart follows in the Baudrillardean line in her insightful treatment of the collection in *On Longing*, 151–66.

38. Baudrillard, *The System of Objects*, 99 and 88.

39. See Naomi Schor's assessment of Baudrillard's "insistently phallocentric theorization of collecting" in her groundbreaking essay "*Cartes Postales:* Representing Paris 1900," *Critical Inquiry* 18 (1992): 202. Susan Pearce suggests that the "concentration

on a sexuality divorced from social practice and the personality as a whole can offer only a fatally limited account of human motive," and she points to empirical evidence showing collectors no more likely to be living solitary lives than anybody else. Pearce, *On Collecting*, 8, 226.

40. Silsbee's memorandum books are among the holdings of the Peabody Essex Museum in Salem, Massachusetts. The passages I mention here are quoted in Marion Kingston Stocking's excellent edition *The Clairmont Correspondence: Letters of Claire Clairmont, Charles Clairmont, and Fanny Imlay Godwin*, 2 vols. (Baltimore: Johns Hopkins University Press, 1995), 2:657.

41. George Edward Woodberry, ed., *The Shelley Notebook in the Harvard College Library* (Cambridge: John Barnard Associates, [1929]), 7, 19.

42. Ibid., 23, 19.

43. Garnett, introduction to *Journal of Edward Ellerker Williams*, 11.

44. Woodberry, *The Shelley Notebook*, 20.

45. Quoted in Evan Charteris, *John Sargent* (New York: Charles Scribner's Sons, 1927), 14.

46. Silsbee's desire for immortality echoed the romantic poets' tendency to imagine for themselves a posthumous fame, to insist that final judgment of their work rested with future, more discerning readers. Andrew Bennett explores this phenomenon in *Romantic Poets and the Culture of Posterity* (Cambridge: Cambridge University Press, 1999).

47. Henry James, preface to *The Aspern Papers*, vol. 12 of *The Novels and Tales of Henry James* (1908; reprint, New York: Augustus M. Kelley, 1971), x. Hereafter cited in text as preface. Quotations from the novel are cited in text after the short title *Aspern*.

48. *The Notebooks of Henry James*, ed. F. O. Matthiessen and Kenneth B. Murdock (New York: George Braziller, 1955), 72. Even before James took up the story of the Clairmont archive and its pursuers, this history was being transformed. William Graham, who claimed to have visited Clairmont one spring day in the early 1880s—that is, four years after she died—fondly recalled her as a woman whom time had bypassed; she still had her "slender willowy figure," her "merry silvery laugh," and a complexion "clear as at eighteen." Graham also claimed that Clairmont, whose middle name was Jane, was the Jane who had received the gift of a guitar from Shelley. He remembered having seen this guitar, the one that had actually been given to Jane Williams, in Clairmont's possession. William Michael Rossetti chronicles Graham's inaccuracies in *Some Reminiscences of William Michael Rossetti*, 2:354–55. As Marion Kingston Stocking reports, Claire Clairmont's name was actually Clara Mary Jane Clairmont, but her family called her Jane. See *The Clairmont Correspondence*, 1:xvii.

49. John Wheeler Williams to Richard Garnett, 4 April 1898, in Thurman, "Letters about Shelley," 418.

50. Ibid., 419.
51. Walter Benjamin, "The Work of Art in the Age of Its Technological Reproducibility: Second Version," in *Walter Benjamin: Selected Writings*, vol. 3, trans. Edmund Jephcott, Howard Eiland et al., ed. Howard Eiland and Michael W. Jennings (Cambridge: Harvard University Press, 2002), 104.
52. See Lisa Fittko's account of Benjamin's last days, "The Story of Old Benjamin," in the English translation of Benjamin's work in progress *The Arcades Project*, trans. Howard Eiland and Kevin McLaughlin (Cambridge: Harvard University Press, 1999), 946–54.
53. Walter Benjamin to Gerhard Scholem, 23 April 1928, in *The Correspondence of Walter Benjamin, 1910–1940*, ed. Gershom Scholem and Theodor W. Adorno, trans. Manfred R. Jacobson and Evelyn M. Jacobson (Chicago: University of Chicago Press, 1994), 333.
54. Walter Benjamin to Gerhard Scholem, 15 March 1929, ibid., 348.
55. Walter Benjamin, "Enlargements," in *One-Way Street*, vol. 1 of *Walter Benjamin: Selected Writings*, ed. Marcus Bullock and Michael W. Jennings (Cambridge: Harvard University Press, 1996), 465. See Bill Brown's comments on Benjamin's writing about children and their things, "How to Do Things with Things," 954–56. For an excellent discussion of Benjamin's comments on collecting, see Esther Leslie, "Telescoping the Microscopic Object: Benjamin the Collector," in *The Optic of Walter Benjamin*, ed. Alex Coles (London: Black Dog Publishing, 1999), 58–89.
56. Benjamin, *The Arcades Project*, 207–8.
57. Ibid., 207. Susan Pearce, too, describes the collection as an act of the imagination, as "a metaphor intended to create meanings which help to make individual identity and each individual's view of the world." Pearce, *On Collecting*, 27.
58. The photographs are reproduced in the English translation of Benjamin's *Arcades* project; I am referring to the caption provided in that edition. Benjamin, *The Arcades Project*, 889.
59. Ibid., 210.
60. Walter Benjamin, "Arrested Auditor of Books," in *One-Way Street*, 456.
61. Howard Eiland and Kevin McLaughlin, "Translators' Foreword," in Benjamin, *The Arcades Project*, xi.
62. Rolf Tiedemann, "Dialectics at a Standstill: Approaches to the *Passagen-Werk*," ibid., 931.
63. Walter Benjamin, "Principles of the Weighty Tome, or How to Write Fat Books," in *One-Way Street*, 457.
64. Susan Sontag, *On Photography* (New York: Farrar, Straus and Giroux, 1977), 80, 77, 181. Ann Rigney, in her study of imperfection as a structural feature of historical writing, notes that the fascination of many contemporary historians with what es-

capes them can be seen as a late manifestation of romantic historicism, since romantic historians such as Carlyle laid as much emphasis on the limitations of history as on its possibilities. She notes that contemporary theoretical reflections on the limits of representability have impinged very little on the way in which histories get written, and she points to the need for new discursive forms. Ann Rigney, *Imperfect Histories: The Elusive Past and the Legacy of Romantic Historicism* (Ithaca: Cornell University Press, 2001), esp. 102–3 and 139. James Chandler, too, addresses this issue in his discussion of the generic hybridity of W. G. Sebald's four fictions. Chandler writes, "If history is necessary to the purposes of human memory, and history needs a form, and if its forms have degenerated into cliché, then the forms of historiography as we know it must be revitalized by rhetorical genre crossing." Chandler, "About Loss," 258.

65. Benjamin, "The Work of Art in the Age of Its Technological Reproducibility," 104.

66. Walter Benjamin, "Little History of Photography," in *Walter Benjamin: Selected Writings*, vol. 2, trans. Rodney Livingstone et al., ed. Michael W. Jennings, Howard Eiland, and Gary Smith (Cambridge: Harvard University Press, 1999), 518.

67. Henry James, *The Sense of the Past*, vol. 26 of *The Novels and Tales of Henry James* (New York: Charles Scribner's Sons, 1917), 42 and 49.

68. Lucy Derby Fuller to E. W. B. Nicholson, MS. Shelley adds. d. 2, The Bodleian Library, University of Oxford.

69. Edward Silsbee to E. W. B. Nicholson, ibid.

70. Richard Garnett to E. W. B. Nicholson, 23 January 1898, ibid.

71. Lucy Derby Fuller to E. W. B. Nicholson, 22 May 1900, ibid. Newspapers on the day following the guitar transfer wrongly reported Silsbee at the ceremony, the event having been described by Garnett in advance of press deadlines.

72. See the catalogues to exhibitions of Beckford's and Hamilton's collections: Derek E. Ostergard, ed., *William Beckford, 1760–1844: An Eye for the Magnificent* (New Haven: Yale University Press, 2001); and Ian Jenkins and Kim Sloan, eds., *Vases and Volcanoes: Sir William Hamilton and His Collection* (London: British Museum Press, 1996). Walpole's collections were painstakingly reassembled by Wilmarth Lewis at his Farmington, Connecticut, home, now part of the Yale University library system.

73. Susan Pearce calls the surge of material manufacture and the consequent rise in numbers of objects "one of the most significant, and most neglected, aspects of what we can loosely call capitalism." Pearce, *On Collecting*, 111. See also James H. Bunn, "The Aesthetics of British Mercantilism," *New Literary History* 11.2 (1980): 303–21.

74. Elizabeth Jones, "Writing for the Market: Keats's Odes as Commodities," *Studies in Romanticism* 34.3 (1995): 343.

75. Andrea Henderson, "Passion and Fashion in Joanna Baillie's 'Introductory Discourse,'" *PMLA* 112.2 (1997): 198–213.

76. Colin Campbell, *The Romantic Ethic and the Spirit of Modern Consumerism* (Oxford: Basil Blackwell, 1987).

77. William Bullock, *A Companion to the London Museum*, 17th ed. (London, 1816), 56 and 59.

78. Alan Liu analyzes the romanticism of most recent cultural criticism, pointing out its proclivity for "constructing micro-worlds each as intricately detailed, yet also as expansive in mythic possibility, as a Wordsworthian Lakeland, Blakean ordered space, [or] Keatsian Grecian Urn." Liu characterizes the "miraculously sustained bubbles of recreated or created context" as a "mock reality," and he notes how "the discourses of particularity" tend to lean heavily on a rhetoric of inexpressibility or incompletion." Liu, "Local Transcendence," 91 and 80.

79. Rigney, *Imperfect Histories*, 103.

80. Hayden White, "The Politics of Historical Interpretation: Discipline and De-Sublimation," in *The Content of the Form: Narrative Discourse and Historical Representation* (Baltimore: Johns Hopkins University Press, 1987), 74.

81. Walter Jackson Bate led me to this Wordsworth passage, which was published in *The Friend* (1809). Walter Jackson Bate, *The Burden of the Past and the English Poet* (Cambridge: Harvard University Press, 1970), 70–71.

82. A wonderful exception is Laurel Thatcher Ulrich, *The Age of Homespun: Objects and Stories in the Creation of an American Myth* (New York: Alfred A. Knopf, 2001); see, too, Ann Rosalind Jones and Peter Stallybrass, *Renaissance Clothing and the Materials of Memory* (New York: Cambridge University Press, 2000).

83. Walter Benjamin, "Fancy Goods," in *One-Way Street*, 463.

84. Baudrillard, *The System of Objects*, 91; Benjamin, *The Arcades Project*, 206.

85. Months after the Bodleian ceremony that Silsbee missed, the *Pall Mall Gazette* picked up his story. In an article titled "An International Episode: American Generosity to Oxford," the newspaper informed its readers of his gift: "It met with cordial acceptance from the governing body of Bodley's Museum, and the guitar was installed in a glazed case, with a record of the donor's benefaction and nationality. Mr. E. W. Nicholson, librarian, when formally acknowledging the gift to Mr. Silsbee, expressed on behalf of the curators a desire for a personal remembrance of him in the shape of a likeness of some description." A clipping of the article in the Bodleian Library holdings has been annotated by Nicholson with a handwritten "§" placed between the two sentences so as to lead the reader to this marginal notation: "Quite a mistake." It is unclear whether the reporter was mistaken in his assertion that the Bodleian would record Silsbee's benefaction and nationality, or in his claim that the curators cherished a desire for Silsbee's portrait. *Pall Mall Gazette*, 20 November 1899, 4.

1. Hummingbird Collectors and Romantic Poetry

1. William Bullock, *Six Months Residence and Travels in Mexico* (1824; reprint, Port Washington, N.Y.: Kennikat Press, 1971), 263. Hereafter cited in text as *Travels in Mexico*.

2. For the most thorough account of Bullock's life and career, see Edward P. Alexander, "William Bullock: Little-Remembered Museologist and Showman," *Curator* 28 (1985): 117–147. See also the excellent treatment of Bullock's career, especially his 1824 London exhibition of Mexican artifacts and natural history specimens (including hummingbirds) in Robert D. Aguirre, *Informal Empire: Mexico and Central America in Victorian Culture* (Minneapolis: University of Minnesota Press, 2005).

3. William Bullock to the earl of Liverpool, 24 April 1813, Add. 38,252 f. 265, British Library.

4. Advertisement in *Aris's Birmingham Gazette*, 26 May 1794, quoted in Lucy Wood, "George Bullock in Birmingham and Liverpool," in *George Bullock Cabinet-Maker* (London: John Murray, 1988), 40

5. Ibid., 40.

6. *Catalogue of the Exhibition, Called Modern Mexico* (London: William Bullock, 1824), 26.

7. *A Companion to the Liverpool Museum*, 4th ed. (Liverpool: Printed for the Proprietor by J. Nuttall, 1805), 33; *A Companion to Mr. Bullock's Museum*, 8th ed. (London: William Bullock), 37.

8. *A Companion to the London Museum and Pantherion*, 13th ed. (London: William Bullock, 1812), 62.

9. These museum signs were observed in the spring of 2002.

10. *A Companion to the Liverpool Museum*, 6th ed. (Hull: J. Ferraby, 1808), [v].

11. Anne Laurine Larsen, " 'Not since Noah': The English Scientific Zoologists and the Craft of Collecting, 1800–1840" (Ph.D. diss., Princeton University, 1993), 151. See also Laura Rigal's discussion of Alexander Wilson's deployment of poetry in his *American Ornithology* (1807–1814), in *The American Manufactory: Art, Labor, and the World of Things in the Early Republic* (Princeton: Princeton University Press, 1998), 159.

12. Colin Campbell, *The Romantic Ethic and the Spirit of Modern Consumerism* (Oxford: Blackwell, 1987). James B. Twitchell, the author of *Lead Us Into Temptation: The Triumph of American Materialism* (New York: Columbia University Press, 1999), and an enthusiastic proponent of consumerism, is a romanticist who repeatedly compares the activity of shopping to Keatsian reverie, for example, when he conjures up Keats at the grocery store: "Each aisle tells a different story. Like a modern Keats you can stop and consider every aspect of the commercial life, ponder history and taste, pause to figure out the cost per ounce, comparison shop, touch and feel everything"

(124). See also Andrea Henderson's reading of Joanna Baillie's *Plays on the Passions* in the context of trends in romantic era consumerism that fueled the desire to shop. Andrea Henderson, "Passion and Fashion in Joanna Baillie's 'Introductory Discourse,'" *PMLA* 112.2 (1997): 198–213.

13. Colin Campbell, "The Romantic Ethic and the Spirit of Modern Consumerism: Reflecting on the Reception of a Thesis concerning the Origin of the Continuing Desire for Goods," in *Experiencing Material Culture in the Western World*, ed. Susan M. Pearce (London: Leicester University Press, 1997), 37.

14. *The Keats Circle: Letters and Papers, 1816–1878*, 2 vols., ed. Hyder Edward Rollins (Cambridge: Harvard University Press, 1948), 2:65.

15. *John Keats: Complete Poems*, ed. Jack Stillinger (Cambridge: Harvard University Press, 1978), 468. Hereafter cited in text.

16. Allen Tate, "A Reading of Keats (II)," *American Scholar* 15 (1946): 189.

17. H. W. Garrod, *Keats*, 2nd ed. (Oxford: Clarendon Press, 1939), 111.

18. Richard Harter Fogle, "Keats's 'Ode to a Nightingale,'" *PMLA* 68.1 (1953): 217.

19. Andrew J. Kappel, "The Immortality of the Natural: Keats' 'Ode to a Nightingale,'" *ELH* 45 (1978): 276–77. This article provides an excellent survey of critical responses to the bird's supposed immortality.

20. *Companion to the Liverpool Museum*, 4th ed., 33–34.

21. Informational posting for the O. T. Baron hummingbird display at the Walter Rothschild Zoological Museum, Tring. The Zoological Museum is part of the Natural History Museum in London.

22. George-Louis Leclerc, comte de Buffon, *History of Birds*, vol. 16 of *Natural History, General and Particular*, trans. William Smellie (London: T. Cadell and W. Davies, 1812), 337.

23. *Companion to the Liverpool Museum*, 4th ed., 34; John Gould, *Introduction to the Trochildae, or Family of Humming-Birds* (London: Printed for the Author by Taylor and Francis, 1861), 20 and 19.

24. *Companion to the Liverpool Museum*, 5th ed. (Liverpool, 1807), 17.

25. William Swainson, *On the Natural History and Classification of Birds*, vol. 1 of *The Cabinet of Natural History*, 2 vols., ed. Dionysius Lardner (London: Longman, Rees, Orme, Brown, Green, & Longman, 1836), 274.

26. William Bullock, *A Descriptive Catalogue of the Exhibition, Entitled Ancient and Modern Mexico* (London: Printed for the Proprietors, [1825]), 9.

27. Susan Stewart, *On Longing: Narratives of the Miniature, the Gigantic, the Souvenir, the Collection* (1984; reprint, Durham: Duke University Press, 1993), 55.

28. Charlotte Smith, *Conversations Introducing Poetry: Chiefly on Subjects of Natural History*, 2 vols. (London: J. Johnson, 1804), 2:46–47. Stuart Curran identified Catherine Anne Dorset as the likely author of the poem.

29. David Garnett, "Current Literature: Books in General," *The New Statesman and Nation*, June 10, 1933, 763. Garnett is quoting from a letter that Joseph Ritchie wrote to Garnett's father in 1818. I am grateful to Alan Bewell for drawing my attention to this article.
30. Buffon, *History of Birds*, 330.
31. William Swainson, *Taxidermy, Bibliography, and Biography*, in *The Cabinet Cyclopaedia*, ed. Dionysius Lardner (London: Longman, Orme, Brown, Green, and Longmans, 1840), 4–5.
32. William Bullock, *A Concise and Easy Method of Preserving Objects of Natural History* (London: Printed by the Proprietor, 1817), 7.
33. Ibid., iv. Mrs. R. Lee (Formerly Mrs. T. Edward Bowdich), *Taxidermy; or, The Art of Collecting, Preparing, and Mounting Objects of Natural History, for the Use of Museums and Travellers*, 6th ed. (London: Longman, Brown, Green, and Longmans, 1843), 84.
34. Josiah Nuttall to William Swainson, 4 August 1819, W. Swainson Correspondence, MS no. 272, Linnean Society of London.
35. Swainson, *On the Natural History and Classification of Birds*, 1:278.
36. "Memoirs of Charles Willson Peale From his original Ms. with Notes by Horace Wells Sellers," typescript, 217, American Philosophical Society, Philadelphia.
37. W. H. Hudson, *Idle Days in Patagonia* (New York: E. P. Dutton, 1917), 180.
38. Bullock, *Companion to the Liverpool Museum*, 4th ed., 33.
39. Buffon, *History of Birds*, 326.
40. Gould, *Introduction to the Trochildae*, [i].
41. Ibid., 12, 13.
42. Charles Dickens, "The Tresses of the Day Star," *Household Words*, no. 65 (1851): 65.
43. Queen Victoria's 1851 manuscript journal is quoted in Isabella Tree, *The Ruling Passion of John Gould: A Biography of the Bird Man* (New York: Grove Weidenfeld, 1992), 173. I am grateful for Tree's biography, which led me to many sources of hummingbird information.
44. *The Works of John Ruskin*, 39 vols., ed. E. T. Cook and Alexander Wedderburn (London: George Allen, 1908), 34:670.
45. Frances Trollope, *Domestic Manners of the Americans*, ed. Donald Smalley (1832; reprint, New York: Alfred A. Knopf, 1949), 51 and 67.
46. The practice of collecting engraved portrait heads in albums produced and sold for that purpose was popularized by the Reverend James Granger, who inspired his fellow enthusiasts to slice frontispiece portraits out of magazines and volumes of poetry so as to affix them in the precursors of photo albums. One can see evidence of this practice in the many books left with vestigial page nubs where authors' portraits or other illustrations were once positioned. On portrait collecting, see Marcia Pointon, *Hanging the Head: Portraiture and Social Formation in Eighteenth-Century England* (New Haven: Yale University Press, 1993), 54. Trollope's depiction of Bullock as the

sole aesthete among the rubes was colored by the failure of her own business ambitions. She built a vast shopping emporium called the Bazaar, whose Egyptian exterior mirrored the façade of Bullock's London Museum, and whose panoramic exhibitions conflated shopping with museum-going. Trollope ignored the range of luxury goods already available to Cincinnati shoppers. The shoppers did not entirely ignore Trollope's Bazaar, but they did their purchasing elsewhere. See Donald Smalley, "Introduction: Mrs. Trollope in America," in *Domestic Manners of the Americans*, xlv.

47. Samuel Taylor Coleridge, "Constancy to an Ideal Object," in *Poetical Works I: Poems (Reading Text)*, vol. 16 of *The Collected Works of Samuel Taylor Coleridge*, ed. J.C.C. Mays (Princeton: Princeton University Press, 2001), no. 2, 777.

48. Ibid., 778.

49. Samuel Taylor Coleridge, "A Description of a Nightingale, in *Poetical Works I*, no. 2, 953. Walter Jackson Bate notes Coleridge's tendency to compare himself or his poetry to awkward, unattractive birds, to an oblivious ostrich, or to "a metaphysical Bustard, urging its slow, heavy, laborious earth-skimming Flight, over dreary & level Wastes." Walter Jackson Bate, *Coleridge* (New York: Macmillan, 1968), 111. "A Description of a Nightingale" represents a return to the bird Coleridge had addressed in his earlier and more finished poems, "To the Nightingale" and "The Nightingale: A Conversation Poem."

50. William Bullock, *Sketch of a Journey through the Western States of North America* (London: John Miller, 1827), xi.

51. Cynthia Wall has suggested that late-eighteenth-century auction catalogues "create a sum of parts greater than their previous whole." Bullock's catalogue, which was issued in five parts which were barely printed in time to be available for the sales they described, served to underscore the scope and range of his collections. Cynthia Wall, "The English Auction: Narratives of Dismantlings," *Eighteenth-Century Studies* 31 (1997): 10.

52. Quoted in Jessie M. Sweet, "William Bullock's Collection and the University of Edinburgh, 1819," *Annals of Science* 26 (1970): 27.

53. Hummingbird catalogue descriptions are from the listing for the nineteenth day of sale, in part four of Bullock's sale catalogue. See *Catalogue of the Roman Gallery, of Antiquities and Works of Art, and the London Museum of Natural History* (London: Bullock, 1819), 118–20

54. "The late Mr. George Loddiges," *Journal of the Horticultural Society of London* (1846): 224–25; "Loddiges Collection of Hummingbirds," typescript, 3, Walter Rothschild Library, Tring.

55. George Loddiges, manuscript notebook no. 1, 1826–28, 3, and manuscript notebook no. 2, 18 April 1828–24 April 1829, entry for 5 July 1829, 89, Walter Rothschild Library, Tring. By permission of the Trustees of the Natural History Museum.

56. Bullock dwelt on the advisability of keeping certain large cases intact, recommending that the "fine and unique perfect *Genera* of Birds of Paradise, Humming Birds, Echini, &c. &c. should be offered for sale unbroken, so as to ensure to Science and Art, the benefit of their formation according to their present arrangement." *Catalogue of the Roman Gallery*, 4.

57. George Loddiges, manuscript notebook no. 5, 10 February 1831 to 24 December 1832, entry for 11 June 1831, 344, Walter Rothschild Library, Tring. By permission of the Trustees of the Natural History Museum.

58. Clemency Fisher, ed., *A Passion for Natural History: The Life and Legacy of the 13th Earl of Derby* (Liverpool: National Museums & Galleries on Merseyside, 2002). See the entry for the White Swamp-hen in this excellent catalogue, published to coincide with "The Earl & the Pussycat" exhibition at the Liverpool Museum (123).

59. Loddiges form letter, Walter Rothschild Library, Tring. By permission of the Trustees of the Natural History Museum.

60. "Loddiges Collection of Hummingbirds," 2. The Loddiges birds are in the ornithological research collection of the Natural History Museum at Tring.

61. A few Gould bird cases remain intact in the library of the Natural History Museum and can be seen on request. I am grateful to Mrs. Ann Datta, Zoology Librarian, for allowing me to see these original Gould display cases, and for sharing her knowledge of their history. Six to ten birds are arranged in each case around a centerpiece of foliage. The birds are often posed in flying positions. In case number 1, which is labeled "*Eutoxeres heterura*" and contains seven dull brown birds with hooked beaks, some of the birds soar downward on extended wing. The Natural History Museum also has a hundred or so nineteenth-century hummingbirds from the O. T. Baron collection on display at the Walter Rothschild Zoological Museum at Tring. The birds perch on tiers of pins in an octagonal case that resembles a revolving cake display. Bereft of even the questionable habitat foliage of the possible Bullock display, the hummingbirds look like an array of ornamental hatpins. Still, one cannot help lingering over their Lilliputian details.

2. Queen Charlotte, Collector and Collectible

1. See Oliver Millar's definitive study *Zoffany and his Tribuna* (New York: Pantheon Books, 1967); and also David H. Solkin's discussion of the painting's 1780 exhibition, part of his introduction to the catalogue of an exhibit that reproduced the experience of attending a Royal Academy exhibition. David H. Solkin, " 'This Great Mart of Genius': The Royal Academy Exhibitions at Somerset House, 1780–1836," in *Art on the Line: The Royal Academy Exhibition at Somerset House, 1780–1836*, ed. David H. Solkin (New Haven: Yale University Press, 2001), 1–2.

2. *The Diaries of Colonel the Hon. Robert Fulke Greville*, ed. F. McKno Bladon (London: John Lane, 1930), 128 and 130.

3. Marcia Pointon writes, "The English royal lineage is constructed in Zoffany's conversation piece of Queen Charlotte and her two eldest sons from a mass of imported and gifted goods—forms of cultural annexation." Marcia Pointon, *Hanging the Head: Portraiture and Social Formation in Eighteenth-Century England* (New Haven: Yale University Press, 1993), 162.

4. John Watkins, *Memoirs of Her Most Excellent Majesty Sophia-Charlotte, Queen of Britain* (London: Henry Colburn, 1819), 235. For a discussion of the way in which an aesthetic of accumulating exotic goods materialized as a side effect of mercantilism, see James H. Bunn, "The Aesthetics of British Mercantilism," *New Literary History* 11 (1980): 303–21.

5. Queen Charlotte, 8 September 1789, manuscript diary (23 August–18 September 1789), Add 43/1, Royal Archives, Windsor Castle, Windsor. See Harriet Ritvo's discussion of private menageries in chapter 5 of *The Animal Estate: The English and Other Creatures in the Victorian Age* (Cambridge: Harvard University Press, 1987), 205–42.

6. Elizabeth (Seymour) Percy, *The Diaries of a Duchess: Extracts from the Diaries of the First Duchess of Northumberland (1716–1776)*, ed. James Greig (London: Hodder and Stoughton, 1926), 31. See Marcia Pointon's fascinating work on the association of royal femininity and jewelry, "Intriguing Jewellery: Royal Bodies and Luxurious Consumption," *Textual Practice* 11.3 (1997): 493–516, and "Intrigue, Jewellery and Economics: Court Culture and Display in England and France in the 1780s," in *Art Markets in Europe, 1400–1800*, ed. Michael North and David Ormrod (Aldershot, Hampshire: Ashgate, 1999), 201–19.

7. Percy, *Diaries of a Duchess*, 28–29.

8. Ibid., 31.

9. Horace Walpole, *Memoirs of the Reign of King George III*, 4 vols., ed. Derek Jarrett (New Haven: Yale University Press, 2000), 1:50.

10. Mrs. [Charlotte Louisa Henrietta] Papendiek, *Court and Private Life in the Time of Queen Charlotte*, 2 vols., ed. Mrs. Vernon Delves Broughton (London: Bentley & Sons, 1887), 1:10.

11. Olwen Hedley, *Queen Charlotte* (London: John Murray, 1975), 11. Hedley's biography served as a crucial source of biographical and chronological details.

12. *Gentleman's Magazine* (December 1808): 1068.

13. Quoted in Hedley, *Queen Charlotte*, 47.

14. Ibid., 310 and 25.

15. *The Autobiography and Correspondence of Mary Granville*, ed. Lady Llanover, vol. 2 (London: Richard Bentley, 1862), 578.

16. Charlotte became an object of collectors' desire by the mere fact of becoming queen, but

she also fueled the early-nineteenth-century vogue for collecting through her association with Josiah Wedgwood. She participated in the marketing of Wedgwood's creamware pottery, which became known as "Queen's ware" in what Asa Briggs calls one of the earliest instances of product branding. Asa Briggs, *The Age of Improvement* (London: Longman, Green, and Co., 1959), 28. Wedgwood encouraged his customers to see the purchase of a teapot as the beginning of a pottery collection. His catalogues featured creamware pieces artfully arranged against a white background so that serving bowls and pitchers became aesthetic objects of desire. A page from his 1817 catalogue depicts nine ornate teapots, each of a different design; the text announces, "There are all the other pieces to make up complete sets with the above Teapots." Reprinted in Wolf Mankowitz, *Wedgwood* (London: Spring Books, 1953), plate 30. New developments in pottery manufacturing, which Wedgwood innovated and capitalized on, also led to the mass production of commemorative statuary. An occasion such as the death of Lord Nelson could cause the marketplace to be flooded with memorial ceramics, but these souvenir objects most often marked royal occasions such as coronations and jubilees. See Gillian Russell's commentary on Nelson's "crypto-royalist mystique" in *The Theatres of War: Performance, Politics, and Society, 1793–1815* (Oxford: Clarendon Press, 1995), 82.

George III's temporary recovery from the illness that had the nation on tenterhooks, precariously poised between the delusional aspirations of an aging king and the eager overtures to the throne of his irresponsible son, inspired an outpouring of celebratory souvenirs, such as a pearlware bowl embellished with profiled heads of the king and queen, encircled by the caption "A King Revered A Queen Beloved." Lincoln Hallinan, *Royal Commemoratives* (Princes Risborough, Buckinghamshire: Shire Publications, 1997), 7. Charlotte's image in these productions often served to mirror and dramatize the nation's relief, but even events to which the queen was less directly linked inspired souvenir tokens featuring her image. See, for example, the creamware teapot Wedgwood produced in order to commemorate the capture of Cuba (pictured in Hallinan, *Royal Commemoratives*, 6). The aspiring collector could emulate the collector queen by buying the Wedgwood dishes she endorsed, or by collecting her image on dishes and figurines commemorating the birthdays, jubilees, and deaths of royal family members.

17. Hedley, *Queen Charlotte*, 309–10.
18. Charles Greville, *The Greville Memoirs, 1814–1860*, vol. 2, ed. Lytton Strachey and Roger Fulford (London: Macmillan & Co., 1938), 193–94.
19. This form of insanity, Stewart notes, is, "like anal retentiveness, an urge toward incorporation . . . , an attempt to erase the limits of the body that is at the same time an attempt, marked by desperation, to 'keep body and soul together.'" Susan Stewart, *On Longing: Narratives of the Miniature, the Gigantic, the Souvenir, the Collection* (1984; reprint, Durham: Duke University Press, 1993), 154.

20. Steven Mullaney, "Strange Things, Gross Terms, Curious Customs: The Rehearsal of Cultures in the Late Renaissance," *Representations* 3 (1983): 42–43. See also Stephen Greenblatt's discussion of wonder in *Marvellous Possessions: The Wonder of the New World* (Oxford: Clarendon Press, 1991), and in "Resonance and Wonder," in *Exhibiting Cultures: The Poetics and Politics of Museum Display*, ed. Ivan Karp and Stephen D. Lavine (Washington, D.C.: Smithsonian Institution Press, 1991), 42–56.

21. See especially Harriet Ritvo, *The Platypus and the Mermaid and Other Figments of the Classifying Imagination* (Cambridge: Harvard University Press, 1997). Ritvo discusses a wide range of eighteenth- and nineteenth-century British taxonomic practices.

22. Tony Bennett, *The Birth of the Museum: History, Theory, Politics* (New York: Routledge, 1995), 6 and 19.

23. Queen Charlotte, manuscript diary, GEO/Add 43/3, Royal Archives, Windsor Castle, Windsor. Jean André de Luc, a Swiss geologist, was reader to the queen.

24. Cornelia Knight, who took part in the queen's Frogmore interludes, recalled: "The queen used often to call for me between ten and eleven on her way to Frogmore, where she liked to spend her mornings. She was fond of reading aloud, either in French or English, and I had my work. Her library there was well furnished with books in those languages and in German, and she was so good as to give me a key, with permission to take home any that I liked. Sometimes we walked in the gardens of that pleasant place, Princess Elizabeth being usually of our party, and not unfrequently Princess Mary." *Autobiography of Miss Cornelia Knight*, 2 vols., 4th ed. (London: W. H. Allen and Co., 1861), 1:170.

25. Queen Charlotte to Prince Augustus, 25 March 1791, *The Later Correspondence of George III*, 5 vols., ed. Arthur Aspinall (Cambridge: Cambridge University Press, 1962), 1:525.

26. On William's housecleaning, see Christopher Hibbert, *George IV* (Harmondsworth, Middlesex: Penguin Books, 1976), 784. Lytton Strachey, *Queen Victoria* (New York: Harcourt, Brace and Company, 1921), 400.

27. Ibid., 401. Strachey's source is *The Private Life of the Queen by a Member of the Royal Household*. The anonymous author describes the queen's insistent desire to "fix the picture": "This idea of the Queen's . . . extends to every article in her possession, which in the mass—that is to say, in the various apartments where the things may be kept—as well as singly, are all photographed. Every piece of plate and china, every picture, chair, table, ornament, and articles of even the most trivial description, all pass through the photographer's hands, and are 'taken' from every point of view." *The Private Life of the Queen* (New York: D. Appleton and Company, 1901), 119.

28. James Pope-Hennessy, *Queen Mary, 1867–1953* (New York: Alfred A. Knopf, 1960), 408.

29. Mary Delany, *The Autobiography and Correspondence of Mary Granville, Mrs. Delany*, ed. Lady Llanover, 2nd ser., 3 vols. (London: Richard Bentley, 1862), 2:371.

30. Horace Walpole, *The Duchess of Portland's Museum* (New York: Grolier Club, 1936), 6–7.

31. *Diaries of Robert Fulke Greville*, 57.

32. *A Catalogue of the Portland Museum, Lately the Property of the Duchess Dowager of Portland, Deceased* (London, 1786), iv.

33. Delany, *Autobiography and Correspondence*, 2nd ser., 2:578–79.

34. Mary Delany, *The Autobiography and Correspondence of Mary Granville, Mrs. Delany*, ed. Lady Llanover, 3 vols. (London: Richard Bentley, 1861), 3:439.

35. Delany, *Autobiography and Correspondence*, 2nd ser., 2:372, 373.

36. Walpole, *Duchess of Portland's Museum*, 7.

37. Joseph Banks quoted in Bernard Smith, *European Vision and the South Pacific* (New Haven: Yale University Press, 1985), 53. See p. 123 for terms of agreement. See also Charles Mitchell, "Zoffany's *Death of Captain Cook*," *Burlington Magazine* 84 (1944): 56–62.

38. Horace Walpole to Horace Mann, 20 September 1772, *Horace Walpole's Correspondence with Sir Horace Mann*, ed. W. S. Lewis, Warren Hunting Smith, and George L. Lam (New Haven: Yale University Press, 1967), 7:436.

39. Horace Walpole to Horace Mann, 12 November 1779, ibid., 8:527.

40. Horace Mann to Horace Walpole, 10 December 1779, ibid., 8:540.

41. C. S. Matheson, "'A Shilling Well Laid Out': The Royal Academy's Early Public," in *Art on the Line*, 49.

42. John Stuart, Third Earl of Bute, *Botanical Tables, Containing the Different Familys of British Plants*, 9 vols. (London, 1786), 1:1–6.

43. This was the status of the queen's herbarium during the spring of 1999.

44. Quoted in Margot Walker, *Sir James Edward Smith* (London: Linnean Society, 1988), 24.

45. Watkins, *Memoirs of Her Most Excellent Majesty Sophia-Charlotte*, 458–61.

46. Ann Bermingham, "The Aesthetics of Ignorance: The Accomplished Woman in the Culture of Connoisseurship," *Oxford Art Journal* 16.2 (1993): 3–20.

47. Lucy Kennedy manuscript diary, 15 [October 1793], Royal Library, Windsor Castle, Windsor.

48. Papiendiek, *Court and Private Life in the Time of Queen Charlotte*, 2:201.

49. Ibid., 1:83.

50. Ibid., 1:85.

51. On the exhibition of *The Tribuna of the Uffizi*, see Solkin, "Introduction: 'This Great Mart of Genius,'" 1.

52. Quoted in Hedley, *Queen Charlotte*, 162.

53. *Diaries of Robert Fulke Greville*, 130.

54. *Autobiography of Miss Cornelia Knight*, 2:276.

55. Ibid., 277–80.

56. William Cowper, *The Task*, vol. 2 of *The Poems of William Cowper*, ed. John D. Baird and Charles Ryskamp (Oxford: Clarendon Press, 1995), 128–29.

57. Ibid., 215.

58. *Autobiography of Miss Cornelia Knight*, 2:280–81.

59. Queen Charlotte, "A Catalogue of Theatrical Prints," manuscript index, the Royal Library, Windsor Castle, Windsor.

60. Thomas Richards, *The Imperial Archive: Knowledge and the Fantasy of Empire* (London: Verso, 1993), 3–4.

61. Joseph Farington, 11 April 1813, in *The Diary of Joseph Farington*, ed. Kathryn Cave, 16 vols. (New Haven: Yale University Press, 1983), 12:4330.

62. The affidavits of Princess Sophia and Mrs. Beckedorff (mss. 36832 and 36844–45) are gathered with Queen Charlotte's manuscript letters, Royal Archives, Windsor Castle, Windsor.

63. Quoted in Hedley, *Queen Charlotte*, 303.

64. Ibid., 301.

65. *Times* (London), 22 February 1819, 2.

66. See the copy of the catalogue in the British Library. The purchases by Lady Grenville, Mrs. Brande, Mrs. Cockrant, and Mrs. Wilcox are found in the record of the first day's sale. *A Catalogue of the First Part of a Magnificent Collection of Oriental Curiosities and Porcelain* (London, 1819), 9 (May 7, 1819, and three following days). Mrs. Anstey's purchase was made on May 24. See *A Catalogue of the Remaining Part of a Valuable Collection of Curiosities, Comprising Carvings in Ivory, Trinkets, Coins, Porcelain and Furniture* (London, 1819), [3] (May 24, 1819, and two following days).

67. For a discussion of the "rhetorical strategies and cultural implications of the English auction, see Cynthia Wall, "The English Auction: Narratives of Dismantlings," *Eighteenth-Century Studies* 31 (1997): 1–25.

68. Robin Mackworth-Young, "The Royal Archives, Windsor Castle," *Archives* 13 (1978): 117.

69. Cowper's 1798 *Poems* and his 1810 *Poems* are both listed in the auction catalogue of Queen's Charlotte's collections, *A Catalogue of the Genuine Library, Prints, and Books of Prints, of an Illustrious Personage Lately Deceased* (1819).

70. These architectural details are provided by Oliver Millar in *Zoffany and his Tribuna*, 10–12.

71. Tobias Smollett, *Travels through France and Italy*, ed. Frank Felsenstein (Oxford: Oxford University Press, 1979), 238.

72. *Morning Chronicle*, 20 May 1780, quoted in Millar, *Zoffany and His Tribuna*, 34.

3. Travels with Napoleon's Carriage

1. The Waterloo exhibition that went on display at no. 1 St. James Street in 1815 consisted almost entirely of relics from Waterloo, many of them the sad remains of anonymous dead soldiers. Item no. 131 in the catalogue consists of "seventy-eight pounds weight of buttons, from the clothing of French soldiery, slain in battle." *The Waterloo Exhibition* (London, 1815), 9. For a discussion of how Waterloo relics caused Britons to grapple with the fragmentation of history, see Stuart Semmel, "Reading the Tangible Past: British Tourism, Collecting, and Memory After Waterloo," *Representations* 69 (2000): 9–37. For treatments of romantic writers' engagement with Waterloo, see Simon Bainbridge, *Napoleon and English Romanticism* (Cambridge: Cambridge University Press, 1995); and Philip Shaw, *Waterloo and the Romantic Imagination* (New York: Palgrave and Macmillan, 2002).

2. *A Description of the Costly and Curious Military Carriage of the Late Emperor of France* (London: William Bullock, 1816), 4–5; *Napoleon Relics Catalogue* (London: Madame Tussaud's, 1901), 24.

3. For details of George's carriage, see H. Clifford Smith, *Buckingham Palace* (New York: Charles Scribner's Sons, 1931), 67–70. For a discussion of Mary Robinson's carriage, see Judith Pascoe, *Romantic Theatricality: Gender, Poetry, and Spectatorship* (Ithaca: Cornell University Press, 1997), 147–50.

4. *Shelley and His Circle, 1773–1822*, vol. 3, ed. Kenneth Neill Cameron (Cambridge: Harvard University Press, 1970), 174. In an introduction to the letters that passed between Shelley and Charters, Cameron provides a fascinating account of Shelley's carriage and the financial altercations it precipitated.

5. *Catalogue of the Roman Gallery, of Antiquities and Works of Art, and the London Museum of Natural History, Part Fifth* (London: William Bullock, 1819), 164.

6. Ibid., 161–65.

7. J. H. Plumb, *Royal Heritage* (London: British Broadcasting Corporation, 1977), 215.

8. Steven Parissien, *George IV: The Grand Entertainment* (London: John Murray, 2001), 271; Plumb, *Royal Heritage*, 226–27. For a discussion of the evolution of the Louvre during the Napoleonic era, see Andrew McClellan, *Inventing the Louvre: Art, Politics, and the Origins of the Modern Museum in Eighteenth-Century Paris* (Cambridge: Cambridge University Press, 1994), 114–21. George's female descendants carried on his preoccupation with Napoleon. Edward VII's queen, Alexandra, devoted a room at Marlborough House to her Napoleon collection, loading Empire table tops with busts of, and books about, the French conqueror. Queen Alexandra's photo album, labeled "Marlborough House, 1912" (Royal Archives, Windsor Castle), contains two views of this room. The princess Marie Louise claimed Napoleon as her hobby. In her memoirs, she describes a thrilling discovery she made in the lounge of an Orléans

hotel: "There I saw this beautiful coffee set with the 'N' and the well-known bees, all in that heavily encrusted gold always associated with that particular period." Full of trepidation, Marie Louise demanded to know the price. She writes, "Need I tell you that in the shortest time possible—in fact, just the time it took to unlock the show-case—Napoleon's coffee set was mine!" The princess then proceeded to motor through France with Napoleon's coffee set balanced on her knees. Princess Marie Louise, *My Memories of Six Reigns* (New York: E. P. Dutton & Company, 1957), 177 and 178. Marie Louise's grandmother Queen Victoria preserved in an album of photograph portraits a picture of Colonel Basil Jackson, a balding elderly man with a mild expression. A letter pasted in the album identifies the retired colonel as a custodian of Napoleon at St. Helena. "Photographic Portraits," vol. 2, Royal Archive, Windsor Castle. On the subject of Queen Victoria's photo collecting, see Frances Dimond and Roger Taylor, *Crown and Camera: The Royal Family and Photography, 1842–1910* (Harmondsworth: Penguin Books, 1987), 67.

9. *The Diary of Dr. John William Polidori*, ed. William Michael Rossetti (London: Elkin Mathews, 1911), 82.

10. Pryse Lockhart Gordon, Esq., *Personal Memoirs; or Reminiscences of Men and Manners at Home and Abroad, During the Last Half Century*, 2 vols. (London: Henry Colburn and Richard Bentley, 1830), 2:328.

11. Gordon, *Personal Memoirs*, 2:329 and 328. *Diary of Dr. John William Polidori*, 211. Marguerite Gardiner, the countess of Blessington, considered Byron's carriage evidence of bad taste. She described it as "having an affectation of finery, but *mesquin* in the details, and tawdry in the *ensemble*." The editor of Gardiner's memoirs of Byron, however, notes that her own carriage was similarly equipped and equally ostentatious. *Lady Blessington's Conversations of Lord Byron*, ed. Ernest J. Lovell Jr. (Princeton: Princeton University Press, 1969), 154. I am grateful to Doucet Devin Fischer for drawing my attention to Lady Blessington's comments.

12. *Diary of Dr. John William Polidori*, 62, 65.

13. *Childe Harold's Pilgrimage, A Romaunt*, vol. 2 of Lord Byron, *The Complete Poetical Works*, ed. Jerome J. McGann (Oxford: Clarendon Press, 1980), 191. For a fascinating account of Elgin's tragic history, see Gillen D'Arcy Wood, "Mourning the Marbles: The Strange Case of Lord Elgin's Nose," *Wordsworth Circle* 29 (1998): 171–77.

14. Byron, *Childe Harold's Pilgrimage*, 191.

15. Byron, *The Curse of Minerva*, in vol. 1 of Lord Byron, *The Complete Poetical Works*, 326.

16. Willard Bissell Pope, ed., *The Diary of Benjamin Robert Haydon*, 5 vols. (Cambridge: Harvard University Press, 1960), 1:89.

17. Ibid., 1:88, 1:89, and 1:87–88.

18. Byron, *Childe Harold's Pilgrimage*, 307.

19. Richard Altick states with assurance that Byron visited Bullock's exhibition, citing

Leslie Marchand's biography, but Marchand does not confirm Byron's attendance. Nevertheless, since Byron was living at 13 Piccadilly Terrace, and since Bullock's museum was on the north side of Piccadilly, near the foot of Old Bond Street (and given Byron's fascination with Napoleon), Altick is surely correct. Richard Altick, *The Shows of London* (Cambridge: Harvard University Press, 1978), 241.

20. Joseph Farington, *The Farington Diary*, ed. James Greig, vol. 8 (London: Hutchinson & Co., 1928), 88. For an excellent survey of Bullock's curatorial career, see Edward P. Alexander, "William Bullock: Little-Remembered Museologist and Showman," *Curator* 28 (1985): 125.

21. *Description of the Costly and Curious Military Carriage*, 9.

22. For detailed descriptions of these drawings, see Mary Dorothy George, *Catalogue of Prints and Drawings in the British Museum*, vol. 9, *1811–1819* (London: Printed by Order of the Trustees, 1949), 627–28.

23. *Description of the Costly and Curious Military Carriage*, 3.

24. William Jerdan, *The Autobiography of William Jerdan*, 4 vols. (London: Arthur Hall, Virtue, & Co., 1852), 2:87; William Jerdan, *Men I Have Known* (London: George Routledge and Sons, 1866), 82.

25. Jerdan, *Autobiography*, 2:87.

26. Ibid.

27. Mary Dorothy George, *Catalogue of Prints and Drawings in the British Museum*, vol. 9, *1811–1819*, 628.

28. Susan M. Pearce, *On Collecting: An Investigation into Collecting in the European Tradition* (1995; reprint, New York: Routledge, 1999), 133.

29. Ibid., 127.

30. Margreta de Grazia, *Shakespeare Verbatim: The Reproduction of Authenticity and the 1790 Apparatus* (Oxford: Clarendon Press, 1991).

31. R. Bearman, "Sharp Practice," *Equilibrium* 2 (2000): 2464–68.

32. *Napoleon Relics Catalogue*, 28. The Fowler Collection of "Napoleana," a small and unimpressive compilation of association objects featured on the Web site of the Museum of Jurassic Technology in Los Angeles, perfectly replicates the Napoleon collector's preoccupation with material remains, no matter how tenuously linked to the object of his obsession. The paltry remains on display include ferns from Napoleon's tomb, a fragment of Napoleon's tent, a frame made from a shelf taken from the library of Josephine in the palace of Malmaison, mortar from the tomb of Napoleon, and a framed engraving of an amaryllis flower labeled "Amaryllis, a favorite flower of Josephine" (http:///www.mjt.org/exhibits/gallery7.html, accessed 2 May 2002). Lawrence Weschler explores the exhibition spaces of the MJT, its re-creation of the wonder-inspiring displays and hallowed atmosphere of the nineteenth-century museum through the exacting curation of whimsical and possibly manufactured "arti-

facts." Lawrence Weschler, *Mr. Wilson's Cabinet of Wonder* (New York: Vintage Books, 1996).

33. *Diary of Benjamin Robert Haydon,* 3:452.

34. Martin Levy, *Napoleon in Exile: The House and Furniture Supplied by the British Government for the Emperor and his Entourage on St. Helena* ([England]: Furniture History Society, 1998), 12.

35. Byron to John Murray, 27 June 1816, in *Byron's Letters and Journals,* 12 vols., ed. Leslie A. Marchand (Cambridge: Harvard University Press, 1973–82), 5:82.

36. William Godwin, *Essay on Sepulchres: or, A Proposal for Erecting Some Memorial of the Illustrious Dead in All Ages on the Spot Where Their Remains Have Been Interred* (London: W. Miller, 1809), 6. Hereafter cited in text as *Sepulchres.*

37. Jean Baudrillard, *The System of Objects,* trans. James Benedict (London: Verso, 1996), 85.

38. *The Narrative of Jean Hornn, Military Coachman to Napoleon Bonaparte* (London: London Museum, 1816), [iii]. Hereafter cited in text as *Narrative.*

39. Christopher Flint, "Speaking Objects: The Circulation of Stories in Eighteenth-Century Prose Fiction," *PMLA* 113.2 (1998): 212–26.

40. "Not only one carriage, but eight were taken [by Blücher's men] and the accounts of what they contained make one think of the Arabian nights," writes the battle historian Ernest F. Henderson. "One of the coaches, we are told, had been destined for the grand entry that Napoleon had intended to make into Brussels, and was to have been drawn by eight cream-coloured stallions." Ernest F. Henderson, *Blücher and the Uprising of Prussia against Napoleon, 1806–1815* (New York: G. P. Putnam's Sons, 1911), 312.

41. Sir James Paget, quoted in L. W. Proger, "A Napoleonic Relic," *Annals of the Royal College of Surgeons of England* 26 (1960): 3.

42. Edwin Wolf, *Rosenbach: A Biography* (Cleveland: World Publishing Company, 1960), 204. Rosenbach's relics came from the collection of the abbé Vignali, a Corsican priest who conducted Napoleon's funeral at St. Helena. Wolf seems to be quoting from a catalogue description, but he does not specify a source.

43. Ibid., 275. Wolf quotes from a New York newspaper article about the exhibition without specifying a source.

44. Mary Monica Maxwell Scott, *Abbotsford: The Personal Relics and Antiquarian Treasures of Sir Walter Scott* (London: Adam and Charles Black, 1893), 28. Relics of Napoleon's nemesis the duke of Wellington are not nearly as sought after. For a comparison of the auction prices fetched by Napoleon versus Wellington relics up to the beginning of the twentieth century, see Harold MacFarlane, "Napoleon v. Wellington: The Comparative Value of Relics," *Connoisseur* 8 (April 1904): 225–30. The discrepancy can be partly explained by Philip Shaw's observation that Waterloo

is overwhelmingly recalled as a scene of defeat instead of a scene of victory. The vanquished Napoleon fascinates far more than the victorious (and comparatively stolid) Wellington. Shaw, *Waterloo and the Romantic Imagination*, 1.

45. Scott, *Abbotsford*, 29.

46. *Diary of Dr. John William Polidori*, 34.

47. Ralph Milbanke, *Astarte: A Fragment of Truth Concerning George Gordon Byron*, new ed., ed. Mary, Countess of Lovelace (London: Christophers, 1921), 17. I am grateful to Leslie Marchand's biography of Byron for leading me to this source.

48. *The Harcourt Papers*, ed. Edward William Harcourt, 14 vols. (Oxford: James Parker and Co., [1880–1905]), 6:190.

49. *Don Juan*, vol. 5 of Lord Byron, *The Complete Poetical Works*, ed. Jerome J. McGann (Oxford: Clarendon Press, 1986), 482.

50. Leslie A. Marchand, *Byron: A Biography*, 3 vols. (New York: Alfred A. Knopf, 1957), 3:971. Byron's general staginess was not lost on his fellow poets. Keats once proposed a theory of personality that divided people into one of two tempers of mind— "the worldly, theatrical and pantomimical" and the "unearthly, spiritual and etherial." Into the first category he put Byron and Napoleon Bonaparte. John Keats to the George Keatses, 14 October 1818, in *The Letters of John Keats, 1814–1821*, 2 vols., ed. Hyder Edward Williams (Cambridge: Harvard University Press, 1958), 1:395.

51. John Clubbe, "Napoleon's Last Campaign and the Origins of *Don Juan*," *Byron Journal*, no. 25 (1997): 12, 13.

52. Ibid., 17.

53. Byron, *Childe Harold's Pilgrimage*, 82.

54. Mrs. Pryse Lockhart Gordon was having a run of good luck in her autograph collecting. She had already managed to get Sir Walter Scott to inscribe a few lines from "The Field of Waterloo," lines that Byron read out loud on the evening he was cajoled into taking an ice with the Gordons after dinner:

> The sound of Cressy none shall own,
> And Agincourt shall be unknown,
> And Blenheim be a nameless spot
> Long ere thy glories are forgot.

Scott was anointing Waterloo as the battle site to beat all battle sites, as one that would be remembered long after other war scenes faded in memory. Byron, unwilling to concede Scott's poetic point, struck the page with his hand and cried, "I'll be d—d if they will, Mr. Scott, be forgot!" Gordon, *Personal Memoirs*, 2:327.

55. Byron to Douglas Kinnaird, 26 October [1819], in *Byron's Letters and Journals*, ed. Leslie A. Marchand, 12 vols. (Cambridge: Harvard University Press, 1976), 6:232.

56. By the time Byron wrote the lines about *Don Juan*, the paint on his carriage was

starting to chip, and his illegitimate daughter Allegra had come to live with him. "My green carriage has lost much of it's [*sic*] splendour and consequently I am shorn of one of the principal seductive qualities of an accomplished gentleman," Byron wrote to Lord Kinnaird in July 1819. Ibid., 6:176. When Percy Shelley visited Byron's palazzo at Ravenna, he was met on the staircase by five peacocks, two guinea hens, and an Egyptian crane, all part of what Byron referred to as his flourishing family. "Besides my daughter Allegra," he wrote, "here are two Cats—six dogs—a badger—a falcon, a tame Crow—and a Monkey.——The fox died—and a first Cat ran away." Byron to Augusta Leigh, [18?] October 1820, Ibid., 7:208–9. It is unclear how many of the animals were driven about in the Napoleonic carriage; when his caravan of carriages departed Ravenna in October 1821, Byron left the four-year-old Allegra, and some of the less satisfactory pets, behind.

57. A. M. Broadley, *Napoleon in Caricature, 1795–1821*, 2 vols. (London: John Lane, 1911), 1:22.

58. *The Coach That Napoleon Ran From: An Epic Poem in Twelve Books* (London: Juvenile Library, London Museum, 1816), 12.

59. Pearce, *On Collecting*, 395.

60. E. J. Trelawny, *Recollections of the Last Days of Shelley and Byron* (London: Edward Moxon, 1858), 134. Eventually buried in the Shelley family vault at Bournemouth, the heart resided for years in Mary Shelley's writing desk before being installed by her daughter-in-law in a sanctum dimly lit by a red lamp and with a blue ceiling studded with stars. When Byron's lungs were preserved at Missolonghi after his body was sent back to England for burial, this grisly saga in relic worship was repeated.

61. *The Autobiography of Leigh Hunt*, 2 vols. (New York: Harper & Brothers Publishers, 1850), 2:130.

62. Ibid., 2:131.

63. Byron to Charles F. Barry, 24 July 1823, in *Byron's Letters and Journals*, 10:214; Marchand, *Byron: A Biography*, 3:1094.

64. Byron, *Childe Harold's Pilgrimage*, 3 and 6.

65. Ernestine Hill, *The Territory* (Sydney: Angus and Robertson, 1951), 109. My thanks to Mary Lynn Grant and to Dino Felluga for drawing my attention to a posting on the North American Society for the Study of Romanticism (NASSR) list serve that took up the final sighting of Byron's carriage. And thanks to the author of that posting, Paul Douglass, who passed along a citation he had received from Graham Pont, for alerting me to Ernestine Hill's book.

66. I thank William Kupersmith for helping me puzzle over Byron's Latin motto.

67. Maurice Willson Disher, *Pharaoh's Fool* (London: Heinemann, 1957), 244.

68. John Theodore Tussaud, *The Romance of Madame Tussaud* (London: Odhams, 1920), 199.

4. Belzoni in Ruins

1. See Alberto Siliotti, "Giovanni Belzoni in Nineteenth-Century Egypt," in Siliotti's splendid edition of *Belzoni's Travels* (London: British Museum Press, 2001), 21–77. For accounts of Belzoni's career, see Stanley Mayes, *The Great Belzoni* (London: Putnam, 1959); Colin Clair, *Strong Man Egyptologist* (London: Oldbourne, [1957]); Maurice Willson Disher, *Pharaoh's Fool* (London: Heinemann, 1957); and Peter A. Clayton, *The Rediscovery of Ancient Egypt: Artists and Travellers in the Nineteenth Century* (New York: Portland House, 1982). See also Gillen D'Arcy Wood, *The Shock of the Real: Romanticism and Visual Culture, 1760–1860* (New York: Palgrave, 2001). Wood uses Belzoni's exhibition as an example of a "real copy," a term that describes an emerging class of visual media in late Georgian England that Romantic writers such as Coleridge and Wordsworth disdained (4).

2. G[iovanni] Belzoni, *Narrative of the Operations and Recent Discoveries within the Pyramids, Temples, Tombs, and Excavations, in Egypt and Nubia; and of a Journey to the Coast of the Red Sea, in Search of the Ancient Berenice; and Another to the Oasis of Jupiter Ammon* (London: John Murray, 1820), 248. Hereafter cited in text.

3. William Turner, *Journal of a Tour in the Levant*, 3 vols. (London: John Murray, 1820), 2:377.

4. My attention was drawn to Flaubert's infuriation by Avital Ronell, who reads the inscription on Pompey's column as a monument to stupidity. See Avital Ronell, *Stupidity* (Urbana: University of Illinois Press, 2002), 12; I quote her translation. Flaubert wrote to Parain (6 October 1850): "À Alexandrie, un certain Thompson, de Sunderland, a sur la colonne de Pompée écrit son nom en lettres de six pieds de haut. Cela se lit à un quart de lieue de distance. Il n'y a pas moyen de voir la colonne sans voir le nom de Thompson, et par conséquent sans penser à Thompson. Ce crétin s'est incorporé au monument et se perpétue avec lui." Vol. 2 of the *Correspondance, Oeuvres complètes de Gustave Flaubert* (Paris: Louis Conard, 1926), 243.

5. Emma Hamilton to Horatio Nelson, 8 September 1798, reprinted in Hugh Tours, *The Life and Letters of Emma Hamilton* (London: Victor Gollancz, 1963), 121.

6. Lady Hamilton to Nelson, 26 October 1798, in *Nelson's Letters to His Wife and Other Documents*, ed. George P. B. Naish ([Greenwich]: Navy Records Society, 1958), 420.

7. Robert Southey, *Letters from England*, 3 vols. (London: Longman, Rees, and Orme, 1807), 3:305. On the popularization of Egyptian design in the romantic era, see Jean-Marcel Humbert, Michael Pantazzi, and Christiane Ziegler, *Egyptomania: Egypt in Western Art, 1730–1930*; Richard G. Carrott, *The Egyptian Revival: Its Sources, Monuments, and Meaning, 1808–1858* (Berkeley: University of California Press, 1978); and James Steven Curl, *Egyptomania: The Egyptian Revival, A Recurring Theme in the History of Taste* (London: George Allen and Unwin, 1982).

8. John Soane, *Lectures on Architecture*, ed. Arthur T. Bolton (London: Sir John Soane's Museum, 1929), 21.

9. Thomas Willson, *The Pyramid* (1824).

10. I am indebted to Richard G. Carrott's discussion of the building's architectural details in *The Egyptian Revival: Its Sources Monuments, and Meaning, 1808–1858*, 34–35.

11. Leigh Hunt, *A Saunter Through the West End* (London: Hurst and Blackett, 1861), 43.

12. Ibid., 43.

13. Jean Baudrillard, *The System of Objects*, trans. James Benedict (London: Verso, 1996), 90.

14. On the association between aristocratic patrons and early museum formation, see Inderpal Grewal, *Home and Harem: Nation, Gender, Empire, and the Cultures of Travel* (Durham: Duke University Press, 1996), 90.

15. Keats to Benjamin Bailey, 8 October 1817, in *The Letters of John Keats*, ed. Hyder Edward Rollins, 2 vols. (Cambridge: Harvard University Press, 1958), 1:170.

16. William Wordsworth, *The Prelude, 1799, 1805, 1850*, ed. Jonathan Wordsworth, M. H. Abrams, and Stephen Gill (New York: W. W. Norton & Company, 1979), ix and 522. The editors quote a manuscript letter that Wordsworth's daughter Dora wrote in February 1832. "Mother and he work like slaves from morning to night—an arduous work—correcting a long Poem written thirty years back and which is not to be published during his life—The Growth of his own Mind—The ante-chapel as he calls it to *The Recluse*."

17. Andrew Bennett, *Romantic Poets and the Culture of Posterity* (Cambridge: Cambridge University Press, 1999), 200. On a related subject, see Bruce Haley, *Living Forms: Romantics and the Monumental Figure* (Albany: State University of New York Press, 2003).

18. William Wordsworth, "Lines composed a few miles above Tintern Abbey," in *The Poetical Works of William Wordsworth*, 2nd ed., vol. 2 (Oxford: Clarendon Press, 1952), 259.

19. Eric George, *The Life and Death of Benjamin Robert Haydon, Historical Painter, 1786–1846*, 2nd ed. (London: Oxford University Press, 1967), 172.

20. William Hazlitt, "Haydon's 'Christ's Agony in the Garden,'" in vol. 8 of *The Complete Works of William Hazlitt*, ed. P. P. Howe, 21 vols. (London: J. M. Dent and Sons, 1930–34), 142; Hazlitt, "Mr. Coleridge," in *The Spirit of the Age*, vol. 11 of *The Complete Works*, 29.

21. Classic surveys of sublime experience and the aesthetics of the infinite include Marjorie Hope Nicolson, *Mountain Gloom and Mountain Glory: The Development of the Aesthetics of the Infinite* (Ithaca: Cornell University Press, 1959); Samuel H. Monk, *The Sublime* (Ann Arbor: University of Michigan Press, 1960); and Thomas Weiskel, *The Romantic Sublime: Studies in the Structure and Psychology of Transcendence* (Baltimore: Johns Hopkins University Press, 1976).

22. Edmund Burke, *A Philosophical Enquiry into the Origin of our Ideas of the Sublime and Beautiful*, in vol. 1 of *The Writings and Speeches of Edmund Burke*, ed. T. O. McLaughlin and James T. Boulton (Oxford: Clarendon Press, 1997), 242.

23. Immanuel Kant, *Observations on the Feeling of the Beautiful and Sublime*, trans. John T. Goldthwait (Berkeley: University of California Press, 1965), 48–49.

24. Immanuel Kant, *Critique of the Power of Judgment*, ed. Paul Guyer, trans. Paul Guyer and Eric Matthews (Cambridge: Cambridge University Press, 2000), 136.

25. Ibid., 138.

26. Burke, *Philosophical Enquiry*, 225–26.

27. "Giovani Baptista Belzoni. The Celebrated Patagonian Sampson," Harvard Theatre Collection, Nathan Marsh Pusey Library, Houghton Library, Harvard University.

28. John Thomas Smith, *A Book for a Rainy Day* (London: Richard Bentley, 1845), 171–72.

29. I. W., "Belzoni at Oxford," *Notes and Queries*, 16 July 1864, 44.

30. Wordsworth, *The Prelude* (1805), 7.293–97.

31. The holdings of the Department of Prints and Drawings at the British Museum include three prints purportedly showing Belzoni with Patrick Cotter (also known as Patrick O'Brian). One, published by Hogg and Co. in October 1804, titled "Patrick O'Brian, The Wonderful Irish Giant 8 ft 7 in high," shows Belzoni leaning on a cane and staring up at Cotter. Catalogue no. 1872–10–12–4542.

32. Walter Scott to Anna Seward, summer 1803, *The Letters of Sir Walter Scott*, 12 vols., ed. H. J. C. Grierson (London: Constable and Co., 1932–37), 6:189. For an account of giant and dwarf performers, see the chapter "Freaks in the Age of Improvement" in Richard D. Altick, *The Shows of London* (Cambridge: Harvard University Press, 1978), 253–65. For an eloquent account of Caroline Crachami's reign as "The Smallest of All Persons Mentioned in the Records of Littleness," see Gaby Wood's book of that name (London: Profile Books, 1998).

33. Walter Scott to Cornet Walter Scott, October 1820, *The Letters of Sir Walter Scott*, 1:276. Scott's comment on the quixotic nature of public renown inadvertently foreshadows the circumstances of Haydon's death, a suicide which was attributed to the painter's despair at lack of public recognition. On the morning of June 22, 1846, Haydon's wife and daughter heard a heavy thud in his studio and thought he had dropped one of the large canvases he was in the habit of moving. Haydon had killed himself by gunshot wound, they discovered later that afternoon, after returning from a ride to Brixton. He was reportedly incensed at having his paintings passed by in the Egyptian Hall by people who were rushing to see P. T. Barnum's exhibition of the thirty-one-inch-tall General Tom Thumb.

34. William Wordsworth, Preface to *Lyrical Ballads*, in *The Prose Works of William*

Wordsworth, 3 vols., ed. W. J. B. Owen and Jane Worthington Smyser (Oxford: Clarendon Press, 1974), 1:128–30. Burke, *Philosophical Enquiry*, 210.

35. *The Collected Writings of Thomas De Quincey*, vol. 5, ed. David Masson (1890; reprint, New York: Johnson Reprint Corporation, 1968), 325.

36. John Ritchie Findlay, *Personal Recollections of Thomas De Quincey* (Edinburgh: Adam & Charles Black, 1886), 48.

37. Susan Stewart, *On Longing: Narratives of the Miniature, the Gigantic, the Souvenir, the Collection* (1984; reprint, Durham: Duke University Press, 1993), 73.

38. Burke, *Philosophical Enquiry*, 306.

39. Samuel Smiles, *A Publisher and His Friends: Memoir and Correspondence of the Late John Murray*, 2 vols. (London: John Murray, 1891), 2:97. Belzoni once left a party in a huff when he thought someone had made an allusion to his early career. On New Year's Eve 1822, Belzoni joined a reception at the home of his publisher, John Murray. Murray presented each of his guests with a pocket book, and while a special bowl of punch was being prepared, Isaac D'Israeli took a pencil and wrote the following words:

> Gigantic Belzoni at Pope Joan and tea,
> What a group of mere puppets we seem beside thee;
> Which, our kind host perceiving, with infinite zest,
> Gives us Punch at our supper, to keep up the jest.

Belzoni read the last lines twice over and decided that they contained an insulting allusion to his early career as a showman. "His eyes flashing fire, he exclaimed, 'I am betrayed!' and suddenly left the room," recalled Smiles. See *Publisher and His Friends*, 2:97–98.

40. The preamble to the "Act . . . to deprive her Majesty Caroline Amelia Elizabeth of the Title, Prerogatives, Rights, Privileges and Exemptions of Queen Consort of this Realm, and to dissolve the Marriage between his Majesty and the said Caroline Amelia Elizabeth" alleged that the queen had acted toward Pergami, "a foreigner of low station," "with indecent and offensive familiarity and freedom, and carried on a licentious, disgraceful and adulterous intercourse" with him. Quoted in Flora Fraser, *The Unruly Queen: The Life of Queen Caroline* (New York: Alfred A. Knopf, 1996), 400.

41. Ibid., 256, 276.

42. Cyrus Redding, *Past Celebrities Whom I Have Known*, 2 vols. (London: Charles J. Skeet, 1866), 2:273.

43. *Plates Illustrative of the Researches and Operations of G. Belzoni in Egypt and Nubia* (London: John Murray, 1820).

44. Burke, *Philosophical Enquiry*, 230.

45. Sarah Atkins, *The Fruits of Enterprize Exhibited in the Travels of Belzoni in Egypt and Nubia* (London: Harris & Son, 1821), 44 and 111.

46. Wordsworth, *The Prelude* (1850), 6.591–94, 617, 608.

47. Ibid., 6.609–16.

48. For a reading of this passage in the context of Napoleon's pursuit, see Alan Liu, *Wordsworth: The Sense of History* (Stanford: Stanford University Press, 1989), 21–31.

49. John Whale, "Sacred Objects and the Sublime Ruins of Art," in *Beyond Romanticism: New Approaches to Texts and Contexts, 1780–1832*, ed. Stephen Copley and John Whale (London: Routledge, 1992), 224.

50. Mayes, *The Great Belzoni*, 258.

51. Ibid., 261.

52. [Marguerite Gardiner, countess of Blessington], *The Magic Lantern; or Sketches of Scenes in the Metropolis*, 2nd ed. (London: Longman, Hurst, Rees, Orme, and Brown, 1823), 58, 61, 69.

53. *Description of the Egyptian Tomb, Discovered by G. Belzoni* (London: John Murray, 1822), 4.

54. Ibid., 5–6.

55. Belzoni, *Narrative*, 236.

56. Belzoni to the Honourable Trustees of the British Museum, CE 4/4, 1681a (10 September 1821), Original Letters and Papers, vol. 4, 1816–1821, British Museum Central Archives. By kind permission of the Trustees of the British Museum.

57. Henry Ellis to Belzoni, CE 4/4, 1693 (12 December 1821), Original Letters and Papers, vol. 4, 1816–1821, British Museum Central Archives. By kind permission of the Trustees of the British Museum.

58. J. J. Hall, *The Life and Correspondence of Henry Salt*, 2 vols. (London: Richard Bentley, 1834), 2:374–75.

59. *The Diary of Benjamin Robert Haydon*, 5 vols., ed. Willard Bissell Pope (Cambridge: Harvard University Press, 1960), 2:478. Hereafter cited in text.

60. Byron to John Murray, 16 February 1821, in *Byron's Letters and Journals*, 12 vols., ed. Leslie A. Marchand (Cambridge: Belknap Press of Harvard University Press, 1978), 8:79.

61. Helen Dorey, "Sir John Soane's Acquisition of the Sarcophagus of Seti I," *Georgian Group Journal* (1991): 28.

62. John Summerson, "Sir John Soane and the Furniture of Death," in *The Unromantic Castle and Other Essays* ([London]: Thames and Hudson, 1990), 140.

63. George, *The Life and Death of Benjamin Robert Haydon*, 139.

64. William Boyd, "Skeletons in the Closet," *Art and Antiques* (November 1988): 86.

65. William Hazlitt, "Mr. Coleridge," in *The Spirit of the Age*, 30.

66. George, *The Life and Death of Benjamin Robert Haydon*, 139.

67. Letter from G. A. Browne to John Soane, 9 February 1825, Sir John Soane's Museum Archive, London, Spiers Box, letters relating to the purchase of the Belzoni sarcophagus.

68. Belzoni was married to "an English consort of Amazonian proportions," states the *Dictionary of National Biography*, in a passage without clear attribution, but one that

every writer on Belzoni seems to quote, however skeptically. Whatever Sarah Belzoni's measurements, she was a formidable woman. Once, while Belzoni was off excavating a temple, his wife was attacked by robbers intent on stealing their boat. "They were rather impertinent to her, and attempted to go on board in spite of all she could say to them," Belzoni writes (*Narrative*, 100). Pushed to the limits of her tolerance, Mrs. Belzoni brandished a pistol and chased the men up a hill.

69. Sarah Belzoni's manuscript notebook, 129, Bristol Museums and Art Gallery, Bristol, England.

70. Sarah Belzoni's marginalia in copy of Edward J. Cooper's *Views in Egypt and Nubia*, Bristol City Museum and Art Gallery.

71. "Mrs. Belzoni was present, and received every attention from the guests of her kind patron," according to an account of Soane's reception in the 26 March 1825 *Literary Gazette*. Sir John Soane's Museum Archive, Newscuttings volumes, 1825, vol. 1.

72. Redding, *Past Celebrities*, 2:299–300.

73. Jane Porter to James Morier, 15 March 1845, Porter Family Papers, POR 1397, reproduced by permission of the Huntington Library, San Marino, California. I am grateful to Thomas McLean for discovering and transcribing this letter.

74. Pryse Lockhart Gordon, Esq., *Personal Memoirs; Reminiscences of Men and Manners at Home and Abroad, During the Last Half Century*, 2 vols. (London: Henry Colburn and Richard Bentley, 1830), 2:405.

75. For detailed descriptions of the drawings, now in the holdings of the Bristol City Museum and Art Gallery, and for an account of their provenance, see Susan M. Pearce, "Giovanni Battista Belzoni's Exhibition of the Reconstructed Tomb of Pharaoh Seti I in 1821," *Journal of the History of Collections* 12.1 (2000): 109–25.

76. William Wordsworth to Henry Taylor, 23 October 1826, in vol. 4 of *The Letters of William and Dorothy Wordsworth*, 2nd ed., ed. Alan G. Hill (Oxford: Clarendon Press, 1978), 488.

77. Clayton, *The Rediscovery of Ancient Egypt*, 43.

78. William Wordsworth, "A slumber did my spirit seal," in *The Poetical Works of William Wordsworth*, 2nd ed., vol. 2, ed. Ernest de Selincourt (Oxford: Clarendon Press, 1952), 216.

79. I quote Stuart Curran in a classroom lecture. See his discussion of the poem's inscrutability in "Romantic Poetry: Why and Wherefore," in *The Cambridge Companion to British Romanticism*, ed. Stuart Curran (Cambridge: Cambridge University Press, 1993), 234–35. The poem has been taken up as part of a discussion of eighteenth-century object narratives and modern theories of sympathy in Jonathan Lamb, "Modern Metamorphoses and Disgraceful Tales," *Critical Inquiry* 28 (2001): 133–66.

80. Erik Iversen, *Obelisks in Exile*, 2 vols. (Copenhagen: G. E. C. Gad Publishers, 1972), 2:85.

81. Donald A. Baker, *John Keast Lord: Materials for a Life* (Leiden: Backhuys Publishers, 2002), 23.

5. Mary Anning Recollected

1. From the description accompanying the specimen in the London Natural History Museum display cabinet, specimen no. 2003, Hawkins Collection, purchased in 1834. See S. R. Howe, T. Sharpe, and H. S. Torrens, *Ichthyosaurs: A History of Fossil 'Sea Dragons,'* pamphlet to an exhibition in the Department of Geology at the National Museum of Wales.

2. Maria Hack, *Geological Sketches and Glimpses of the Ancient Earth* (London: Harvey and Darton, 1833), 24; Thomas Hawkins, *The Book of the Great Sea-Dragons, Ichthyosauri and Plesiosauri* (London: William Pickering, 1840), 10.

3. For an account of Anning's early discoveries, see George Roberts, *The History of Lyme Regis* (Sherborne: Printed for the author by Langdon and Harker, 1823), 288.

4. On romantic poets' interest in geological and archaeological discoveries, see John Frederick Wyatt, *Wordsworth and the Geologists* (New York: Cambridge University Press, 1995); Anne D. Wallace, "Picturesque Fossils, Sublime Geology? The Crisis of Authority in Charlotte Smith's *Beachy Head*," *European Romantic Review* 13.1 (2002): 77–93; and Charles J. Rzepka, "From Relics to Remains: Wordsworth's 'The Thorn' and the Emergence of Secular History," *Romanticism on the Net* 31 (August 2003).

5. On Mary Anning's religion, see Thomas W. Goodhue, "The Faith of a Fossilist: Mary Anning," *Anglican and Episcopal History* 70 (March 2001): 80–100. I am grateful to Tom Goodhue for generously sharing his Anning findings.

6. Hannah More, *Poems* (1816; reprint, London: Routledge/Thoemmes Press, 1996), 118, 107–8.

7. W. H. Edwards to W. D. Lang, 30 April 1947, NHMS XXXVII/2/b, Dorset County Museum. My thanks to the Dorset Natural History and Archaeological Society for permission to quote from materials in the Dorset County Museum.

8. W. D. Lang, "More about Mary Anning. Including a Newly-Found Letter," *Proceedings of the Dorset Natural History and Archaeological Society* 71 (1949): 188.

9. Harriette Wilson, *The Memoirs of Harriette Wilson Written by Herself*, 2 vols. (London: Eveleigh Nash, 1909), 2:483.

10. Jane Austen, *Persuasion*, ed. John Davie (Oxford: Oxford University Press, 1990), 93.

11. See J. M. Edmonds, "The Fossil Collection of the Misses Philpot of Lyme Regis," *Proceedings [1976] of the Dorset Natural History & Archaeological Society* 98 (1978): 43–48; H. P. Powell and J. M. Edmonds, "List of Type-Fossils in the Philpot Collection, Oxford University Museum," *Proceedings [1976] of the Dorset Natural History and Archaeological Society* 98 (1978): 48–53.

12. John Fowles, *The French Lieutenant's Woman* (London: Jonathan Cape, 1969), 50.

13. John Fowles, "The Blinded Eye," in *Wormholes: Essays and Occasional Writings*, ed. Jan Relf (London: Jonathan Cape, 1988), 260.

14. Naomi Schor, "*Cartes Postales:* Representing Paris 1900," *Critical Inquiry* 18 (1992): 201.

15. Since the symposium, one of the participants, Thomas W. Goodhue, has published two biographies of Anning. One is written for children: *Curious Bones: Mary Anning and the Birth of Paleontology* (Greensboro, N.C.: Morgan Reynolds Publishing, 2002). The other is aimed at an adult readership: *Fossil Hunter: The Life and Times of Mary Anning (1799–1847)* (Bethesda, Md.: Academica Press, 2004). Both biographies are carefully annotated.

16. John Fowles and Liz-Anne Bawden, *Lyme Regis Museum Curator's Report, 1987–1988*, 7.

17. Hugh Torrens, "Mary Anning (1799–1847) of Lyme; 'the greatest fossilist the world ever knew,'" *British Journal for the History of Science* 28 (1995): 281.

18. Ibid., 276.

19. John Haskings's account of "That awful Thunder which made all people for to wonder at Lyme 19th August, 1800," typescript, NHMSXXXVII/9/d, Lang Papers, Dorset County Museum, Dorchester.

20. Typescript of Charles Churchill Anning's account of his aunt, July 1847, NHMS XXXVII/9/c, Lang Papers, Dorset County Museum.

21. Laurence Anholt, *Stone, Girl, Bone Girl: The Story of Mary Anning*, illus. Sheila Moxley (New York: Orchard Books, 1998), unpaginated. Other recent Anning children's books include Catherine Brighton, *The Fossil Girl: Mary Anning's Dinosaur Discovery* (London: Frances Lincoln, 1999) and Jeannine Atkins, *Mary Anning and the Sea Dragon*, illus. Michael Dooling (New York: Farrar Straus Giroux, 1999). Torrens discusses some of the earlier juvenile biographies in "Mary Anning (1799–1847) of Lyme," 276.

22. Mary Anning to Mrs. [Charlotte] Murchison, 11 October 1833, reprinted in W. D. Lang, "Three Letters by Mary Anning, 'Fossilist,' of Lyme," *Proceedings of the Dorset Natural History and Archaeological Society* 66 (1945): 169–73.

23. Thomas Hawkins, *Memoirs of Ichthyosauri and Plesiosauri, Extinct Monsters of the Ancient Earth*, 2nd ed. (London: Relfe and Fletcher, 1834), 26.

24. Mary Anning to Mrs. [Charlotte] Murchison, 25 February [1829], reprinted in Lang, "Three Letters by Mary Anning," 170.

25. William Buckland, *Geology and Mineralogy Considered with Reference to Natural Theology*, 2 vols. (Philadelphia: Lea & Blanchard, 1841), 1:158.

26. This is William Buckland's translation of Cuvier's description of the plesiosaurus in the *Recherches sur les ossemens fossiles*. Buckland, *Geology and Mineralogy*, 1:158.

27. Torrens, "Mary Anning (1799–1847) of Lyme," 278.

28. Idris Bell, manuscript letter, Lang Papers, Dorset County Museum. Tickell writes of the commonplace book's contents, "They do not add much to knowledge about her [Anning]." Crispin Tickell, *Mary Anning of Lyme Regis* (Lyme Regis: Lyme Regis Philpot Museum, n.d.), 23.

29. William St. Clair, "The Impact of Byron's Writings: An Evaluative Approach," in *Byron: Augustan and Romantic*, ed. Andrew Rutherford (London: Macmillan, 1990), 10. See also St. Clair, *The Reading Nation in the Romantic Period* (Cambridge: Cambridge University Press, 2004), 224–29.

30. Austen, *Persuasion*, 106, 96–99.

31. Reprinted in W. D. Lang, "Mary Anning (1799–1847) and the Pioneer Geologists of Lyme," *Proceedings of the Dorset Natural History and Archaeological Society* 60 (1938): 155.

32. Noah Heringman points out the common idiom shared equally by poetry and early earth science, focusing particularly on the rhetoric of landscape aesthetics. See Noah Heringman, *Romantic Rocks, Aesthetic Geology* (Ithaca: Cornell University Press, 2004).

33. Quoted in Gideon Mantell, *Petrifactions and their Teachings* (London: Henry G. Bohn, 1851), 341.

34. "Remarks Introductory to the First American Edition," in Gideon Algernon Mantell, *The Wonders of Geology*, 2 vols. (New Haven: A. H. Maltby, 1839), 2:39.

35. Mantell, *Wonders of Geology*, 2:592 and 591; Gideon Mantell, *The Medals of Creation; or, First Lessons in Geology*, 2 vols. (London: Henry G. Bohn, 1844), 1:8.

36. Hawkins, *Memoirs of Ichthyosauri*, 28.

37. Buckland, *Geology and Mineralogy*, 1:132 and 174. The Milton passage is taken from book 2 of *Paradise Lost*.

38. Cited by Mantell in *Wonders of Geology*, 2:490.

39. Buckland, *Geology and Mineralogy*, 458; Mantell, *Petrifactions and their Teachings*, 367.

40. Oxford English Dictionary, s.v. "memoir."

41. Hawkins, *Memoirs of Ichthyosauri*, v, 13; Henry Thomas De la Beche accused Hawkins of carrying away quarries. He is quoted in Lang, "Mary Anning, of Lyme, Collector and Vendor of Fossils, 1799–1847," *Natural History Magazine* 5 (April 1935): 77.

42. Lang, "Three Letters by Mary Anning," 171.

43. John Fowles, introduction to Crispin Tickell, *Mary Anning of Lyme Regis*, 5.

44. W. D. Lang's handwritten extracts from Anna Maria Pinney diary, Dorset County Museum.

45. Germaine de Staël, *Corinne, or Italy*, trans. Avriel Goldberger (New Brunswick: Rutgers University Press, 1987), 21 and 32.

46. W. D. Lang's handwritten extracts from Anna Maria Pinney diary.

47. Ibid.

48. George Gordon, Lord Byron, "January 22nd 1824. Messalonghi. On this day I complete my thirty sixth year," in vol. 7 of Lord Byron, *The Complete Poetical Works*, ed. Jerome J. McGann (Oxford: Clarendon Press, 1993), 79.

49. Ibid., 80–81.

50. Goodhue, "The Faith of a Fossilist," esp. 83.

51. Henry Kirk White, "Solitude," *The Remains of Henry Kirke White*, 2 vols. (London: Longman, Hurst, Rees, Orme, and Brown, 1821), 2:133.

52. Byron, "Lines and Note by Lord Byron," in *The Remains of Henry Kirke White*, 1:279.

53. See Leah Price's discussion of how anthologies served to create and reinforce a shared cultural currency when, for example, a popular elocution handbook could render a passage from a play immediately recognizable long after that play had ceased being performed. Leah Price, *The Anthology and the Rise of the Novel: From Richardson to George Eliot* (Cambridge: Cambridge University Press, 2000), 80.

54. Quoted in Lang, "Mary Anning and the Pioneer Geologists of Lyme," 151.

55. W. D. Lang, "Mary Anning, of Lyme, Collector and Vendor of Fossils, 1799–1847," 74.

56. Ibid., 81.

57. Lang's transcript in the Dorset County Museum can be compared with the version he published in his article.

58. W. D. Lang's handwritten extracts from Anna Maria Pinney diary.

59. Quoted in Torrens, "Mary Anning (1799–1847) of Lyme," 272.

60. C. G. Carus, *The King of Saxony's Journey through England and Scotland in the Year 1844* (London, 1846), 197.

61. Hugh Torrens, "Early Collecting in the Field of Geology," in *The Origins of Museums: The Cabinet of Curiosities in Sixteenth- and Seventeenth-Century Europe*, ed. Oliver Impey and Arthur MacGregor (Oxford: Clarendon Press, 1985), 213.

62. Mantell, *Medals of Creation*, 1:56.

63. Thomas W. Goodhue, "Mary Anning: The Fossilist as Exegete," *Endeavour* 29 (March 2005): 30.

64. Rosamond Wolff Purcell and Stephen Jay Gould, *Finders, Keepers: Eight Collectors* (London: Pimlico, 1992), 111.

65. Torrens, "Mary Anning (1799–1847) of Lyme," 281.

66. See David Quammen's excellent review essay "The Man Who Knew Too Much: Stephen Jay Gould's Opus Posthumous," *Harper's* (June 2003): 73–80, for a discussion of Gould's dual career as a scientist and a popular essayist. Other conference attendees also saw their work cross over the literary-scientific divide, sometimes without their volition. Jo Draper, a local historian of a feminist bent who led a discussion at the conference, may have been surprised to find her conference session title— "Mary Anning: The Right Woman in the Right Place at the Right Time"—neutral-

ized (so that "woman" became "person") and used in print without attribution by a male paleontologist when Chris McGowan wrote of the symposium, "If the essence of the meeting were distilled into a single sentence it would be that Mary Anning happened to be the right person, in the right place, at the right time." Chris McGowan, *The Dragon Seekers* (Cambridge, Mass.: Perseus Publishing, 2001), 203.

Coda

1. Hyder Edward Rollins and Stephen Maxfield Parrish, *Keats and the Bostonians* (Cambridge: Harvard University Press, 1951), 35.
2. Ibid., 35.
3. *Shelley and His Circle, 1773–1822*, vol. 2, ed. Kenneth Neill Cameron (Cambridge: Harvard University Press, 1961), 911.
4. "Jane Clairmont," in *Literary Anecdotes of the Nineteenth Century*, ed. W. Robertson Nicoll and Thomas J. Wise, 2 vols. (London: Hodder and Stoughton, 1896), 2:461.
5. *The Clairmont Correspondence*, 2 vols., ed. Marion Kingston Stocking (Baltimore: Johns Hopkins University Press, 1995), 2:655.
6. Quoted ibid., 656. Silsbee's claim on the object may have been legitimate. He moved back to America from Florence in 1876, and seems to have subsidized the Clairmont household in the year following. "Mr. Silsbee helped us almost thro' last year," Claire wrote early in 1879. She died in March, and Silsbee wrote to her niece in July to withdraw from the contest for the letters, saying that he could not give the price she was asking.
7. John Collins, *The Two Forgers: A Biography of Harry Buxton Forman and Thomas James Wise* (New Castle, Del.: Oak Knoll Books, 1992),165.
8. *The Library of the Late H. Buxton Forman* (New York: Anderson Galleries, March 15–17, 1920), part 1, 170; part 2, 142.
9. Thomas Wise, *A Shelley Library* (London: Printed for Private Circulation, 1924), 11.
10. Walter Benjamin, "Enlargements," in *One-Way Street*, vol. 1 of *Walter Benjamin: Selected Writings*, ed. Marcus Bullock and Michael W. Jennings (Cambridge: Harvard University Press, 1996), 465.
11. *A Shelley Library*, x.
12. Collins, *The Two Forgers*, 98.
13. Walter Benjamin, "Program for Literary Criticism," in *Walter Benjamin: Selected Writings, 1927–1934*, vol. 2, trans. Rodney Livingstone et al., ed. Michael W. Jennings, Howard Eiland, and Gary Smith (Cambridge: Harvard University Press, 1999), 290.
14. Walter Benjamin, "Unpacking My Library: A Talk about Collecting," ibid., 487. For instances of artists taking inspiration from museum collections, see the cata-

logue of a 1999 exhibition staged at the Museum of Modern Art in New York, Ky-
naston McShine, *The Museum as Muse: Artists Reflect* (New York: Museum of Modern Art, 1999).

15. Susan Sontag comments on the way in which photographs improve with age: "Photographs, when they get scrofulous, tarnished, stained, cracked, faded still look good;
do often look better. (In this, as in other ways, the art that photography does resemble is architecture, whose works are subject to the same inexorable promotion
through the passage of time; many buildings, and not only the Parthenon, probably
look better as ruins." Susan Sontag, *On Photography* (New York: Farrar, Straus and
Giroux, 1977), 79.

INDEX

Judith Pascoe teaches in the English department of the University of Iowa. She is the author of *Romantic Theatricality: Gender, Poetry, and Spectatorship* (Cornell, 1997) and the editor of *Mary Robinson: Selected Poems* (Broadview, 2000).